# Networking Essentials
# Exam 70-058

Microsoft is a registered trademark of Microsoft Corporation in the United States and in other countries.
All other trademarks quoted are the property of their respective editors.

All rights reserved. No part of this publication may be reproduced, stored in a retrieval system, or transmitted, in any form, or by any means, electronic, mechanical, photocopying, recording or otherwise, without the prior permission of the publishers.

Copyright - Editions ENI - January 2000
ISBN: 2-7460-0562-X
Original edition: ISBN : 2-7460-0178-0

## ENI Publishing LTD

500 Chiswick High Road
London W4 5RG

Tel: 020 8956 23 20
Fax: 020 8956 23 21

e-mail: publishing@ediENI.com
http://www.editions-eni.com

## Editions ENI

BP 32125
44021 NANTES CEDEX 1

Tél. 02.51.80.15.15
Fax. 02.51.80.15.16

e-mail : editions@ediENI.com
http://www.editions-eni.com

Collection directed by Joëlle MUSSET
Author: José DORDOIGNE
Translated from the French by Andrew BLACKBURN

# Preparation for the MCSE exam 70-058 Networking Essentials

This book is designed to provide effective assistance to a student preparing for the MCSE exam on the networking essentials.

For optimal assimilation of the topics covered, the book is divided into eleven chapters, which are structured as follows:
- Statement of **objectives**: a precise enumeration of the skills acquired by a student who has completed the chapter.
- A **theoretical exposé** of the topic: defines the terms and concepts involved and gives an overview of the main themes of the chapter.
- **Practical application** of the theory: shows precisely how to set up the configuration on a machine (screen shots and diagrams).
- **Exercises**: grouped together at the end of the book, the exercices provide concrete examples of specific parts of the course, which the student works through on his/her computer.
- **Assessment** of skills: each chapter ends with a set of between 15 and 66 questions either directly related to the chapter, or linking the topic in the current chapter to one discussed earlier, prompting the student to make the synthesis (in a separate section, the questions are reiterated along with their answers and relevant comments). There are almost 415 questions on the topics fundamental to master the essentials of networking.

**Networking**

## Basic network concepts — Chapter 1

- **A.** History . . . . . . . . . . . . . . . . . . 9
- **B.** Overview of network technology . . . 14
- **C.** The principal items of a network . . . . 23
- **D.** Environment protection . . . . . . . . . 32

## Protocol standards — Chapter 2

- **A.** The OSI model . . . . . . . . . . . . . . 57
- **B.** Standards and organizations . . . . . 65

## Data transmission physical layer — Chapter 3

- **A.** Role of the Network Interface Card . . 79
- **B.** Configuration options and parameters 80
- **C.** Network performance . . . . . . . . . . 87
- **D.** Specialized network interface cards . 88
- **E.** Data encoding . . . . . . . . . . . . . . 89

| | | |
|---|---|---|
| F. | Signal conversion | 97 |
| G. | Transmission media | 100 |

## Elements of communication software — Chapter 4

| | | |
|---|---|---|
| A. | Types of configuration | 131 |
| B. | Configuration options for the network interface card | 132 |
| C. | NDIS and ODI | 134 |
| D. | Installing a network interface card driver | 136 |
| E. | Network protocol stack | 146 |

## Network and interconnection architecture — Chapter 5

| | | |
|---|---|---|
| A. | Topologies | 157 |
| B. | Choosing a network topology | 163 |
| C. | Communications management | 164 |
| D. | Interconnecting networks | 172 |
| E. | Choice of connection hardware | 183 |

## Lower layer protocols — Chapter 6

- A. Characteristics of the physical layer . 209
- B. IEEE protocols . . . . . . . . . . . . . . 212
- C. AppleTalk . . . . . . . . . . . . . . . . 227
- D. Arcnet (Attached Resource Computer Network) . . . . . . . . . . . . . . . . 229
- E. FDDI . . . . . . . . . . . . . . . . . . 231
- F. ATM (Asynchronous Transfer Mode from the ATM Forum) . . . . . . . . . . 233
- G. Summary of the capacities of the different physical layers used . . 235

## Medium and higher layer protocols — Chapter 7

- A. TCP/IP and the Internet protocols . . 255
- B. IP protocol . . . . . . . . . . . . . . . 263
- C. File sharing . . . . . . . . . . . . . . 266
- D. Netware and the OSI model . . . . 270

**E.** NetBEUI
(NetBIOS Enhanced User Interface) . 273

**F.** DLC (Data Link Control) . . . . . . . . . 278

# Extended networks  Chapter 8

**A.** Types of connection available . . . . 295

**B.** ISDN
(Integrated Services Digital Network)   297

**C.** SLIP (Serial Line IP) . . . . . . . . . . . 300

**D.** PPP (Point-to-Point Protocol) . . . . . 302

**E.** X.25 . . . . . . . . . . . . . . . . . . . . . 303

**F.** Frame relay . . . . . . . . . . . . . . . . 305

**G.** ATM (Asynchronous Transfer Mode) . 306

# Network administration  Chapter 9

**A.** Accessing resources . . . . . . . . . . . 321

**B.** Accounts management . . . . . . . . . 323

**C.** Security management . . . . . . . . . 328

- D. Monitoring the network . . . . . . . . 333

- E. Choosing a recovery plan
  for different catastrophic scenarios . 337

## Network troubleshooting — Chapter 10

- A. Diagnosing common connectivity problems
  involving network interface cards,
  cables and associated hardware . . 347

- B. Solving connection problems . . . . 350

## Future prospects — Chapter 11

- A. Introduction . . . . . . . . . . . . . . . 365

- B. The global internetwork . . . . . . . . 366

- C. Mobile networks . . . . . . . . . . . 367

- D. Network management . . . . . . . . 369

# Exercises

Exercises relating to chapter 1 .... 373

Exercises relating to chapter 2 .... 381

Exercises relating to chapter 3 .... 383

Exercises relating to chapter 4 .... 385

Exercises relating to chapter 5 .... 388

Exercises relating to chapter 6 .... 391

Exercises relating to chapter 7 .... 395

Exercises relating to chapter 8 .... 400

Exercises relating to chapter 9 .... 406

Exercises relating to chapter 10 .... 413

# Appendices

Glossary .................. 420

Skills measured by exam 70-058 .... 431

Index .................... 433

## Prerequisites for this chapter

☒ General computing knowledge: files, directories.

## Objectives

When you have completed this chapter you will be able to:
☒ Present computing history from centralized computing up to the appearance of networks.
☒ Define network terms, such LAN, MAN and WAN.
☒ Describe the network services: file services, application services and data services.
☒ Distinguish between client/server architecture and peer-to-peer architecture.
☒ Distinguish between user level security and resource level security.
☒ Define the terms confidentiality, security and fault tolerance.
☒ Describe the functioning of RAID levels 0, 1 and 5.
☒ Describe the different types of archiving strategy: full, incremental and differential.

# Basic network concepts

# Summary

- **A. History** . . . . . . . . . . . . . . . . . 9
  1. Beginnings of the computer network . . . . . . . . 9
  2. Heterogeneous networks . . . . . . . . . . . . . 12
  3. Modern computer networks . . . . . . . . . . . 13

- **B. Overview of network technology** . . . 14
  1. Networks . . . . . . . . . . . . . . . . . . . . 14
  2. Resource sharing . . . . . . . . . . . . . . . . 15

- **C. The principal items of a network** . . . 23
  1. Software aspects . . . . . . . . . . . . . . . . 23
  2. Hardware aspects . . . . . . . . . . . . . . . 32

- **D. Environment protection** . . . . . . . . 32
  1. Reliability and confidentiality . . . . . . . . . . 32
  2. Data redundancy . . . . . . . . . . . . . . . 36
  3. Archiving strategies . . . . . . . . . . . . . . 43

This chapter will describe the origins of distributed computing, as we know it today. On the one hand, large centralized proprietary systems were set up. On the other hand, the personal computer concept was established. Personal computers grew in popularity rapidly, particularly after the appearance of local area networks. At the same time, TCP/IP and Unix evolved and, because of their transparency and openness, they quickly became indispensable items in the computing world.

## A. History

### 1. Beginnings of the computer network

#### a. Centralized computing in the 50s and 60s

At this time, data was managed on large centralized computers. The data was accessible from remote terminals. These terminals were equipped with communications hardware that allowed them to exchange characters with the central system.

The idea of sharing information and services gave rise to the networks we know today.

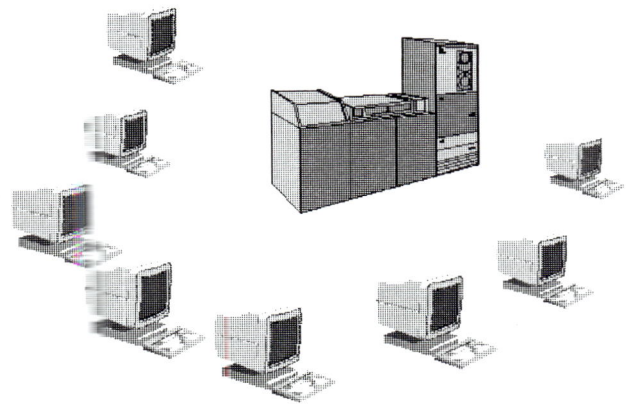

☞ DIGITAL's DECnet and IBM's System Network Architecture, are examples of centralized network architectures.

### b. The first packet switching network

Towards the end of the 60s, it was realized that overall resources were not being used very efficiently. Unofficially, the cold war climate of the time led the American Department of Defense to develop protocols and hardware with the objective of constructing a network with a high fault tolerance (for use in case of a war). This development led to the appearance in 1970 of the first packet switching network (cf. chapter 5 - C - 4 - c). This network was called ARPANET (Advanced Research Project Agency NETwork). This appearance of this network, together with the use of existing telephone lines, formed the basis for the future development of the Internet.

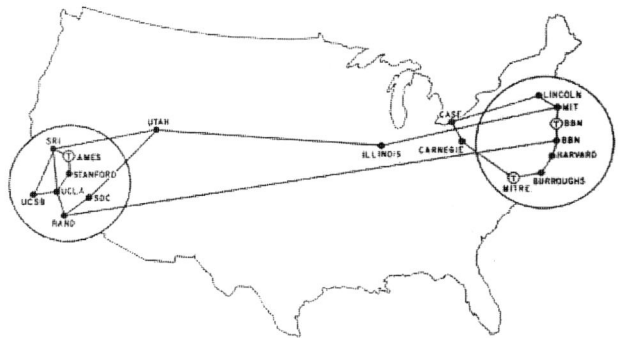

ARPANET grew very rapidly. The above map illustrates the extent of this network in September 1971.

By 1972, approximately 40 institutions were linked together and equipped with electronic mail and remote login services.

The map below illustrates the state of the ARPANET in October 1980. This configuration includes a packet satellite link with London (UCL).

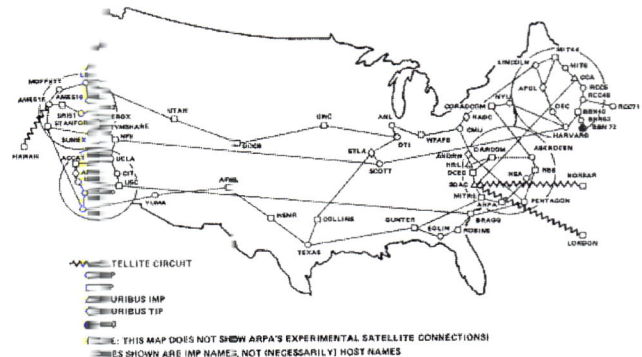

### c. Development of a de facto protocol standard: TCP/IP

1974 saw the origins of the Internet with the appearance of the IP protocol (*Internet Protocol*). The future IP was included in the publication of the TCP protocol (Transmission Control Protocol).

In 1980 the DARPA (Defense Advanced Research Projects Agency), which is responsible for management of the ARPANET, decided that TCP/IP should not be regarded as a military secret. At the same time, Unix operating systems continued their prodigious development. The BSD (Berkeley Software Development) version of Unix even included the TCP/IP sources, which were free for universities. From these beginnings, the world network has never stopped growing at a phenomenal rate.

### d. Distributed computing

The personal computer concept began in 1981, with the appearance of the first IBM PC: the PC XT.

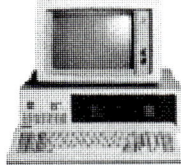

The advent of PCs, led to the creation of a new approach to computing management: that of **distributed computing**.

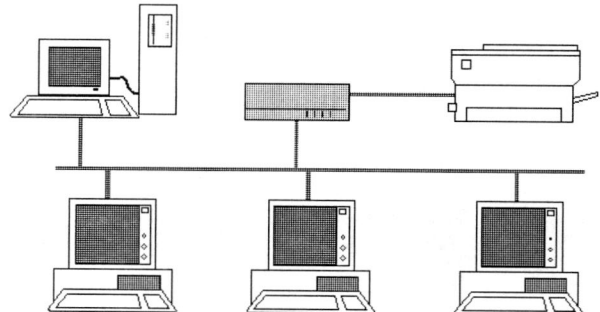

With this approach, global processing is divided into subtasks and distributed on different workstations. The distribution of the information is ensured by network services that provide all the workstations with the same functionalities.

Following the concept of small networks, that of *Local Area Networks* appeared.

## 2. Heterogeneous networks

Gradually, standards were developed that simplified the interconnection of different systems. Organizations such as the IEEE (Institute of Electrical and Electronic Engineers) put forward protocols for physical layers (10Base2, 100BaseT, etc.).

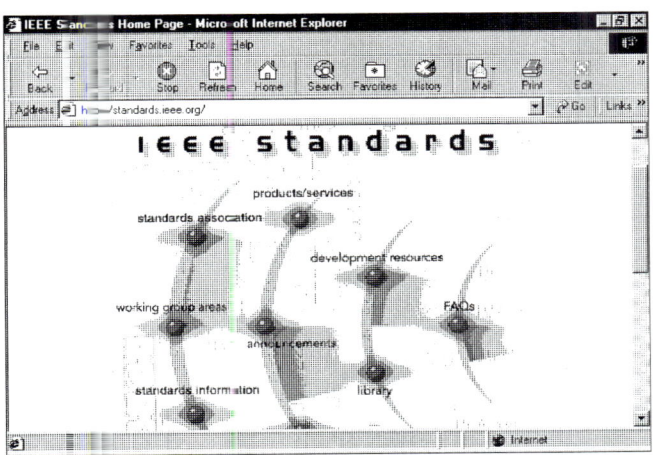

Then, the IEEE provided its support to the ISO (International Standards Organization) and to its network model, which is arranged in seven layers. This is called the OSI (Open System Interconnection) model.

```
7 - APPLICATION
6 - PRESENTATION
5 - SESSION
4 - TRANSPORT
3 - NETWORK
2 - DATA LINK
1 - PHYSICAL
```

## 3. Modern computer networks

Today, networks are composed of computers and operating systems that are based on all computing models. Thus, a typical network can include big systems as well as PCs. In addition, the machines concerned can run different operating systems.

## B. Overview of network technology

This chapter will describe the role of network technology along with the associated terms and concepts. These concepts are based on a number of computing techniques, which we will also cover. Finally, we will discuss the different services that network operating systems make available to the users.

### 1. Networks

A **network** is a means of allowing individuals and groups to share information and services.

Network technology covers the set of tools that allow computers to share information and resources.

Networks are classified according to their size, their extent and their structure.

There are three types of network:
- Local Area Networks,
- Metropolitan Area Networks,
- Wide Area Network.

#### a. Local Area Network (LAN)

A local area network covers a relatively small area such as a building, a company or a site. This type of network does not extend over more than 6 miles (10 kilometers). Generally, a LAN uses only one type of transmission medium and includes a limited number of computers.

#### b. Metropolitan Area Network (MAN)

A metropolitan area network covers a town or a city. It often includes different types of communication media in order to support communications over longer distances.

#### c. Wide Area Network (WAN)

WANs are often composed of several LANs interconnected across different regions of a country, or across different regions of the world.

There are two categories of WAN:
- Company networks, which are composed of a number of LANs each covering a subsidiary of the company concerned.
- Global networks which extend across the world. A global network can group together sites that are spread across different countries and can also include the networks of several companies.

☞ *An example of a WAN is USENET. This is a worldwide system of discussion groups, each of which is concerned with information on a specific theme.*

## 2. Resource sharing

The prime purpose of a network is to pool computing resources. In particular, a network ensures the sharing of information. This is achieved by the implementation of a set of network services, such as file, printing, mail, application and database services.

These services are often managed by the network operating system. The network operating system provides information to applications that are specific to the managed services.

### a. File services

File services are network applications that manipulate data in the form of files. These services include copying and moving files, managing several copies of the same file and backing up important data.

File services have four essential functions:
- File transfer,
- File storage and data migration,
- Synchronization of file updates,
- File archiving.

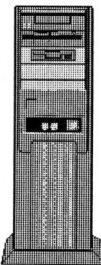
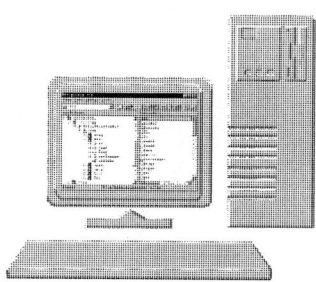

## File transfer

Before you can implement computing utilities that exchange files, you must have the basic means of transmitting information.

Information exchange is greatly assisted by network services such as electronic mail and other file transfer utilities.

In addition to the sharing of information, file access can be made more secure either by the application that authorizes file sharing, or by the file systems themselves that manage access permissions, or by both of these items.

 *For example, an ftp (file transfer protocol) server manages access security by authorizing reading, and possibly writing, from and to certain partitions. In addition, the file system that stores the files can also define specific access permissions. The access that is granted to the user will be defined by the most restrictive combination of these two systems.*

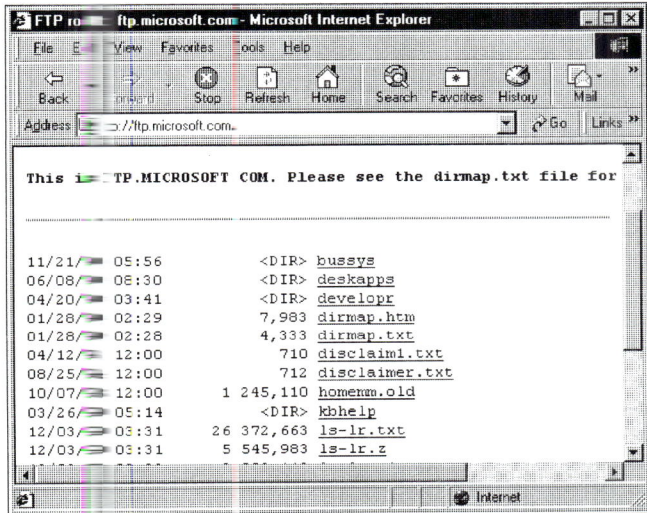

## File storage and data migration

To handle the rapid growth in volume of processed data, many different **storage devices** have been invented. These include fixed online devices, removable **offline devices** and **semi-online** devices (disk arrays). Examples of such devices include magnetic disks, optical disks, erasable optical disks, hard disks, floppy disks and CD-ROMs.

Centralized storage techniques allow you to make expensive equipment more cost-effective. In addition, the storage unit can be chosen according to criteria such as specific needs, access time, reliability and length of life of the device.

Data that is less recent, or used less often, can be transferred from expensive storage units to more economical devices that have a longer service life.

## File update synchronization

Nowadays, the increasing numbers of portable computers have created a new problem. This problem concerns the updating of these computers that are not permanently connected to their corporate networks.

The classical scenario is when two users access the same file on a server. In this case, a copy of this file can be stored on each of these client workstations. When a modification is made to the file on the server, the previous version of the file is replaced by the new version. Consequently, In order to determine whether or not a user has the latest version of a file, it is essential to know when the latest modification was made to the file. The file update and synchronization function operates on this principle. This function must be able to manage the different copies in existence by working with the dates and times concerned. Most current implementations can take into account only the most recent version. However Windows NT and 95 offer the 'My Briefcase' item, which can be used to synchronize two MBD files for updating at record level (the MDB extension is used for Microsoft Access database files).

## Archiving

In order to forestall potential faults, you need to implement a strategy for archiving important data. Archiving involves the backing up of data onto an offline device.

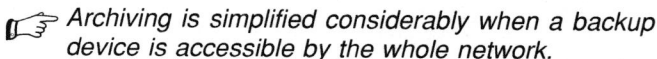
*Archiving is simplified considerably when a backup device is accessible by the whole network.*

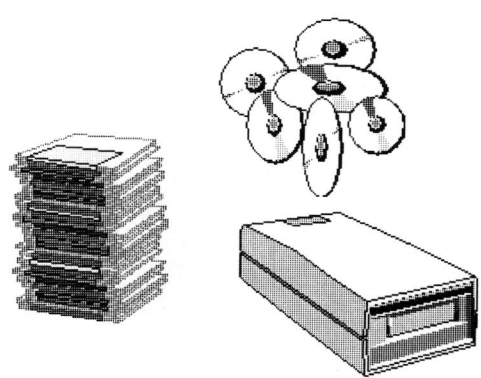

### b. Printing services

Printing services allow you to manage printing devices (such as printers and fax machines).

The objective of printing services is to share these exclusive devices so that printing jobs can be managed coherently. Priority rules and specific printing formats must also be administered.

In addition, the implementation of a spool queue allows you to restrict the overall number of printing devices, whilst ensuring concurrent access to peripherals. At operating system level, spool queue jobs are stored as temporary files.

Furthermore, some printing devices can be relatively expensive, such as an A0 color chart plotter for example. When you share such machines in this way, you make them more cost effective.

Increasingly, fax services are being integrated into corporate networks. This technique allows you to send and receive documents very easily. In addition, managing the queues reduces the waiting time considerably. Furthermore, this technique means that a printed copy of the fax is no longer necessary. In fact, your document is sent to a fictive printer, which is called your fax, and then forwarded to your recipients fax in electronic format.

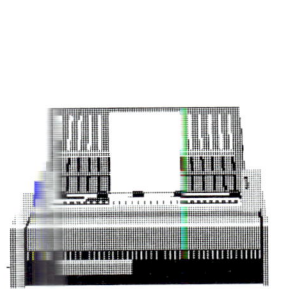

### c. Mail services

This type of service combines the storage, the use and the transmission of information. This information can include multimedia data, thanks to the use of embedded object techniques.

In addition to its file service function, mail services manage direct communication between users, or between applications. One of the functions of such communications is to notify the user when messages arrive.

Electronic mail, fax services and Internet newsgroups are the three fundamental services that are available.

The security and interactivity of these mail services have greatly contributed to their success.

In addition, **groupware** is a relatively recent technology that applies shared document management. This technology allows several users to communicate with each other, and to work together to solve problems.

☞ *Examples of such communication applications are Lotus Notes, Microsoft Exchange Server and Novell Group Wise.*

### d. Application services

Application services not only provide a means of sharing data, but they also offer processing power. These services allow you to divide tasks more efficiently amongst the most suitable machines. This allows selected machines to provide specialist internetwork server functions.

Suppose that you connect as a client to a server, and request the execution of a program on the server. If the server is a file server, the file associated with the program will be transferred across the network, loaded in memory on the client machine and executed on the client machine.

On the other hand, if the server is an applications server, peer-to-peer communication will be established and an exchange of messages will take place between the client and the server. The client will make a request and then await a response from the server. The client will request the execution of the program, the program will be executed on the server and the result of the execution will be returned to the client. In this case, the server processor will work for the client. In order to fulfill its role, an applications server requires a large amount of processing power (typically, an applications processor would be either a multiprocessor or at least a powerful monoprocessor machine). On the other hand, a file server would require plenty of (cached) memory so as to transfer the required data.

> *A network applications development platform must allow you to choose where, on the network, you wish to implement functions and procedures for client/server applications.*

### e. Database services

In client-server data applications it is generally the client that makes the request and processes the response. On the other hand, the server analyses the request and supplies the requested data. In this way, the physical location of the data on the server machine can be chosen in order to ensure data security and to optimize access times.

At the company level, only one database is visible. However, on a physical level, the database can be distributed, and even duplicated, in different locations. These techniques are used to improve response times, as local data can be accessed much quicker. This technique also causes a number of problems. These problems can concern the duplication of the data and, more critically, the update of the information. However, using data reproduction techniques, you can create several copies of a database and synchronize their update on the network.

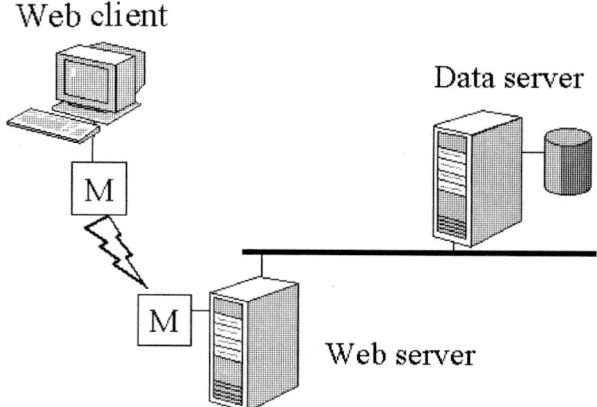

At present, there are two principal methods to ensure database consistency:

The first method involves using a master database that stores all new or modified data. The database management system must ensure that all modifications made to the master database are also implemented on the copy databases.

The second method involves storing modifications locally on each of the databases (which are copies of the master database). In this case, each local database management system is responsible for the consistency of the whole database set.

## C. The principal items of a network

In this section, we will define the main terms that are essential to a thorough understanding of network environments. We will clarify the fundamental differences between networks that have several clients and one server, and networks that function in a peer-to-peer environment. We will discuss the cases in which one of these configurations might be preferred to the other.

### 1. Software aspects

#### a. Principles

The network operating system is made up of different software layers (communications protocols, application layer and so on). It allows several (physically) interconnected people to work with the same **resources**.

It implements **network access checking** (login and resource access security). It also coordinates simultaneous access and manages queues for exclusive devices.

#### b. Definitions

Here is a set of terms that are frequently used in network environments:

**File server**

> File servers distribute files to clients that request them. To fulfill this function the server generally needs large amounts of memory that is often partly cached. This server is also used as a storage point to centralize documents. This helps with the audit, security and backup of data.

File services can be implemented in several ways.

For example, you can use SMB (Server Message Block) protocol. This is the file and print service protocol used by Microsoft networks.

This service is often called the **Server service**. For example, you can access this service on a Windows NT server:

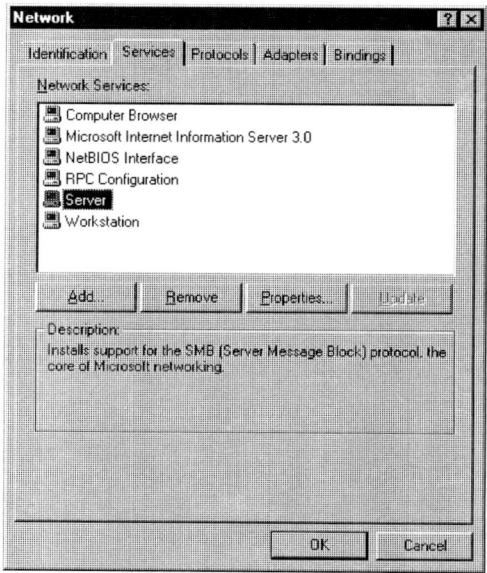

Similarly, on a Novell network, the **NCP** (Netware Core Protocol) protocol is used for Netware file and printing services.

In Unix environments, specific file services are used, such as **NFS** (Network File System), or **FTP** (File Transfer Protocol) or **HTTP** (HyperText Transfer Protocol), which is above all, a file transfer protocol.

### Dedicated server

A dedicated server is a specialized computer that is optimized to respond to requests. It cannot execute applications as a client. For example, the Novell Netware server is a dedicated server. All the commands recognized by these servers are specialized commands. They allow you to manage the server configuration. They also allow you to diagnose problems by monitoring the status of internal memory buffers.

### Non-dedicated server

A non-dedicated server operates in a peer-to-peer environment. It can be used as a server or as a client. The Microsoft NT server is a example of a non-dedicated server. All non-dedicated server applications can run either on a server, or on a client.

### Workstation

A workstation is a machine in a network from which a user can access the resources of a server. A workstation communicates with the server and with other workstations via a network interface card and a cable that links the machines to one another.

From a software viewpoint we speak of a **client**. A client must be associated with a corresponding service.

On a Windows 95 machine, the SMB client is called a **Client for Microsoft Networks**. On the same system an NCP client is called a **Client for Novell Networks**.

On a Windows NT machine, the SMB client is called a **Workstation service** (as shown in the example **Network** window below). On the same system an NCP client is called a **Client service for Netware Networks**.

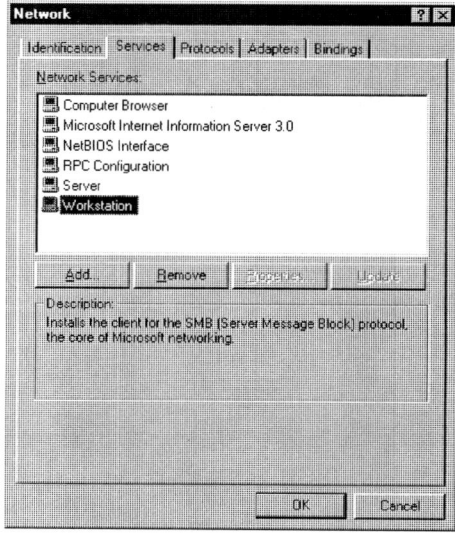

Finally for an ftp service, the client is called either, **ftp client** (ftp.exe program), or **Internet Explorer**, which integrates the management of several clients.

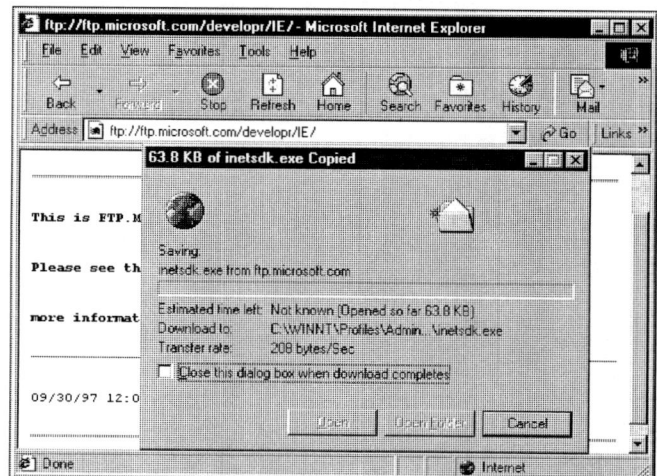

For example, on Microsoft networks, the forwarder concept means that a request sent to a device indicated with a local letter (for example G:) may be forwarded to a network path (for example \\SERVER1\SHARED). The local input/output manager then masks Local Procedure Call access, or Remote Procedure Call access, from the user.

**Print server**

The file server works closely with the print server. The file server stores the jobs that are to be printed on the print server. They are stored as files and organized in a defined file hierarchy. Then, the print server reads the files and transmits the print jobs to the available print devices, taking any priorities into account. In general, the print device is physically attached to the print server. However, the print device may be attached to a remote workstation. It may even be connected directly to a network interface card (for example HP LaserJet 4LM).

c. **The Network Operating System**

i) **Basic principles**

It is often the Network Operating System that defines the network architecture.

Some **network operating systems** are configured around **a central server**, whilst other network operating systems are **based on a peer-to-peer architecture**.

ii) **Differences between a peer-to-peer network and a centralized network**

**Peer-to-peer networks**

In a **peer-to-peer network** all machines have an identical role and act as both clients for some resources and servers for others. In general, there are relatively few machines in such networks. In this type of structure, the whole network shares resources, administrative tasks and security operations. Centralized control is impossible with this type of architecture. The user of each machine is also the machine's administrator.

Users of peer-to-peer networks should not be complete beginners, as they must work in a correctly structured environment.

Another drawback of peer-to-peer networks is that users cannot be managed on a centralized database. This means that access to resources cannot be checked according to the names of the users.

In a Microsoft Windows 95 environment, **workgroups** are used for this type of organization.

### Centralized networks

In a centralized network, each user has a username and a password. These items are entered and checked when the user opens a session. In addition, the user database is centralized.

This means that access to resources can be checked by applying **security at user level**. In this security mode, permissions are individualized for each user and for each available resource. This technique makes it much easier to know who is doing what, and when. One of the users is designated as the administrator, and must manage all the resources in the network. This is the most powerful user on the whole network.

☞ *Novell Netware is an example of a centralized architecture operating system.*

### iii) Resource level security versus user level security

#### Resource level security

With resource level security, the security is based on the resource concerned. In this case, a password is assigned to a given resource, and is independent of all users.

With resource level security, the user does not need to provide username and password identification. On the other hand, each time you request access to a new resource you must input the password for the resource concerned. This is taken as proof that you have the required permission to use the resource. Products such as Windows 3.x use this principle. Passwords associated with resources are memorized so that you do not need to specify them more than once.

In this way, specific permission is associated with a specific shared resource. Access to the resource is granted after verification of a password, which is independent of the users.

☞ *To prevent a user from accessing a resource, the administrator must modify the password to the resource. The administrator can then transmit the new password to the other users (to whom access must be granted).*

The following example shows permissions being assigned to a directory.

### User level security

User level security allows you to attribute permissions to access a given resource, specifically to each user. First the user must identify himself/herself on a reference system (such as a specific server or an NT domain). A session must be opened on the network and a username and password must be supplied. After these details have been checked, the user can access a certain number of resources.

In the following example a Windows NT directory is declared as shared so that the different users can access it. You need do this just once for each resource concerned.

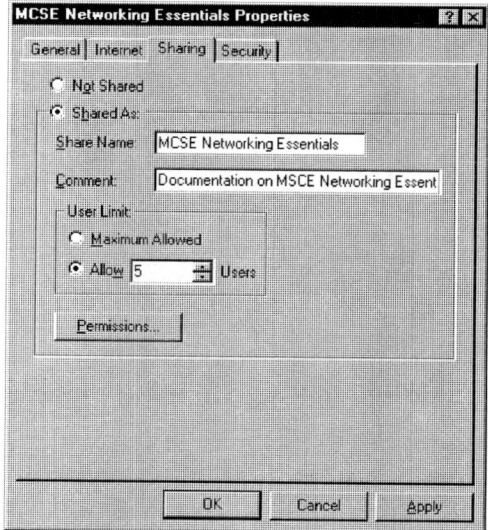

Specific permissions can be associated with this shared resource so as to allow individualized access.

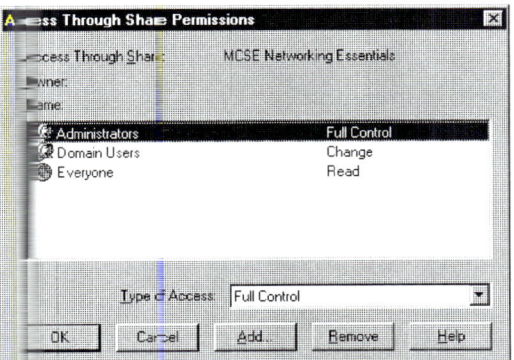

## Examples of network operating systems

Here are a few examples of network operating systems:

### These network operating systems work in a centralized server environment
Microsoft Windows NT
Novell Netware
Banyan Vines
Open VMS
Microsoft Windows 95, in user level security mode.

### These network operating systems work in a peer-to-peer environment
Microsoft Windows 95, in resource level security mode
AppleTalk (Apple Computers)
LANtastic (Artisoft)
Novell Personal Netware.

## 2. Hardware aspects

### a. Physical connections

For a network operating system to be operational, the various hardware items must be physically interconnected. You can connect two machines together using a serial cable (that must be connected to the serial ports of both machines). Alternatively, you can use a network interface card equipped with the necessary connections according to the network topology used (network cabling). The network cards provide the interface between the other network cards and the workstation.

### b. Communication protocols

In addition to the hardware, which ensures specific connectivity and the exchange of signals, certain communication rules must be followed. These rules give a meaning to the electronic signals that are exchanged between the machines. They also manage access to the shared media that link all the machines together.

# D. Environment protection

A company uses computing facilities to store its most important data. This data must be protected from unauthorized modification. In addition, confidentiality must be ensured. In this section, we will discuss how a company can protect its information. We will also discuss fault tolerance and, finally, we will examine the backup strategies that are most commonly used.

## 1. Reliability and confidentiality

Reliability and confidentiality have two basic aspects: the first concerns local considerations and the second concerns data exchange.

### a. Reliability

## Local aspects

### Redundancy

Redundancy is built into a system in order to ensure fault tolerance by duplicating data. You can use RAID (Redundant Array of Inexpensive Disks) techniques RAID and RAID 5, to ensure fault tolerance in this way.

### UPS

It is sometimes necessary to protect key network machines, such as servers, from voltage peaks and power-cuts. You can do this using a UPS (Uninterruptible Power Supply). UPS act as voltage filters. They are able to compensate for any deficiency in the mains power supply by switching the machine onto a battery.

### Transactional file systems

These transactional systems can be implemented explicitly at the system level (as with Novell Netware). Alternatively, they may be implemented implicitly by systematic logging all operations that are carried out (as with Windows NT NTFS).

### Data integrity and CRC

In addition, every file system checks the integrity of its data. CRC (Cyclic Redundancy Checks) is a commonly used technique for this purpose.

## Data exchange aspects

### Reliable physical transmission media

A simple way of ensuring reliability of data exchange is to use a reliable transmission medium that is not susceptible to electromagnetic disturbance. Optical fiber is an example of such a physical transmission medium.

### Synchronization points

When crucial data is being exchanged, such as database update information, you must implement a mechanism that will allow the system to recover if an incident occurs. You can do this by implementing **context backups** or **synchronization points**.

By logging the modifications that are made, these techniques allow you to recover the context that existed before the incident occurred. It is important to identify exactly which modifications had been taken into account by the last transaction that took place before the incident.

### Connection-oriented protocols

Connection-oriented protocols ensure data exchange reliability by using acknowledgement and CRC techniques.

#### b. Confidentiality

## Local aspects

### Secure file systems

The file system of the operating system can be used as a first means of ensuring data confidentiality.

To implement local security, you must be able to identify each access.

So as to identify each access, you must first authenticate the users. On a secure file system, this means you must rely on the initial authentication.

A good secure file system manages customized security at file level, by taking the system users into account.

☞ *Examples of secure file systems include those of Novell and Windows NT (NTFS).*

## Data exchange aspects

### Authentication

Setting up of a connection is often preceded by an authentication that validates access to the remote resources.

☞ *As anyone can dial a number to connect to a remote modem, the access must be checked.*

### Encryption

Information confidentiality is often necessary when data is transmitted. As you cannot ensure that your data frames will not be intercepted and in addition you cannot know when your data frames have been read, it is preferable to ensure that the information you transmit cannot be read by everyone.

☞ *Windows NT includes a network monitor as part of its standard supply. Although it is a limited version, it is nevertheless very powerful and allows you to capture and read data frames, very easily.*

### Internet and confidentiality

Subversive third parties can intercept confidential information, such as a credit card number, if this information is not encrypted.

For this reason encrypting is used for confidential information such a names, passwords and even the data content themselves.

The effectiveness of encryption methods varies from country to country, often according to the commercial legislation in the country concerned.

In the USA however, encryption developed independently and the government has given up pursuing the authors of encryption methods who have made their algorithms available on the Internet.

Increasingly, encryption is being integrated into protocols, such as PPTP (Point to Point Tunneling Protocol).

☞ *The features that are offered by the SSL (Secure Socket Layer) are subject to government legislation in many countries. For example, you can be authorized to encrypt information on the Internet on a certain number of bits (e.g. 128 bits). This encryption may be validated for data transmission only after a transmission certificate has been issued (for which you have to pay). However, security certificates do not authorize payment by credit card. They simply allow you to encrypt data.*

Most sites use this functionality. In many countries, methods that are not officially approved by the government concerned may be considered as war items and may result in serious sanctions. However, such attitudes are gradually changing so as to favor more widespread commercial activity on the Web.

## 2. Data redundancy

### a. Fault tolerance

Fault tolerance is the ability of a hardware or software configuration to accommodate one or more failures that could otherwise prevent correct functioning of the system, or hinder a user or process.

There are several levels of fault tolerance:

### Software fault tolerance

Software fault tolerance involves the implementation of RAID (Redundant Array of Inexpensive Disks). This is the fault tolerance level that is most commonly used. It is also a very flexible method as disks can be changed whilst the system is functioning (hot plug). However, RAID can be expensive to implement.

### Hardware fault tolerance

This fault tolerance level concerns failure of external disk drives. A system has hardware fault tolerance when replacement disks are available in the drive bay.

### Multiple servers

This level concerns the introduction of multiple servers. This means that the environment includes redundant servers.

### Multiple servers with data duplication

The major drawback with the multiple server tolerance level is that data is not available simultaneously on the redundant servers. Consequently, a multi-server environment is required, in which data is duplicated in the network.

### Multiple servers with data mirroring

With this level, the data is duplicated on mirrored disks. This is implemented on a private connection that links up the disks of different servers.

### Server mirroring

With this level, it is the servers that are mirrored. This means that one server can replace its mirror at any moment. Data is automatically duplicated on a fast connection.

### Clustering with RAID hardware

Clustering is the technique of connecting two or more computers together so that they appear to be just one computer. For example, suppose we have two servers clustered together using RAID hardware. The two servers will access the same information on the RAID external rack. In addition, the servers have a special link that allows each of the servers to detect failure of the other server.

### b. Disk mirroring

In mirror mode, two or more hard disks are associated on the same channel. Data blocks are stored simultaneously on the primary disk and on the secondary disk.

The disks carry out the same work, at the same time: they record and update the same files. If one of the disks fails, the other disk continues running without interruption or loss of data.

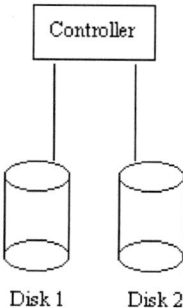

☞ *Mirror mode alone is not sufficient to protect your data. For example, data may still be lost if the computer itself fails, or if both disks fail at the same time (due to channel failure for example). It is advisable therefore, to make backup copies regularly.*

If one of the disks fails, the operating system emits a message to indicate the incident. This is done so that mirror mode protection can be reimplemented as soon as possible. As this mode duplicates data on the same channel, it does not guarantee protection between the hard disks and the server in case of a failure on the channel. In fact, an incident on the channel could lead to failure of both disks.

☞ *Both Windows NT Server and Novell Netware allow you to implement disk mirroring.*

### c. Mirroring controllers and disks

This method of data duplication ensures a better level of data protection. It consists of copying simultaneously, data on two different disks, using two separate channels. This technique is known as duplexing.

In this way, data is protected either in the event of a hard disk failure or in the case of failure of a channel between a hard disk and the server (this channel includes the disk controller and the interface cable). If any part of one channel fails, the other disk continues to function correctly without interruption or loss of data. This is because the data is transmitted on the other channel. The operating system sends a warning message to indicate that one of the units has failed.

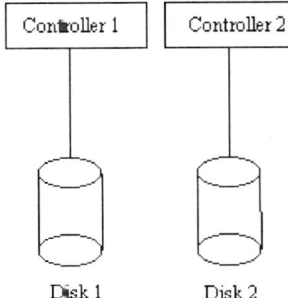

☞ *Duplexing does not guarantee full data protection. For example, data may still be lost if the computer itself fails, or if both channels fail at the same time. It is advisable therefore, to make backup copies regularly.*

In duplexed mode, data is recorded on all the disks simultaneously. As the disks are on different channels, data transfer is quicker than when only the disks are mirrored. This is because with the latter configuration, data is transmitted successively to each disk via the same channel.

Duplexing allows you to make a distributed search request that sends read requests to several disks. Also, if several requests arrive at once they can be divided up among the disks and processed simultaneously.

### d. Mirroring servers

Mirroring servers provides fault tolerance to level SFT III (System Fault Tolerance III). This configuration involves a secondary server, which is identical to the primary server. In case of failure of the primary server, the secondary server takes over immediately.

The two servers that are mirrored should have similar characteristics. It is preferable that both machines have the same CPU speed, memory and disk storage capacity.

The two servers do not need to have the same CPU, nor do they need to have the same CPU version or clock speed. However, it is advisable to use identical servers in order to obtain better performance. If you have two servers at two different speeds, SFT III adjusts itself to the slower of the two.

The servers must be connected directly to each other by a server mirror link. This is a fast link that allows information to be updated via a special card that is installed on each of the servers.

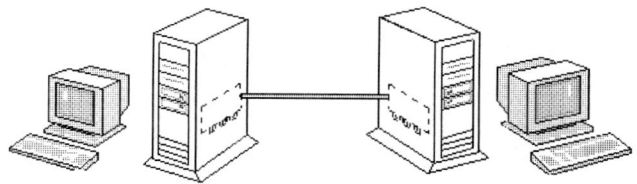

☞ *Novell Netware does not offer server mirroring as a standard functionality.*

### e. Disk striping with parity

**RAID 5**

Disk striping with parity is the fault tolerance technique that is most commonly used. This is implemented using RAID technology. RAID offers a hardware solution and a software solution. With hardware RAID, the operating system sees only one logical disk. On the other hand, with software RAID, the different physical disks are visible to the operating system and can be managed individually.

☞ RAID 3 also implements a version of disk striping with parity. In this case the parity is stored on a specific disk. On the other hand, with RAID 5, parity information is written to a different disk on each stripe set.

**Disk striping**

Disk striping involves reading and writing in parallel from and to several hard disks (at least two hard disks are required for disk striping, plus a further disk for the parity).

☞ RAID 0 does not provide fault tolerance. However, it does improve disk input/output performance.

**Parity**

In addition to disk striping, parity information is written to the last disk. This technique allows you to recover the data in case of failure of any of the disks.

Suppose you have a configuration with n disks. The information that must be stored is split up and shared between n-1 disks.

Suppose we want to write '110 101 001' to the stripe set of four disks.

We calculate the parity as follows: for each bit position on each of the disks, the parity bit is calculated. The parity bit for each position in a stripe is determined so that the total number of '1' for that position is even.

Thus, if we take the first bit position for each of the three disks, we obtain:

'110'. In order that the total number of '1' is even for the four disks, the first bit position on disk 4 must be '0'. Thus, there is an even number of '1' (two of them) for the set of four disks

Similarly, using the symbols in the second position ('100') we must choose '1' for the parity bit in the second position on the fourth disk. Finally, after applying this algorithm to the third position, we obtain '010' as the parity information to be written to the fourth disk.

In case of failure of a disk, for example the third disk, we can now recalculate the data that was lost. We calculate this in exactly the same way as we calculated the parity information.

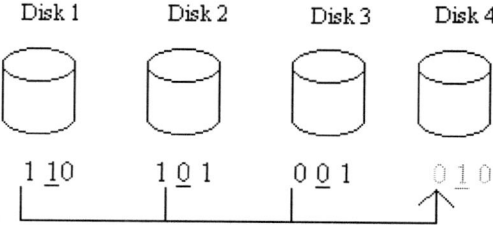

Thus, using the disks 1, 2 and 4, we take all the first bits: '110'. Using these bits we calculate the first bit for disk 3 so as to obtain a parity sum of 1's: this bit then, is '0'.

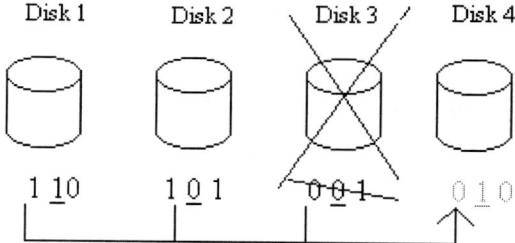

The same operation is applied to the symbols in the second position and to those in the third position. This gives us '001' for the third disk. This technique then, allows us to re-constitute the overall information: '110 101 001', even when one of the disks fails.

> At the lowest level, parity is calculated applying an exclusive OR (XOR) operator. Thus the parity information for the disk 4 in the above example is as follows: d4 = 110 XOR 101 XOR 001 = 010. Using the same method, it is easy to obtain the information for any of the disks. For example, d3 = 110 XOR 101 XOR 010 = 001.

### f. Neutralizing bad sectors

This technique allows you to guarantee correct data storage on a disk ever if it has bad sectors. Every piece of data to be stored on disk, is written in a background task and then checked. This checking consists of making sure that the data in memory is the same as that written on the disk. If a write operation is unsuccessful after a certain number of attempts, the sector concerned is marked as a bad sector and the data is redirected to an area of the disk that reserved for this purpose. Sectors that are marked in this way are no longer used.

> For example, on Novell Netware, by default, 2% of a disk partition is reserved for data that is redirected in this way. This area is called "Hot fix".

### 3. Archiving strategies

For each file that is created or modified, the operating system either sets the **archive attribute to 'A'**, or updates the **last modification date**. Using this information, the operating system can determine which files have been created or modified since a certain date.

> Microsoft and Novell products use an archive attribute. Unix systems work with file timestamps.

The company will determine an archiving strategy by answering the following questions:

Which files must be backed up?

What type of backup must be used?

When must backing up operations take place?

To how many volumes must the backup be made?

Is it more important to backup quickly or to restore quickly?

How many tapes must be used and how should they be used (tape rotation)?

### a. Full backup

When a full backup is made, the archive attribute of the files are reset to '0'. This signifies that the file has been backed up. Systems that work with dates, memorize the last backup date so as to distinguish between those files that have been backed up and those files that have not been backed up (using the last modification date).

### b. Incremental backup

Incremental backups also mark the files as having been recorded. This type of backup is often carried out daily, and records the modifications that were made on the day concerned. A weekly strategy may consist of making a full backup on Fridays and an incremental backup on the other days.

Incremental backups minimize the daily backup time. On the other hand, if a complete restore must be made up to Thursday, for example, the tape of the preceding Friday must be restored followed by the tape corresponding to each of the days from Monday to Thursday.

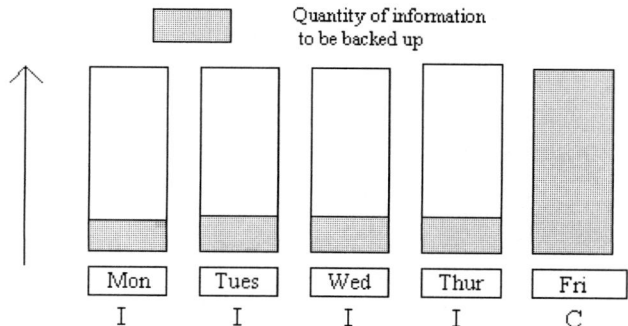

I = Incremental backup
C = Full backup

### c. Differential backup

This type of backup is also often carried out daily. However, differential backups do not mark the files as having been recorded (they do not reset the archive attribute to zero). Because of this, on each new backup, the previous modifications are taken into account, as well as those that have been made on the day concerned.

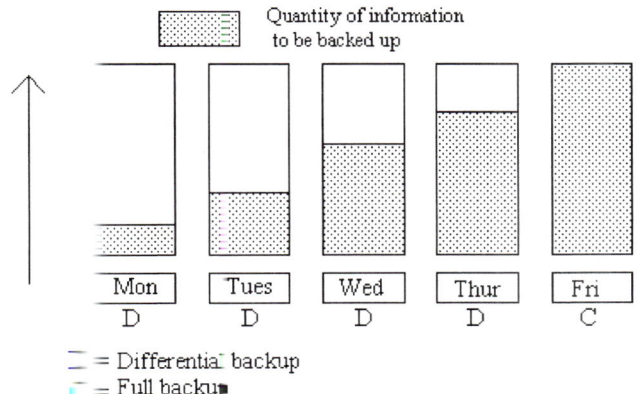

- = Differential backup
- = Full backup

Differential backups minimize the restore time. This is because a restore requires only two tapes (the full backup tape and the last differential tape). On the other hand, the daily backup takes more and more time each day.

## Exercises

To be absolutely sure that you have assimilated this chapter, work through the corresponding exercises. These are set out from page 373.

☒ Networking overview.

## Assessing your skills

Try the following questions if you think you know this chapter well enough.

*History*

1 What is the name of the network that was the initial project at the origin of the Internet? ☐

2 Which family of protocols, became the standard that is used for network interconnection? ☐

3 How did TCP/IP come to be known to the public? ☐

4 Give the names of two standards organizations that took part in creating network standards. ☐

*Overview of network technology*

5 What is a network called that can be used for a company or for a site? ☐

6 Two subsidiaries of a company in London and Paris, are interconnected using an ISDN (Integrated Services Digital Network) link at a speed of 128 Kbps. What is this type of overall network called? ☐

# Essentials

7 What sort of network is the Internet? ❏

8 What are the different types of file storage? ❏

9 Which software item allows you to share the access to a print device? ❏

10 What sort of service allows you to exchange mail messages with other users? ❏

11 Which service allows you to spread processing load over several machines? ❏

12 Which service allows you to manage information and guarantee data integrity? ❏

13 Which resource does a file server use the most heavily? ❏

14 Which resource does an applications server use the most heavily? ❏

## Items of a network

15 Which network operating system can be used to implement a dedicated server? ❏

16 Which service, in its standard version, can be used to make files and printer spool queues available on Microsoft machines in a network? ❏

17 What types of service do ftp and NCP provide?

18 Which protocol is associated with the server service on a Windows NT server?

19 Which program is supplied with Windows 95 as the client for an ftp server?

20 Which protocol refers to the client for Netware networks on a machine running Windows 95?

21 What type of network architecture is used for a network in which security is not essential?

22 Which type of network is composed of machines that can be both clients and servers?

23 With which type of network architecture can each user be considered as the administrator of his/her own machine?

24 What type of security requires initial authentication of the users before they can access resources?

25 Which type of security allows you to define individualized access to resources?

26 Which type of security allows you to manage resource access, using a password for each resource?

27  Give one example of a network operating system that is based on user level security, and another example of a network operating system that is based on resource level security.

28  Which type of network architecture is suitable for environments that include over 10 users?

### Environment protection

29  Which system can be used to protect a computing system in the event of a failure of the mains power supply?

30  Give an example of a transactional file system that offers individualized security for each user.

31  Which method can be used to ensure data exchange reliability?

32  Which method can be used to ensure data exchange confidentiality?

33  Give an example of a protocol that allows you to create a private connection on the Internet.

34  Which fault tolerance technique also improves input/output performance?

35  Which is the more effective fault tolerance technique: mirroring and duplexing?

36 Which weekly archiving strategy allows you to minimize the time required for daily backup?  ☐

_____
_____

## Results

Check your answers on pages 51 to 54. Count one point for each correct answer.

Number of points ⬚ /36

For this chapter you need to have scored at least 27 out of 36.

Look at the list of key points that follows. Pick out the ones with which you have had difficulty and work through them again in this chapter before moving on to the next.

## Key points of the chapter

- ☐ History.
- ☐ Overview of network technology.
- ☐ Items of a network.
- ☐ Environment protection.

# Solutions

## History

1 What is the name of the network that was the initial project at the origin of the Internet?

*ARPANET.*

2 Which family of protocols, became the standard that is used for network interconnection?

*TCP/IP*

3 How did TCP/IP come to be known to the public?

*The TCP/IP sources were diffused to universities as part of Unix BSD. In addition, a little later the American government made it obligatory to use the TCP/IP protocol.*

4 Give the names of two standards organizations that took part in creating network standards.

*The International Standards Organization (ISO) and the Institute of Electrical and Electronic Engineers.*

## Overview of network technology

5 What is a network called that can be used for a company or for a site?

*A LAN (Local Area Network).*

6 Two subsidiaries of a company in London and Paris, are interconnected using an ISDN (Integrated Services Digital Network) link at a speed of 128 Kbps. What is this type of overall network called?

*A company network.*

7 What sort of network is the Internet?

*A WAN (Wide Area Network).*

8 What are the different types of file storage?

*Online, offline and semi-online.*

9 Which software item allows you to share the access to a print device?

*A print queue (print spool).*

10 What sort of service allows you to exchange mail messages with other users?

*The mail service.*

11 Which service allows you to spread processing load over several machines?

*The applications service.*

13 Which service allows you to manage information and guarantee data integrity?

*The database service.*

13 Which resource does a file server use the most heavily?

*The machine memory, as it is cached.*

14 Which resource does an applications server use the most heavily?

*The CPU.*

## Items of a network

15 Which network operating system can be used to implement a dedicated server?

*Novell Netware.*

16 Which service, in its standard version, can be used to make files and printer spool queues available on Microsoft machines in a network?

*The server service (SMB protocol).*

17 What types of service do ftp and NCP provide?

*Ftp provides file services. NCP provides file and print services.*

18 Which protocol is associated with the server service on a Windows NT server?

*The SMB (Server Message Block) protocol.*

19 Which program is supplied with Windows 95 as the client for an ftp server?

*The ftp.exe program.*

20 Which protocol refers to the client for Netware networks on a machine running Windows 95?

*NCP (Network Core Protocol).*

21 What type of network architecture is used for a network in which security is not essential?

*Peer-to-peer architecture.*

22 Which type of network is composed of machines that can be both clients and servers?

*A peer-to-peer network.*

23 With which type of network architecture can each user be considered as the administrator of his/her own machine?

*Peer-to-peer architecture.*

24 What type of security requires initial authentication of the users before they can access resources?

*User level security.*

25 Which type of security allows you to define individualized access to resources?

*User level security.*

26 Which type of security allows you to manage resource access, using a password for each resource?

*Resource level security.*

27 Give one example of a network operating system that is based on user level security, and another example of a network operating system that is based on resource level security.

*Resource level security: Windows 95 (by default).*
*User level security: Windows NT.*

28 Which type of network architecture is suitable for environments that include over 10 users?

*Client-server architecture.*

### Environment protection

29 Which system can be used to protect a computing system in the event of a failure of the mains power supply?

*UPS (Uninterruptible Power Supply).*

30 Give an example of a transactional file system that offers individualized security for each user.

*NTFS (New Technology File System), the Windows NT file system.*

31 Which method can be used to ensure data exchange reliability?

*Connection-oriented protocol with acknowledgements, CRC and synchronization points.*

32 Which method can be used to ensure data exchange confidentiality?

*Encryption.*

33 Give an example of a protocol that allows you to create a private connection on the Internet.

*PPTP (Point to Point Tunneling Protocol).*

34 Which fault tolerance technique also improves input/output performance?

*RAID 3 or 5.*

35 Which is the more effective fault tolerance technique: mirroring and duplexing?

*Duplexing offers more effective fault tolerance as it duplicates entire input/output channels.*

36 Which weekly archiving strategy allows you to minimize the time required for daily backup?

*An archiving strategy that involves a full backup on Fridays and an incremental backup on the other days.*

## Prerequisites for this chapter

- General knowledge of networking.

## Objectives

When you have completed this chapter you will be able to:
- Define the OSI model.
- Define the roles of each layer of the OSI model.
- Explain the encapsulation and the de-encapsulation of a layered network model.
- Describe the role of a protocol.
- Define the different types of standard.
- Give examples of standards organizations.

# Protocol standards

## Summary

**A. The OSI model . . . . . . . . . . . . . . 57**
    1. Overview . . . . . . . . . . . . . . . . . . . . 57
    2. Communications between layers . . . . . . . 58
    3. Encapsulation of the OSI model . . . . . . . . 60
    4. Role of the different layers . . . . . . . . . . . 61

**B. Standards and organizations . . . . . 65**
    1. Protocols . . . . . . . . . . . . . . . . . . . . 65
    2. Types of standard . . . . . . . . . . . . . . . . 66
    3. Standards organizations . . . . . . . . . . . . 66

An important event in the opening of networks was the definition of the OSI reference model. This model is composed of seven layers and must be present on each machine that wishes to communicate on a network. Each layer has its own set of features and provides services to the layers that are immediately adjacent to it.

## A. The OSI model

INTERNATIONAL ORGANIZATION FOR STANDARDIZATION

### 1. Overview

The OSI (Open System Interconnection) model of the ISO (International Organization for Standardization) provided an alternative to proprietary systems. It appeared in 1984 (10 years after TCP/IP). It defines a model in seven layers with the objective of standardizing data exchange between two machines. This model provides a precise definition of the functions associated with each layer. Each layer behaves as a service provider for the layer immediately above it. A layer can send data, or a command, to the corresponding layer on another machine. To do this it must construct a frame and send it via all the layers below it.

Each layer adds a specific header. At the destination, the frame is decoded and data, or the command, is extracted.

```
7 - APPLICATION
6 - PRESENTATION
5 - SESSION
4 - TRANSPORT
3 - NETWORK
2 - DATA LINK
1 - PHYSICAL
```

## 2. Communications between layers

Each layer provides a precise function when data is transmitted. In fact, this is a sort of "divide and rule" approach. Each layer (for example, layer N) uses the layer underneath it (**layer N-1**) and provides services to the layer above it (**layer N+1**).

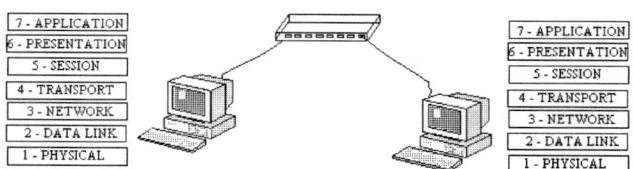

### a. The kings analogy

This mechanism can be compared to two medieval kings who want to exchange messages. The kings rule two kingdoms: A and B. The first king gives a parchment to his chamberlain. The chamberlain gives instructions to his henchman. In turn, the henchman gives instructions to a messenger to forward the precious parchment to the destination kingdom.

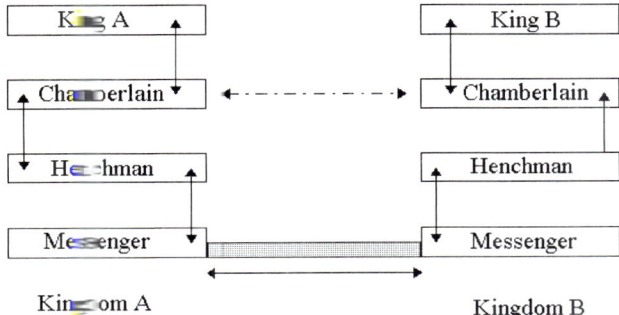

The henchman of kingdom B receives the parchment together with the instructions indicated by the henchman of kingdom A. These instructions request that the parchment is passed up to the chamberlain of king B. Chamberlain B reads the instructions indicated by chamberlain A. These instructions request chamberlain B to give the parchment to king B. King B can now read the message from king A.

Everything functions as if the network layer of one computer communicated directly with the corresponding layer of the other computer (for example, between the two chamberlains).

In reality, the message can be forwarded to its destination because the information goes down to the messenger who can carry the data to the other kingdom (the messenger is the physical layer which transmits the signal containing the data to be sent). When the information reaches the destination machine, it is passed up through the layers and each layer interprets the instructions of the corresponding layer of the sender.

## 3. Encapsulation of the OSI model

When a network layer on one machine wishes to communicate with the corresponding layer on another machine, the only way it can do this is by adding to the data, instructions for the corresponding layer on the destination machine and passing the instructions and the data, down to the layer below it. In this way, the header and the data of layer N become the data of the layer N-1. The layer N-1 then composes a heading (its own instructions for the layer N-1 on the destination machine). This header plus the N-1 data, become the data for layer N-2.

This process, of placing data inside a box together with the instructions for this data, is called **encapsulation**.

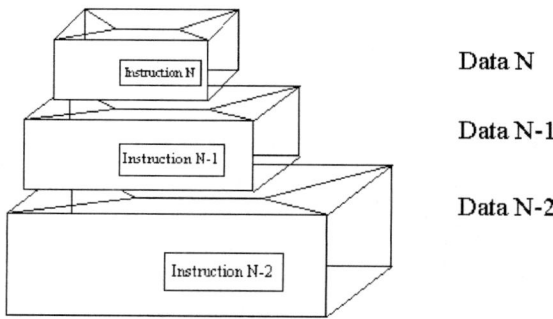

When the box reaches the destination machine, it is opened and the instructions are read. The (smaller) box that is found inside the opened box is transmitted according to these instructions.

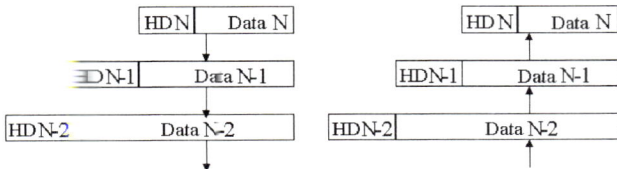

## 4. Role of the different layers

Each network layer defined by the model has a precise role. These roles range from transmission of the signal containing the data, to the presentation of the information to the destination application.

### a. Physical layer

This is the layer on which the signals are transmitted. These signals can be **electrical**, **electromagnetic** or **optical**. These signals contain the coded numerical data (0 and 1). This layer corresponds to all the connecting hardware on the network: network card, cables and so on.

Examples of these connecting items are the RS232C and V24 interfaces

### b. Data link layer

This is the layer that translates the numerical data into signals. The data bits are organized in frames. A header is created which identifies the **physical addresses**, 6 bytes long, of both emitter and receiver.

This layer adds a **CRC** (Cyclic Redundancy Check), which allows the detection of certain transmission problems. This CRC is generally a sum calculated from a high level polynomial. When the data link layer receives this frame, it recalculates this sum and compares it with that which was transmitted. If a difference is found, the frame is rejected.

The OSI model offers an HDLC (High-Level Data Link Control) implementation for this layer.

Other proprietary models offer other protocols. For example, IBM offers the SDLC (Synchronous Data Link Control) protocol, which is part of its SNA (System Network Architecture) protocol suite. Also, ITU offers the LAPB (Link Access Procedure Balanced) protocol for its model. The ITU model uses the X.25 protocol suite.

**c. Network layer**

This layer selects **the best route** to get to the destination address. Whereas the physical address can be used to identify a local device, a **logical address** can be used to identify a global network component. For this purpose, some protocols identify network devices using a number that identifies the network, combined with a number that identifies a machine in this network. Examples of such protocols are IP (Internet Protocol) and IPX (Internetworking Packet eXchange).

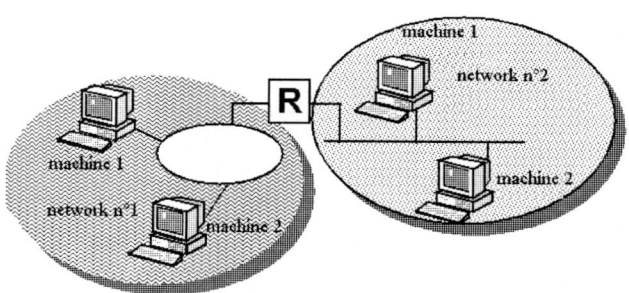

To reach a destination machine, **a cost is calculated**. This cost depends on a number of parameters such as the number of networks that must be crossed, transmission time, communications costs and line congestion. This cost is used as the criteria to decide if one route is better than another.

Other protocols that are used include CLNP (ConnectionLess Network Protocol), CONS (Connection Oriented Network Service) and X.25 PLP (Packet Level Protocol).

# Essentials

### d. Transport layer

This is the heart of the OSI model. This layer ensures a **connection oriented** service. It ensures that all the data has been transmitted without problems. First, acknowledgements must be received for all packets sent. Also, each acknowledgement must be received within a given time limit. (this time limit corresponds to twice the return time that should normally be required). If an acknowledgement is not received within this time limit, then the packet is considered to have been lost and is retransmitted. In addition, connection oriented mode provides a connection service that allows the layer above the transport layer, to consider the connection as if it were a point-to-point link.

Whilst the network layer chooses the best path with a global view of the inter-network, the transport layer ensures the **reliability** of the data that is received.

Protocols such as TCP and SPX (in addition to TP0, TP1, TP2, TP3 and TP4) allow the implementation of these services, from their simplest form (connectionless) to their most elaborate form (connection oriented).

### e. Session layer

The session layer also has a connection-oriented mode. This layer manages synchronization points and context backups to enable recovery in the event of an incident occurring.

This layer generally manages the connection to a shared resource on the network.

☞ *The MAP commands (NET USE for Novell and Microsoft LAN Manager for Windows 3.1, Windows 95 and Windows NT) allow you to set up a connection to a resource such as a directory, by associating a logical letter with the resource concerned.*

## f. Presentation layer

This layer manages the **formatting of the data**. It ensures that the data conforms to international parameters (codes, formats...).

☞ *Typically, this is the role of HTML (HyperText Markup Language).*

This layer also manages encryption and decryption (for example encryption and decryption of names and passwords entered to request the opening of a session). It also manages data compression and decompression.

☞ *It must be remembered that, according to whether the machine is the emitter or the receiver, this layer will either encrypt and compress, or decrypt and decompress.*

The presentation layer works to specifications such as ANS.1 (Abstract Syntax Notation 1 of the ITU), BER (Basic Encoding Rules) and MIME (Multipurpose Internet Mail Extensions).

## g. Application layer

This layer is the communication interface with the user. This can be in either graphical or text mode. It can be implemented in the form of specific **programs**. Alternatively, it can take the form of as a set of **commands** of the network operating system, which can be entered directly by the user.

This layer also manages **communication between applications** such as electronic mail.

Example implementations of the application layer include the following:
- FTAM (File Transfer Access and Management),
- CMIP (Common Management Information Protocol), which allows you to monitor or administer resources, remotely,
- MHS (Message Handling Systems or X.400), which is an international standard method of transmitting messages,
- X.500 or Directory Services, which is a standard relating to the management of distributed databases.

## B. Standards and organizations

In this section we will define the protocol concept and describe existing standards. Then, we will describe the main networking standards organizations, together with a few examples of the standards for which these organizations have been responsible.

### 1. Protocols

The OSI model specifies the functions concerned by each of seven networking layers.

In practical terms, the model is implemented to perform its different functions using a set of **protocols**.

A protocol is a set of communication rules that specify the format in which data must be transmitted across a network.

One or more protocols are used to describe each of the layers, or functions, from the physical layer, to the application layer. Ideally, there would be one protocol per layer.

In practice however, some protocols operate on several layers; some protocols operate on one specific layer and some protocols operate on parts of layers, as defined by the OSI model.

In this context, it must not be forgotten that many protocols existed already when this model appeared. Certain manufacturers adapted their protocols to the model, whilst others continued to use their protocols without modifying them.

☞ *At present, TCP/IP is resisting and even gaining ground with respect to the OSI model.*

## 2. Types of standard

A distinction is made between the legal standards and those offered by manufacturers. The former are called **de jure** standards, whilst the latter are **de facto** standards, because of their widespread use.

In addition, there are **proprietary** standards, which are those that have been invented or are controlled by a commercial organization, and **non proprietary** standards, which are those that have been developed by a standards organization.

## 3. Standards organizations

Standards do not have a unique source. In general, a standards organization coordinates the specification of different hardware and software solutions. Amongst these organizations, there is a relatively small number that have set up the majority of national and international network standards. Each of these organizations specializes in a different area of network activity.

### a. ANSI (American National Standards Institute)

ANSI was created by North American business groups and industrial organizations. This organization develops standards relating to commerce and communications. It works essentially on codes, alphabets, signalization models, programming languages and the SCSI interface.

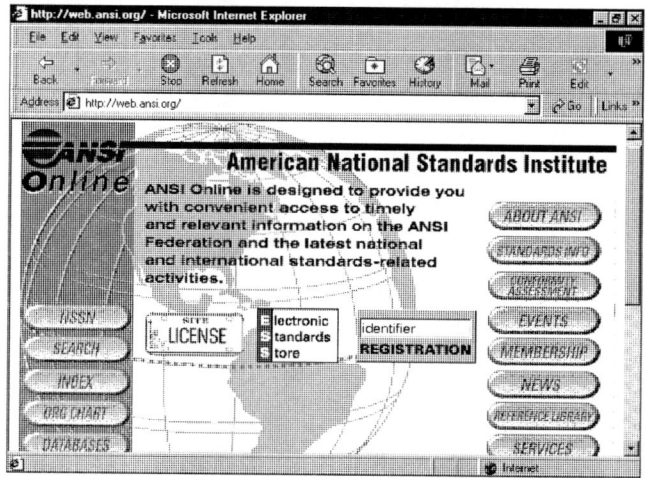

☞ *The ANSI represents the USA at the ISO and the ITU.*

**Examples of standards developed by ANSI:**
- ANSI/IEEE 802.3: CSMA/CD (Carrier Sense Multiple Access/Collision Detection).
- ANSI X3.135: standardization of SQL (Structured Query Language)
- ANSI X3T9.5: FDDI (Fiber Distributed Data Interface) specification.
- Standards for porting programming languages such as FORTRAN, COBOL and C.

### b. COSE (Common Open Software Environment)

This is a consortium that includes HP, IBM, Santa Cruz Operation (SCO), SunSoft (Sun Microsystems), Univel (Novell) and USL (part of Novell). Its purpose is to standardize the Unix desktop and applications environment and development. This group was launched by OSF (Open Software Foundation) in March 1993. The main product of this work is **CDE** (Common Desk Environment).

COSE's objectives include:
- The specification of application program interfaces (AFI) for common graphical environments.
- The specification of a common network environment.
- The definition of system management and distributed systems administration.

### c. CCITT

CCITT is part of the ITU (*International Telecommunications Union*) which in turn is part of the UNO (United Nations Organization). The CCITT committee studies and recommends the use of communications standards from all over the world. It publishes its recommendations every four years.

The CCITT protocols concern modems, networks and fax transmission.

It comprises fifteen working groups, which are referenced for A to U. Each group develops standards in a different field.

**Examples of standards developed by CCITT:**

### The V Series

This covers a set of standards for the design and functionality of modems:
- V.32bis is the standard for synchronous and asynchronous transmission up to 14 400 bauds.
- V.42bis defines the compression of modem data using the Lempel Ziv algorithm.

### The X Series

This concerns OSI standards:
- X.200 defines the OSI reference model.
- X.25 specifies the packet-switching network interface.
- X.400 standardizes message processing (email).
- X.500 defines the management of directories in a distributed environment (for example Novell 4 directories).

### d. COS (Corporation for Open Systems)

COS ensures compatibility between products that adhere to OSI and ISDN standards. This organization supplies standards for OSI products. Amongst the services it offers are compliancy testing, certification and promotion of OSI products.

### e. EIA (Electronic Industries Association)

This association groups together North American manufacturers of electronic parts and equipment. It develops industrial standards for interfaces between data processing and communications devices. EIA works closely with ANSI and CCITT.

#### Example of a standard developed by EIA:
- RS232 is a standard for serial connections using DB9 or DB25 connectors.

## f. IEEE (Institute of Electrical and Electronics Engineers)

The IEEE publishes sets of standards on data communications. The 802 committees form a subgroup of the IEEE that has been developing standards since February 1980 (hence the name: 80 for 1980 and 2 for February). This is a set of 14 committees, each active in a different field.

### Examples of standards developed by IEEE:
- 802.3 concerns bus networks that use CSMA/CD (Carrier Sense Multiple Access/Collision Detection)
- 802.5 concerns token-ring networks.
- 802.11 concerns wireless LANs.

## g. ISO (International Standards Organization)

The ISO is an international organization. In the computing field, the ISO defines international standards for all open network environments.

### Example of an ISO standard:
- The OSI model.

## h. OMG (Object Management Group)

OMG is concerned with a set of standards on programming languages, interfaces and protocols. It groups together over 300 companies including DEC, HP and SunSoft.

### Example of OMG work:
- Development of OMA (Object Management Architecture). OMA is a model for object oriented applications and environments.

## i. OSF (Open Software Foundation)

OSF's objective is to develop computing environments by combining technologies from different manufacturers.

### Example of OSF work:
- OSF/user graphical interfaces.

**j. SAG (SQL Access Group)**

This consortium groups together 39 companies including HP, Digital, Oracle Corporation and Sun Microsystems. Its role is to work with ISO in order to ensure compatibility between front end and back end systems.

SAG aims to promote compatibility amongst SQL (Structured Query Language) standards, relational databases and SQL utilities.

# Exercises

To be absolutely sure that you have assimilated this chapter, work through the corresponding exercises. These are set out from page 381.

☒ Types of communication.

# Assessing your skills

Try the following questions if you think you know this chapter well enough.

### The OSI model

1 How many layers does the OSI model define? ☐

2 What are the names of the OSI model layers? ☐

3 What does horizontal communication signify in the context of the OSI model? ☐

**Essentials**

4 Why is vertical communication necessary in the context of the OSI model? ❏

5 Which model is the more recent: OSI or TCP/IP? ❏

6 At which level does data transmission actually take place? ❏

***Role of the different layers***

7 Which layer ensures the formatting of the data? ❏

8 Which layer introduces the physical addressing? ❏

9 On which layer of the OSI model does IPX operate? ❏

10 On which layer of the OSI model does TCP operate? ❏

11 Which layer introduces the logical addressing? ❏

12 Which layer introduces a CRC to detect any transmission errors? ❏

13 Which layer transmits a digital signal? ❏

14 Are TCP segments encapsulated in IP, or the inverse? ☐

## Types of standard

15 What is a protocol? ☐

16 What is a de facto standard? ☐

17 What is a non proprietary standard? ☐

## Standards organizations

18 Which organization developed the CDE? ☐

19 Which organization was responsible for standards such as V.32, X.25 and X.500? ☐

20 Which organization was responsible for the RS232 standard? ☐

# Results

Check your answers on pages 74 to 76. Count one point for each correct answer.

Number of points ☐ /20

For this chapter you need to have scored at least 15 out of 20.

Look at the list of key points that follows. Pick out the ones with which you have had difficulty and work through them again in this chapter before moving on to the next.

# Key points of the chapter

- ☐ The OSI model.
- ☐ Role of the different layers.
- ☐ Types of standard.
- ☐ Standards organizations.

# Solutions

## The OSI model

1 How many layers does the OSI model define?

*7.*

2 What are the names of the OSI model layers?

*Physical, Data Link, Network, Transport, Session, Presentation and Application.*

3 What does horizontal communication signify in the context of the OSI model?

*This signifies that each layer on one computer communicates with the corresponding layer on the other computer.*

4 Why is vertical communication necessary in the context of the OSI model?

*Each layer requires the services of layer that is immediately below it so that it can carry out its functions.*

5 Which model is the more recent: OSI or TCP/IP?

*The TCP/IP model was created in 1970, whilst the OSI model was created in 1983.*

6 At which level does data transmission actually take place?

*At the lowest level: the physical level.*

## Role of the different layers

7 Which layer ensures the formatting of the data?

*The presentation layer.*

8 Which layer introduces the physical addressing?

*The data link layer.*

9 On which layer of the OSI model does IPX operate?

*The network layer.*

10 On which layer of the OSI model does TCP operate?

*The transport layer.*

11 Which layer introduces the logical addressing?

*The network layer.*

12 Which layer introduces a CRC to detect any transmission errors?

*The data link layer.*

13 Which layer transmits a digital signal?

*The physical layer.*

14 Are TCP segments encapsulated in IP, or the opposite?

*TCP segments are encapsulated in the IP data.*

## Types of standard

15 What is a protocol?

*A protocol is a set of communication rules that specify the format in which data must be transmitted across a network.*

16 What is a de facto standard?

*This is a standard that is adopted by common agreement rather than being imposed by legislation.*

17 What is a non proprietary standard?

*This is a standard that was developed by a Standards Organization.*

## Standards organizations

18 Which organization developed the CDE?

*COSE.*

19 Which organization was responsible for standards such as V.32, X.25 and X.500?

*The CCITT (ITU-T).*

20 Which organization was responsible for the RS232 standard?

*EIA (Electronic Industries Association).*

**Essentials**  Chapter 3 - Page 77

## Prerequisites for this chapter

- General knowledge of computer components: memory, bus, peripheral devices.

## Objectives

When you have completed this chapter you will be able to:

**Characteristics of a network peripheral**
- Define the role of a network interface card.
- Describe the different configuration parameters of a network interface card and the options available, such as IRQ, I/O address, connector type, DMA channel and memory address.
- Describe the different types of bus and their functionalities.
- Describe the options of the network interface card, which allow you to improve network performance.

**Data encoding**
- Describe the different encoding used in networks.
- Describe the two different types of multiplexing: time division and frequency division.
- Describe the two different system types: baseband and broadband.
- Explain the respective signal conversion roles of modems and codecs.

**Network media**
- Describe the characteristics of the different types of media that are used in networking, such as twisted-pair cables, coaxial cables and fiber optic cables.
- Choose the appropriate media for a given situation.
- Explain the three types of wireless networks: LANs, extended LANs and portable computer networks.

# Data transmission physical layer

# Summary

- **A. Role of the Network Interface Card** . . 79
    1. Introduction . . . . . . . . . . . . . . . . . . 79
    2. Data preparation . . . . . . . . . . . . . . . 79

- **B. Configuration options and parameters** 80
    1. Physical address . . . . . . . . . . . . . . . 80
    2. IRQ (Interrupt ReQuest lines) . . . . . . . . . . 81
    3. Input/output address . . . . . . . . . . . . . 82
    4. Base memory address . . . . . . . . . . . . . 83
    5. Direct Memory Access (DMA) channels . . . . 83
    6. Bus width . . . . . . . . . . . . . . . . . . . 84
    7. Bus type (taking control of the bus by the peripheral device) . . . . . . . . . . . . 86
    8. Types of connector . . . . . . . . . . . . . . 86
    9. Types of transceiver . . . . . . . . . . . . . . 87

- **C. Network performance** . . . . . . . . . . 87

- **D. Specialized network interface cards** . 88

- **E. Data encoding** . . . . . . . . . . . . . . 89
    1. Types of data and signal . . . . . . . . . . . 89
    2. Data encoding . . . . . . . . . . . . . . . . . 91
    3. Multiplexing signals . . . . . . . . . . . . . . 94

- **F. Signal conversion** . . . . . . . . . . . . 97
    1. Definitions . . . . . . . . . . . . . . . . . . . 97
    2. Modem . . . . . . . . . . . . . . . . . . . . 97
    3. CODEC . . . . . . . . . . . . . . . . . . . . 98

- **G. Transmission media** . . . . . . . . . . . 100
    1. Cables . . . . . . . . . . . . . . . . . . . . . 100
    2. Wireless media . . . . . . . . . . . . . . . . 109

First, this chapter will describe the different parameters that allow you to configure the peripheral devices of a PC. We will pay particular attention to Network Interface Cards.

Then, we will discuss the main encoding methods that are used in Local Area Networks, and we will examine the roles of multiplexers, modems and codecs.

Subsequently, we will describe the most commonly used transmission media: twisted-pair cables, coaxial cables and fiber optic cables.

Finally we will describe the different types of wireless networks.

## A. Role of the Network Interface Card

### 1. Introduction

The network interface card provides the interface between the computer and the network cable. This card is inserted in an expansion slot of the computer. It allows you to communicate with other items on the network.

The operating system communicates with the network interface card via a device driver. This is a software component provided by the LLC (Logical Link Control) and MAC (Media Access Control) layers (these layers correspond to the data link layer of the OSI model).

### 2. Data preparation

The physical layer converts the bytes of data to be transmitted, into signals. Data is exchanged in parallel between the computer and the network interface card. The network interface card converts the data to serial form before transmitting it on the physical medium.

## B. Configuration options and parameters

Each input/output point in a network must be identified so that the frame will be accepted by the right peripheral. Each network interface card and serial port must have a number that allows it to be identified at the lowest level of the OSI model.

### 1. Physical address

The physical address is composed of 6 bytes. It is the IEEE address that identifies peripheral devices such as network interface cards. The IEEE assigns the three leading bytes of this address so that they identify the hardware manufacturer. For example, 00AA00 is used for Intel and 00A024 is used for 3Com. The three remaining bytes are left at the disposal of the manufacturer. The manufacturer must ensure that no peripheral device can have the same physical address on the same local network.

☞ *In theory, nothing prevents the operating system from working with physical addresses that are different from those of the manufacturer. For example, the Novell client allows you to use a different physical address. This must be specified in the NET.CFG file using an entry of the form: NODE ADDRESS <new_MAC_address>.*

This address is used each time the network access card of a workstation has to send a frame to another network access card. It is also possible to send a packet to several cards simultaneously. You can do this by replacing the unique destination address by a multiple address (for example, you can use a broadcast address such as FFFFFFFFFFFF, in which all the bits in the six bytes are set to 1).

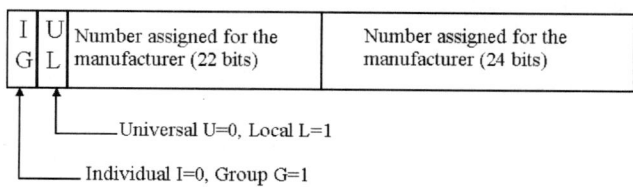

Thus, you can address several hosts by setting the MSB to 1, for example FFFFFF.FFFFFF. Alternatively, you can address one host by setting the MSB to 0, for example 00AA00.123456 (the MSB, or Most Significant Bit, is the first on the left).

An address attributed by the IEEE has its MSB set to 0. Conversely, an MSB of 1 indicates that the address is not a standard one.

☞ For example, in Token Ring networks, a host address has the following structure:

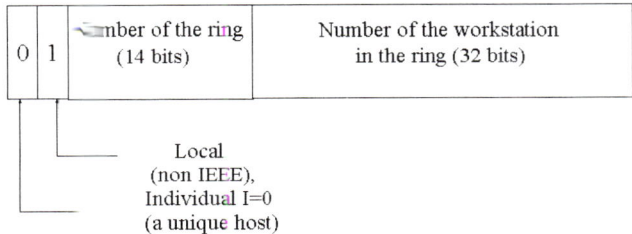

|0|1| Number of the ring (14 bits) | Number of the workstation in the ring (32 bits) |

Local
(non IEEE),
Individual I=0
(a unique host)

☞ You can also create token ring groups (G=1)

## 2. IRQ (Interrupt ReQuest lines)

Every peripheral device on a PC is connected to the microprocessor by a dedicated line. This is known as an interrupt request line or IRQ. When the peripheral device needs the services of the microprocessor, it sends a signal to the microprocessor using this line (the line voltage goes low to digital zero). In all there are 16 IRQ (2x8 lines arranged in cascade). Some lines are assigned by default and others are available so as to accommodate supplementary peripheral devices. The microprocessor manages these lines according to priority (the lower the interruption number, the higher the priority). The following table shows how IRQ are generally used.

| IRQ | Normal use on a PC |
|---|---|
| 0 | reserved for the internal system timer |
| 1 | reserved for the keyboard |
| 2 | reserved for the cascade to the second interrupt controller |
| 3 | used for COM2 or for COM4 (for example, for a modem) |
| 4 | used for COM1 or for COM3 (for example, for a mouse) |
| 5 | available, unless used by LPT2 or MIDI (musical instrument digital interface) |
| 6 | reserved for the floppy disk controller |
| 7 | available, unless used by LPT1 (for example, for a first parallel printer) |
| 8 | reserved for the realtime clock (CMOS) |
| 9 | available, unless used by a sound card |
| 10 | available, unless used by a first SCSI host adapter |
| 11 | available, unless used by a second SCSI host adapter |
| 12 | available, unless used by a PS/2 mouse |
| 13 | reserved, for a Maths coprocessor |
| 14 | reserved, for a primary IDE channel |
| 15 | reserved, for a secondary IDE channel |

## 3. Input/output address

A peripheral interrupts the microprocessor each time data must be exchanged. This data, is sent or received via a local input/output port with a specific address that is called the input/output address. This address points to a maximum memory area of 32 bytes. This area allows the storage of the data and an indication of what must be done with this data.

☞ *The input/output address of 3F8-3FF corresponds to the first serial port. This is often used to manage a mouse.*

The table below indicates some of the input/output addresses that are generally used:

| I/O address | Peripheral device that generally uses this address area |
|---|---|
| 1F0-1F8 | hard disk controller |
| 2F8-2FF | second serial port |
| 278-27F | second parallel port |
| 378-37F | first parallel port |
| 3B0-3DF | VGA, SVGA |
| 3F0-3F7 | floppydisk controller |
| 3F8-3FF | first serial port |
| | |
| 280-310 | available for a new peripheral device (for example, a network interface card in 300-31F) |

## 4. Base memory address

These are addresses in volatile memory (high memory between 640 Kbytes and 1 Mbyte). Their purpose is to provide input/output buffers for the reception and emission of frames via the network.

Buffer addresses must be a multiple of 16. Consequently, they are often written in hexadecimal without the final hexadecimal symbol, which is understood. For example, a network interface card that uses the buffer D000-D7FF, refers to the memory area D0000-D7FFF.

☞ *A0000 corresponds to 640 Kbytes in hexadecimal. This is the upper limit of conventional memory (low memory).*
*100000 corresponds to 1 Mbyte in hexadecimal. This is the beginning of extended memory.*

## 5. Direct Memory Access (DMA) channels

In most cases, peripheral devices depend on the microprocessor to transfer information from their buffer to conventional memory or vice-versa. However, on some machines, special channels exist that allows peripheral devices to exchange information directly with conventional memory, without using the microprocessor.

Some peripheral devices, in particular network interface cards, have several DMA channels, numbered from 1 to 7.

☞ *For example, you may notice that your system does not slow down when you listen to an audio CD on your CDROM drive as a background task. This is due to the action of a DMA channel.*

## 6. Bus width

All data is exchanged between the peripheral devices and the computer via the data bus. The wider this bus, the quicker the data exchange will take place (this is because, a wider bus has more elemental lines on which to transmit the information). Different manufacturers have defined different types of bus, as each manufacturer tried to set up its own standard. A key characteristic of a bus is the bus width. This is the number of elementary lines that are used by the bus to transfer the data, in parallel.

Here are the main types of buses that are used:

### a. ISA (Industry Standard Architecture)

This standard was defined for first generation machines (starting in the 80's with the IBM XT). It authorizes data transfer on 8 or 16 bits (8-bit cards can be inserted into 16-bit slots). This type of bus is still used today in modern machines.

### b. EISA (Extended Industry Standard Architecture)

EISA buses are 32 bits wide. They were developed in 1988 by Compaq and HP. EISA is compatible with 8-bit and 16-bit ISA cards. EISA also provides **bus mastering**. This feature allows cards that are connected on the bus, to communicate with each other without using the microprocessor.

### c. MCA (Micro Channel Architecture)

The MCA bus was created in 1987 for its PS/2 computers. These are 16-bit and 32-bit proprietary buses. They are incompatible with ISA and EISA. MCA also supports bus mastering.

### d. VLBus (Video Electronics Standard Association Local Bus)

The VLBus was developed to standardize the video. Its initial objective was to create an open standard. The VLB offers the performance of 32-bit buses, whilst adapting to the CPU clock rate.

VLBs are available for video and disk controllers. They also support bus mastering. VLBs are becoming less and less common.

### e. PCI (Peripheral Component Interconnect)

The PCI standard has made the VLB obsolete because it offers better performance, and compatibility with other bus standards. PCI has a 32-bit Plug and Play architecture that was developed by Apple. Most modern PCs and Macintosh computers use this architecture.

### f. PC Card (PCMCIA)

The PC Card was developed by the PCMCIA (Personal Computer Memory Card International Association). This standard was developed for devices having the dimensions of a credit card, and is independent of the operating system used. It uses a Plug and Play architecture, which cuts out the need for manual configuration. All modern portable computers use PCMCIA cards to support Ethernet and Token Ring network adapters.

### g. AGP (Accelerated Graphics Port)

AGP has a 32-bit bus width. Its most common use is for video cards.

### h. USB (Universal Serial Bus)

This standard is used for the connection of a variety of peripherals including keyboards, mice, speakers, video cameras, joysticks and digital telephones.

### i. IEEE 1394

This bus looks likely to supercede the USB. This architecture will be a standard feature of Sony, Apple, Compaq, Epson and Kodak computers. This type of bus supports a wide variety of peripherals including keyboards, modems, monitors and printers. IEEE 1394 is much quicker than USB (400 Mbps instead of 12 Mbps). In addition it offers Plug and Play features. Development possibilities of this technology promise speeds of up to 3 Gbps, thereby providing a bridge between computing and electronics.

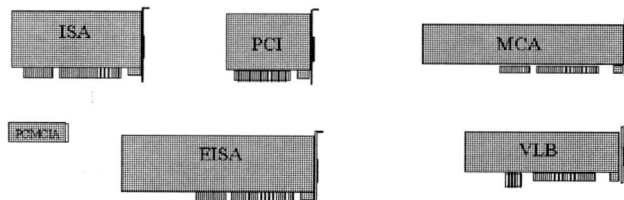

## 7. Bus type (taking control of the bus by the peripheral device)

Some peripheral devices can take control of the data bus in order to exchange data with the central memory more rapidly.

## 8. Types of connector

An important aspect of network interface card configuration is the type of connector that is used to connect the cable to the card.

Here are the principal connectors used:
- RJ45 for twisted-pair cables,
- AUI (Attachment Unit Interface) specifies how to connect a cable to an Ethernet card. It involves the connection of a coaxial cable to a transceiver. The transceiver then connects to the network interface card.
- BNC (British Naval Connector) is used with coaxial cables,
- DB9 is used for Token Ring connections,

- ST is used for a fiber optics connection in an Ethernet or Token Ring network,
- MIC is used for an FDDI (Fiber Distributed Data Interface).

## 9. Types of transceiver

A transceiver is a component that is able to transmit and receive data. It is connected directly to the cable. In the case of a thin-wired Ethernet, the transceiver is often integrated into the network interface card (a thin-wired Ethernet is an Ethernet implemented using thin-wired coaxial cables). On the other hand, when a thick-wired coaxial cable is used, the transceiver is usually situated on the cable.

## C. Network performance

Network performance depends on a number of factors. The network interface card itself plays a crucial role, especially if the server is heavily used.

There are a number of different types of network interface card, offering different performance possibilities. Some cards are equipped with a DMA channel. Some offer shared memory. Others offer **Bus Mastering** that allows them to take control of the data bus (so as to exchange data without using the CPU).

☞ *Although Bus Mastering is an expensive feature, it can improve performance from 20 to 70% (EISA, MCA).*

## D. Specialized network interface cards

In wireless networks, an external transceiver equipped with a small aerial is used.

On some workstations where security is a priority, the network operating system is loaded when the machine is started, from a program written in a PROM (Programmable Read Only Memory). This means that the workstation concerned does not need to have local external storage devices (hard or floppy disks).

This implementation ensures that no data exchange will take place from these workstations. It also ensures improved confidentiality of data and avoids any risk of introducing a virus.

Most network interface cards are equipped with a location where a **boot PROM** can be added. When it is started, the card sends a diffusion frame including its own physical address that will be recognized by a server (a diffusion frame is a frame that is addressed to all machines on the network). The server receives the frame and knows which configuration to associate with the physical address concerned.

☞ *The BOOTP protocol is used for the diffusion.*

# E. Data encoding

In this context, **data** refers to the information that must be exchanged.

However, this data may be transmitted via one or more communication channels before it reaches its destination. For example, the human voice can be transmitted by radio or by the telephone switching network after it has been digitized.

☞ *In addition, digital data can be encoded into an analog signal.*

A signal is information that is transmitted on a communications channel. Passing a signal from one channel to another often involves transformations being made.

## 1. Types of data and signal

Analog data is distinguished from digital data. A digital signal is one that is represented by a finite number of values at discrete intervals (for example, by voltage pulses with widths of 20 ms). An analog signal is represented by a continuous sinusoidal wave made up of an infinite number of values.

### a. Analog signals

When you drop a stone into water, an omnidirectional sinusoidal wave is generated. Sound travels in the same way. However, in the case of sound, the wave takes the form of pressure variations in the air.

You can easily reproduce this type of signal on material media such as cables.

A wave, then, is a **periodic analog signal**. It can be defined by three characteristics: its **amplitude**, its **frequency** (number of cycles per second, or Hertz) and its **phase** (the lead or the lag of the sinewave with respect to the origin).

### b. Digital signals

Digital signals are **synchronized with the internal system timer**. Digital information can be encoded by varying the amplitude of the signal.

The transmission rate of the signal is expressed in **Bauds** (the number of signaling elements per second).

☞ *N.B. According to the algorithm that is used to transform the data, one Baud may or may not correspond to one bit per second. For example, the Manchester algorithm encodes an elementary bit in the form of two successive voltages. In this case, for a transmission rate of 10 Mbits/s, the peripheral devices must have a bandwidth of 20 MHz (20 million symbols per second). This is the case for an Ethernet network, for example.*

### c. Advantages of digital signals

Digital equipment is simpler and less expensive than analog equipment.

### d. Disadvantages of digital signals

Digital signals are more prone to attenuation over distances than analog signals are.

### e. Data and signals

|         | Analog | Digital |
|---------|--------|---------|
| Analog  | radio stations (music, voice) | CD (0 and 1 are decoded into frequencies) |
| Digital | dialing a telephone number (pulse mode)<br><br>modem (analog telephone signals) | terminal and computer |

## 2. Data encoding

In order to convert data into a signal that can be transmitted, certain operations must be carried out.

The method of encoding data is called the **encoding scheme** or **encoding technique**.

The application of the encoding scheme to specific data is called **encoding**.

### a. Encoding digital data into analog signals

The objective is to distinguish the 0s from the 1s, so as to transform the data into an analog signal.

The three characteristics of an analog signal can be used to represent the elements of data.

#### Amplitude modulation

1: amplitude A

0: amplitude 1/2A

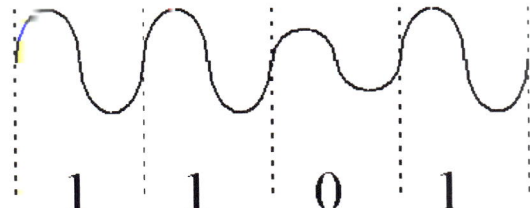

#### Frequency modulation

1: frequency 1/2 f

0: frequency f

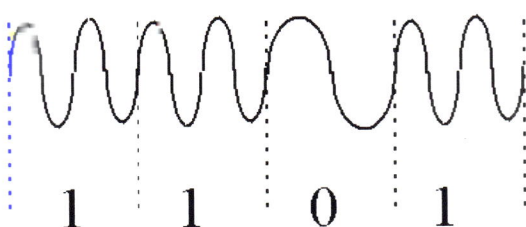

*Phase modulation*

1: phase change

0: no phase change

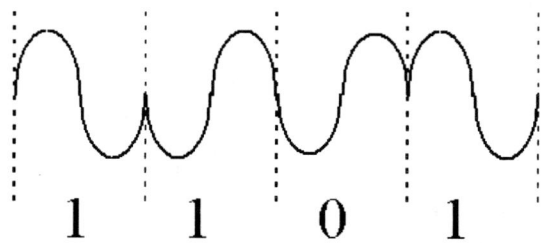

**b. Encoding digital data into digital signals**

Digital data is encoded into digital signals by transforming binary symbols into a certain number of square waves (digital pulses).

There are two ways of encoding digital data into digital signals. **Online encoding** transforms the data bit by bit, so as to produce the signal as it goes along. **Complete encoding** transforms on a set of bits into a specific signal.

**c. Examples of online encoding**

*Manchester*

1: low voltage followed by high voltage

0: high voltage followed by low voltage

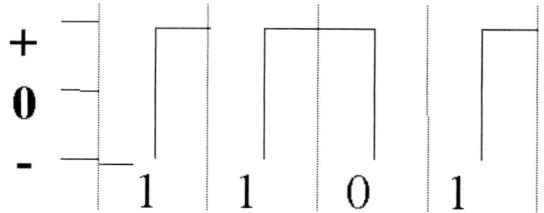

This method is used for Ethernet networks (802.3, 10base2, 10base5 and 10baseT).

Ethernet cards that support transmission rates of 10Mbit/s run at 20MHz. The encoding efficiency of these cards then, is 50%. This is measured with respect to the bandwidth available which indicates encoding capacity. One symbol is encoded into two square voltages.

## Manchester differential

0: the previous signal is repeated

1: the previous signal is inversed

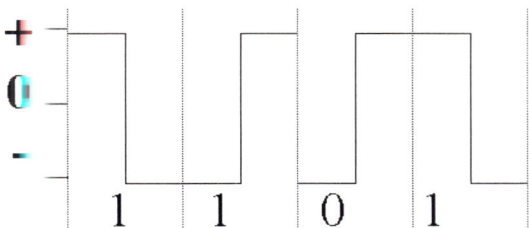

☞ This method is used for Token Ring and 802.5 networks.

## NRZ1 (Non Return to Zero, Invert on One)

0: the previous signal is repeated

1: the previous signal is inversed

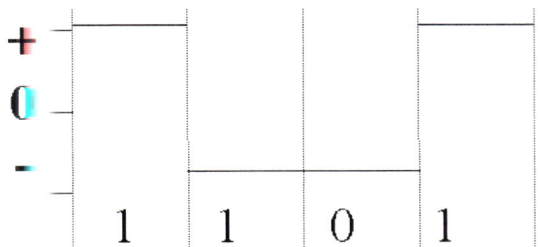

☞ This method is used for FDDI and 100baseFX networks.

### d. Examples of complete encoding

Complete encoding requires better transmission quality than online encoding. For this reason, complete encoding is generally used with optical fibers. An example of complete encoding is 4B/5T (4 bits for 5 transitions). This encoding is used in FDDI networks. This encoding scheme offers an efficiency of 80% (4/5), in contrast to the Ethernet encoding efficiency of 50%.

## 3. Multiplexing signals

### a. Baseband systems

In a baseband network, each medium carries only one signal and each peripheral device uses bidirectional communication. Digital signals are exchanged.

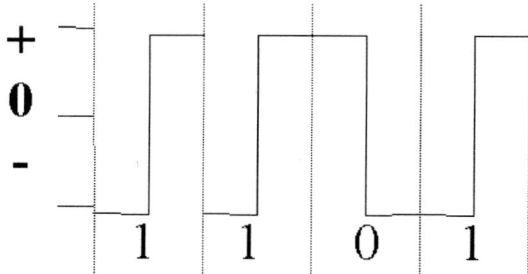

☞ *Attenuation, distortion and noise can destroy digital signals very quickly. Repeaters can be used to regenerate signals that have suffered such transmission losses.*

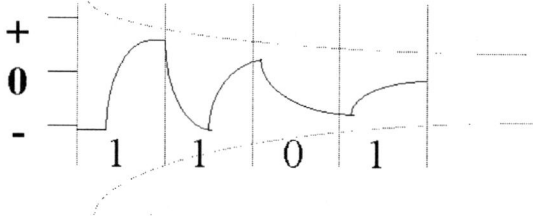

### b. Broadband systems

Each peripheral device uses unidirectional communication and exchanges analog signals.

> Broadband signals suffer very little transmission loss compared to baseband signals. Amplifiers are used to regenerate analog signals.

It is preferable to use analog signals to transmit data over large distances (for example on telephone switching networks via modems).

### c. Multiplexing

The purpose of multiplexing is to share a communication channel between several peripheral devices. In order to do this, the capacity (bandwidth) of the channel is divided up so as to produce several channels.

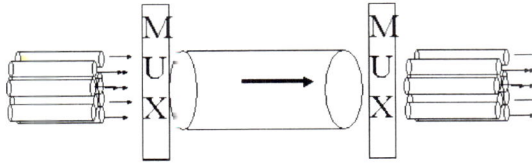

> For example, a 64bit Transfix line including compression can be multiplexed into a telephone line, a terminal line and an X25 line.

With frequency division multiplexing, the channel transports analog signals, whilst with time division multiplexing the channel transports digital signals.

### Frequency division multiplexing (FDM)

The input data is transformed according to carefully chosen frequency components (with one carrier per frequency).

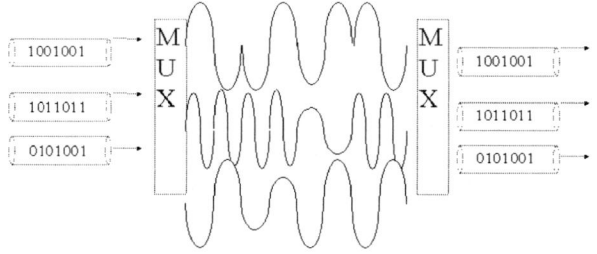

☞ *As an example of multiplexing, 500 MHz television cables can be used to transmit 80 multiplexed channels, each with a bandwidth of 6MHz. Within each of these channels, the sound and the video are also multiplexed.*

## Time division multiplexing (TDM)

With time division multiplexing, several data streams are transmitted sequentially in a set of timeslot channels. Each data stream is assigned to a different time slot channel in the set.

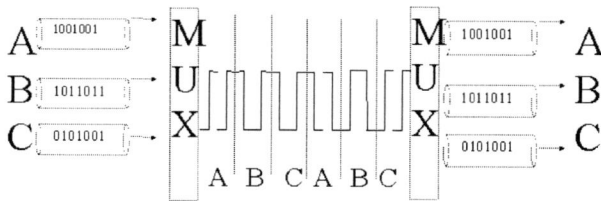

A disadvantage of this method is that if one of the channels is not used then the capacity associated with it is lost.

# F. Signal conversion

## 1. Definitions

At the physical level, signals are transmitted between two points. On one side of the connection there is Data Terminal Equipment (DTE), and at the other side there is the Data Communications Equipment (DCE).

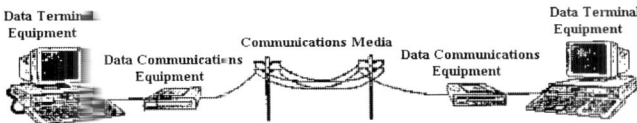

A DCE can be a computer or a router, whilst a DCE can be a modem, a switch or a multiplexor.

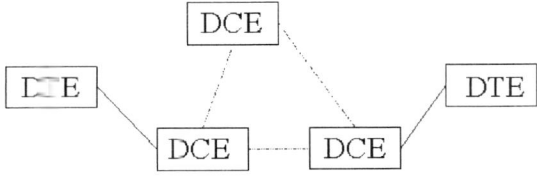

## 2. Modem

An example of a DCE is a modem.

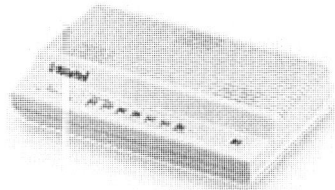

The purpose of a modem is to **MOD**ulate and to **DEM**odulate. A modem encodes (modulates) digital data into analog signals to enable them to be transmitted over long distances.

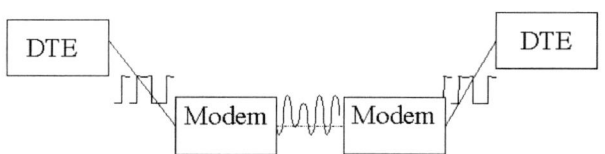

☞ *A modem can be used to share a canal that transmits analog signals. To do this, carriers are used that operate at different frequencies.*

A modem is not necessary for transmission over short distances, within an office for example. In this case you can use digital signals (and RS232-C interfaces for example).

Modems are generally used to transmit from point to point, between two remote sites over the telephone network.

## 3. CODEC

CODEC is short for **COD**er/**DEC**oder. It is used to code an analog signal that represents analog data, into a digital signal. Its role is to sample a signal, which means to digitize it. All good sound cards have an integrated CODEC.

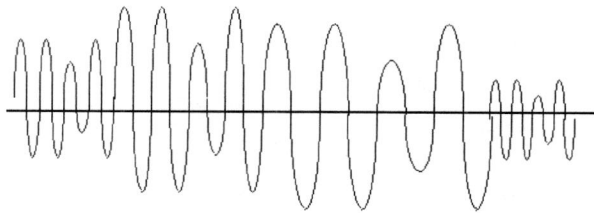

After digitization:

### Digitized signal

(7,9,8,5 1,0,1 8,9,7 1,0,1 5,7,7,6 2,1,2 8,9,7,6 1,0,1)

Suppose the data is coded into 8 bits (to represent values from 0 to 255). In this case each decimal value is coded into 8 binary symbols. When you have done this, all that remains is to apply the encoding scheme so as to encode the 0 and 1 symbols into signals.

### Digitized binary signals

(00000111,00001001,00001000, ...,00000001,00000000,00000001)

☞ *You can use a codec to sample (digitize) analog data, and then use a modem to transmit this digital data via an analog signal.*

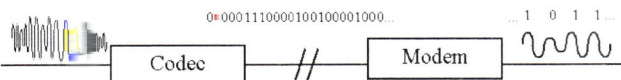

## G. Transmission media

A transmission medium is used to transport data between network interfaces in the form of signals.

There are several types of medium. These media vary in terms of price, simplicity of installation, transmission speed and resistance to interference.

There are two categories of medium: **cables** and **wireless media**.

### 1. Cables

Cables transport either electricity or light.

The main types of cable are **twisted-pair** cables, **coaxial cables** and **fiber optic** cables.

#### a. Twisted-pair cables

In its simplest form, a twisted pair cable is composed of two insulated copper wires twisted around each other. There are two types of twisted pair: **unshielded twisted pair** (UTP) and **shielded twisted pair** (STP).

The number of pairs per cable varies. The twisting of the wires reduces electrical interference coming from adjacent pairs and the environment.

#### b. Unshielded twisted pair (UTP)

This is the type of twisted pair that is most commonly used in local area networks. UTP cable segments can be up to 100 meters long.

Most telephone systems use UTP. The popularity of this type of cable is due to the fact that many buildings are precabled for telephone systems. However, the telephone system must respect computing network characteristics so as to ensure required transmission quality (these characteristics include specification of the number of twists per unit of cable length).

## c. Shielded twisted pair (STP)

UTP cables are particularly prone to interference coming from adjacent pairs. STP cables allow improved transmission. This is because they are equipped with a braided copper sheath that is of higher quality and more protective than that used for UTP cables. In addition, a further aluminium sheath provides a cable jacket for each pair.

STP cables support higher transmission speeds over greater distances than unshielded pairs.

## d. Connectors

A variety of connectors are used with twisted pairs. Here are the main connector types used:

| | |
|---|---|
| RJ-11 | telephone cable with 2 twisted pairs |
| RJ-14 | telephone cable with 3 twisted pairs |
| RJ-45 | network cable with 4 twisted pairs. |

For large networks, you can organize the connections using a cable distribution cabinet.

## e. Categories and types

Commercial standards have been defined for UTP.

The Electronic Industries Association (EIA) and the Telecommunication Industries Association (TIA) have set up the following five categories.

| Category | Characteristics | Data type |
|---|---|---|
| 1 | traditional UTP telephone wire | voice |
| 2 | 4 pair UTP, able to transmit up to 4 Mbits/s | data |
| 3 | 4 pair UTP with 3 twists per foot (25.4 cm) able to transmit up to 10 Mbits/s (current standard) | data |
| 4 | 4 pair UTP, able to transmit up to 16 Mbits/s | data |
| 5 | 4 pair UTP, able to transmit up to 100 Mbits/s | data |

The price of these cables increases progressively from category 1 to category 5. Each component or connector used must support the same transmission rate and conform to the same constraints. Consequently, all components used in category 5 cabling must be certified as being category 5 compliant. Strict installation and certification procedures have been defined, which require special training to implement.

As an example of cabling implementation, IBM have introduced their Token Ring network, ICS (IBM Cabling System):

IBM Cabling System

| Types | Standard denomination | Description | Use |
|---|---|---|---|
| 1 | shielded twisted pair (STP) | 2 pairs contained in a braided jacket shielding | for computers and MAU |
| 2 | voice transmission | 4 pairs with wires to 26 AWG | |
| | data transmission | 2 shielded pairs with braided jacket and wires to 22 AWG | |
| 3 | voice transmission | 4 unshielded pairs | |
| 4 | not defined | | |
| 5 | fiber optics | multimode fibers | |
| 6 | connector cable for data transmission | 2 cables composed of 2 STP, 26 AWG with aluminium shielding and braided jacket | |
| 7 | not defined | | |
| 8 | undercarpet cable | contained in a flat jacket, 2 cables, each with 2 STP to 26 AWG

Length limited to half that of a type 1 cable | |
| 9 | plenum cable | fire resistant, 2 STP pairs | |

*AWG (American Wire Gauge) is a specification for wire sizes. Larger AWG codes indicate smaller wire diameters.*

### f. Quality evaluation of twisted pair cables

Electrical signals can suffer two types of attenuation: **linear attenuation** and **Near End Cross Talk (NEXT) attenuation**. Linear attenuation is expressed in dB/km and characterizes losses of signals over distances. NEXT attenuation occurs in twisted pair cables and is due to electrical interference between one pair and other pairs in the same cable.

Attenuation causes signals to gradually weaken as they travel along the cable. Higher cable impedances cause greater attenuation of the signal. Cables with smaller wire diameters have greater impedances.

NEXT attenuation is a measure of losses between pairs. It is the aptitude of a pair not to be disturbed by an adjacent pair. The higher the NEXT parameter, the better the cable quality.

In summary then, a twisted pair cable is of high quality when the attenuation is low and the NEXT parameter is high.

The quality of twisted pair cables is also determined by how well protected they are against parasite signals, either by limiting these parasite signals, or by not generating them for adjacent pairs.

The shielding of STP cables provides a first level of protection from the environment.

A further method is to use a **balanced** circuit. In balanced mode each wire in the pair has the same voltages, but with opposite polarities. As one signal in the pair is the opposite of the other, their effects on adjacent pairs tend to cancel each other out.

Balanced circuits can be achieved on Token Ring circuits using a frequency filter called a **balun** (balanced/unbalanced).

Care must be taken to protect circuits from motors, neon and florescent tubes. Metallic enclosures can be used so as to provide a **Faraday cage** effect.

## g. Coaxial cables

### Composition

A coaxial cable is composed of a central copper conductor **(core)** that is surrounded by insulation followed by a second conductor (a grounded shield made up of braided wire) and finally a plastic outer cover, which provides mechanical protection.

Coaxial cables are classified according to their impedance characteristics (impedance is the ac equivalent of the resistance of dc circuits). Thus 50 Ohms in digital transmission corresponds to 75 Ohms in analog transmission.

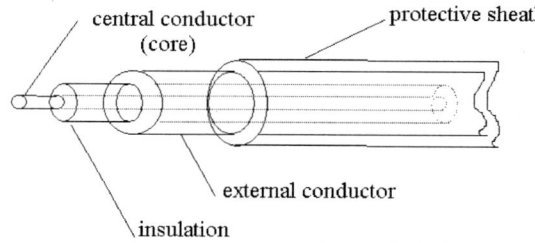

**Coaxial cable**

| | |
|---|---|
| RG-8, RG-11 | thick coaxial cable (12 mm diameter) for thick Ethernet, 50 Ohms, 10base5. |
| RG-58 | thin coaxial cable (6 mm diameter) for thin Ethernet 10base2 (thinnet). |
| /U | general utility, single central wire (not very suitable for networks). |
| A/U | twisted central wire (used for thin coaxial Ethernet). |
| C/U | military specification for A/U. |
| RG-59 | coaxial TV cable (75 Ohms). |
| RG-62 | ArcNet cable (93 Ohms). |

☞ *The thicker the central conductor, the greater the distance that signals can travel along the cable. RG-58 allows cable segments of up to 185 meters, whereas with RG-8 and RG-11 allow segments of up to 500 meters. This latter type of cable is often used as a backbone to interconnect sites that are relatively close to each other.*

### Categories of coaxial cable

There are **two categories of coaxial cables**. The first category has its protective sheath in PVC. These are the most common and the cheapest types of coaxial cable. However, in the case of fire, they emit toxic fumes (at low temperatures of around 100 degrees celsius).

The second category includes cables that are fire resistant. The outer sheaths of these cables are made of **Teflon**. Consequently, they are more expensive than those of the first category. They are called **plenum cables**. A plenum refers to the area under a raised floor, or above a false ceiling, that can accommodate cabling.

### h. Fiber optics

Fiber optic cables are composed of a fiber that can conduct light. This fiber can be in glass or in plastic and is extremely fine (approximately 10 microns in diameter). The fiber transmits digital data as modulated luminous pulses. The signal is emitted at one end of the cable by a laser diode and received at the other end of the cable by a photodiode. The photodiode then transforms the luminous signal into an electrical signal.

Unlike electrical signals, luminous signals transmitted through fiber cables cannot be intercepted.

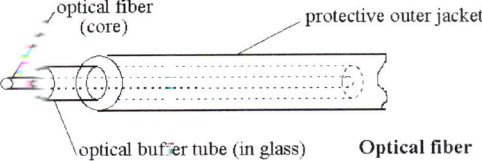

Optical fiber

These cables can be composed of one fiber.

**Simplex cable**

Alternatively, they can be made up of a double fiber with two separate connectors at either end.

There are two types of fiber. **Monomode** fibers have small core diameters (between 2 and 8 microns). They are used to transmit a single signal. **Multimode** fibers have larger core diameters (between 50 and 125 microns). They are used to transmit several signals.

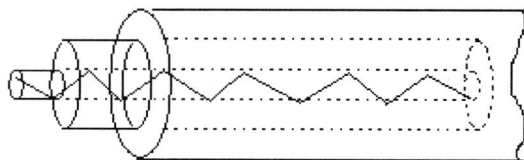

The luminous pulse is reflected by the glass optical buffer tube. Multimode fibers can be **graded index fibers** or **step index fibers**. Graded index fibers allow light to travel in sine waves. This is because the refractive index of graded index fibers decreases from the center to the outside of the fiber core. Step index fibers have a uniform refractive index, which means that the light rays travel along them in zigzag lines.

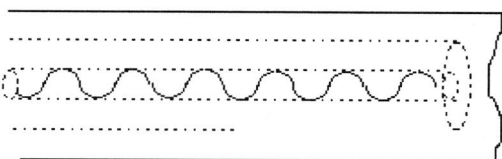

☞ Fibers are often used to interconnect Ethernet LANs. With Ethernet 10BaseFL, which transmits through fiber at 10 Mbits/s, mixed repeaters can be used (fiber/coaxial or fiber/twisted pair).

Fibers allow signals to be transmitted in one direction only. For this reason, fiber cables are often constructed with two fibers, one for emission and one for reception. These are constructed, either with a double core in one cable, or with two cables stuck together.

Fibers are ideal for transmitting large volumes of data at high speeds (from 100 Mbps to 200 Gbps). This is possible because fibers transmit pure signals that are not prone to attenuation and are unaffected by electrical interference. They can be used to transmit data over distances of up to 2000 meters. However, their installation can be quite expensive, as it requires highly qualified installation personnel.

### i. Criteria for choosing media

A number of criteria can be used to choose the most appropriate media for a given application.

Such criteria include **cost**, **bandwidth**, **signal attenuation**, **resistance to electromagnetic interference** from the environment and **simplicity** of **installation**. The environment and the type of signal that must be transmitted may introduce a certain number of constraints. Examples of such constraints are the maximum length of a cable segment and the number of peripheral devices that must be connected (network nodes will be discussed later).

The following table provides a summary of the different media that are used mainly in Ethernet and Token Ring networks.

| Characteristic | Thin coaxial | Thick coaxial | Unshielded twisted pair: UTP | Shielded twisted pair: STP | Fiber optics |
|---|---|---|---|---|---|
| Cable price | Less expensive than UTP cat.5 | More expensive than UTP cat.5 | To cat 5, more expensive than thin coaxial, and to cat.3, less expensive than thin coaxial (not taking into account the fact that the building may be precabled). | More expensive than thin coaxial or UTP. | The most expensive medium, although costs are progressively decreasing. |
| Length of segment | 185 m | 500 m | 100 m | 105 m (similar to UTP but with higher transmission speeds) | 2000 m |
| Transmission speeds | 2.5 Mbps (ArcNet) 10Mbps (Ethernet) | 2.5 Mbps (ArcNet) 10 Mbps (Ethernet) | 10 Mbps (cat.3) 100 Mbps (cat.5) | 4 and 16 Mbps (Token Ring). Speeds of up to 500 Mbps, although in practice they do not exceed 155 Mbps. | 100 Mbps or more (2 Gbps) |
| Installation | Simple | Simple | Very simple | Very simple | Each connection must be made taking care not to obstruct the passage of the light. In addition, curvatures must not exceed certain limits. |
| Attenuation | Average | Low | High | Low | None |
| Sensitivity to interference | Less sensitive than UTP | Less sensitive than UTP | Sensitive | Low sensitivity (equivalent to coaxial) | None |
| Common use | Sites of average size, with high security requirements | As a backbone in an Ethernet network | Small networks and to suit low budgets | Suitable for Token Ring and large networks | Installations of all sizes that require high security and high transmission speeds. |

## 2. Wireless media

Wireless networking technology has not yet reached the stage where it can replace technologies based on cable media. This is because of the high price and low bandwidth that is currently associated with wireless technology.

In practice, "wireless networks" are often composed of mixed components connected together (for example this could be a cabled LAN including a wireless workstation that interfaces with other wireless components).

The main purposes of wireless networks are to provide for **portable workstations** and to interconnect sites where the use of cables would not be viable (treacherous or uncertain ground, or very busy areas that prohibit work being carried out).

There are three categories of wireless network: LANs, Extended LANs and Mobile Computing.

### a. LANs

A wireless network looks like a cabled network and functions like one, except that it uses a different medium.

A wireless network interface card is installed on each computer and the users communicate across the network in the same way as they would if the network was cabled. Wireless LANs are linked to cabled networks by small wall-mounted transceivers.

This type of network transmits data by **infrared**, **laser** or **radio** (narrowband, or wideband on frequencies ranging from 3 MHz to 3 GHz).

### Infrared

Infrared light waves are used to transmit data. These signals are very sensitive to bright light. However, speeds of up to 10 Mbps can be attained over distances of up to 330 meters.

☞ *Infrared communications can be implemented by direct visibility or by diffusion (the signal rebounds off light colored walls, whereas dark colored walls tend to absorb light).*

The advantage of this technique is that the equipment is not expensive as it is manufactured on large scales. This solution is suitable for indoor applications. It is not suitable for outdoors as the equipment is sensitive to atmospheric conditions.

## Laser

In common with direct visibility infrared implementations, this technique requires a direct field of visibility. It is sensitive to any misalignment between the laser and the photodiode. Lasers are resistant to interference and disruptions, but they are sensitive to atmospheric conditions.

## Radio

### Narrowband

The user tunes the transceiver to a given frequency. The waves are omnidirectional and can cover an area of up to 1650 $m^2$. However, as signals are transmitted at high frequencies, they cannot pass through load-bearing or steel walls.

Implementation requires the involvement of a service provider, such as Motorola, in order to obtain a transmission license. Transmission speeds of up to 4.8 Mbps can be attained.

### Wideband

This technique allows you to transmit signals on a range of frequencies. Transmission speeds between 250 Kbps and 2 Mbps can be attained over distances of up to 130 meters indoors, and 3200 meters outdoors.

### b. Extended LANs

Networks can be interconnected without using cables, by using wireless bridges.

In general, a wireless bridge uses wideband radio waves to connect together two LANs in two buildings. The buildings concerned can be up to 4800 meters apart.

 *There are also long range wireless bridges (Ethernet or Token Ring), which can span distances of up to 40 kms.*

### c. Mobile computing

This technique provides communication services to travelers with mobile computers. It provides these people with access to electronic mail and any other available services.

Implementation of such networks often requires the involvement of telecommunications companies and public services. These organizations allow you to emit and receive signals using radio-communications by packets, cellular networks or satellites.

Transmission speeds can range from 8 Kbps and 19.2 Kbps.

## Radio-communications by packets

Messages are divided up into packets and transmitted via satellites.

## Cellular networks

These networks use the transmission technology of cellular telephone systems.

They allow you to transfer data on existing analog voice networks, between calls, when the system is not busy. Data is transferred very rapidly and waiting times are less than one second.

## Satellites

Microwave systems allow you directly to interconnect buildings that are relatively close to one another. This is also the most commonly used method in the USA for long distance transmissions. Excellent results are obtained by direct communications between two points that are directly visible to one another (for example, between an earth station and a satellite in stationary orbit with respect to the earth; between two buildings or across vast expanses).

You need the necessary authorization, two radio transceivers and directional antennae that must be precisely positioned.

☞ In the case of microwave systems by satellite, you can use mobile earth stations (such as airplanes or boats).

### d. Comparison of wireless media

| Type of media | Area covered | Attenuation | Transmission speed | Sensitivity to electromagnetic interference |
|---|---|---|---|---|
| Terrestrial microwaves | Directional beam | 80 km (fog, rain) | 1 to 10 Mbps | High |
| Satellite microwaves | Narrow or wide beam | Thousands of kms | 1 to 10 Mbps | High |
| Laser | Directional beam | Several kms | | None |
| Point to point infrared | Directional beam | Less than 1 km | 4 to 16 Mbps | None |
| Broadcast infrared | Omnidirectional over small areas | Less than 1 km | 1 Mbps | None |
| Narrowband radio | Omnidirectional over small or large areas | Hundreds of kms | 1 to 10 Mbps | High |
| Wideband radio | Omnidirectional over small or large areas | Hundreds of kms | 2 to 6 Mbps | Average |

## Exercises

To be absolutely sure that you have assimilated this chapter, work through the corresponding exercises. These are set out from page 383.

☒ Troubleshooting connectivity problems.

## Assessing your skills

Try the following questions if you think you know this chapter well enough.

*Characteristics of network peripheral devices*

1 What is the purpose of a network interface card?

☐

2 On which layer of the OSI model does the driver of the network interface card operate?

☐

3 Is the data transmitted between the different elements of the computer in series or in parallel?

☐

4 Which are the three most important pieces of information that you need to know in order to configure a network interface card? Give an example of each.

☐

5 How many bytes are contained in a MAC address?

☐

6 What is the purpose of the two most significant bits of the physical address?

7 Which IRQ is used by the first serial port?

8 Which IRQ is used by the first parallel port?

9 In which circumstances is IRQ 11 available?

10 My system has two IDE hard disks. Is IRQ 15 available?

11 Which IRQ must be specified for a network interface card of a server?

12 If two requests arrive simultaneously from two peripherals, one on IRQ 5 and the other on IRQ 4, which of them will have priority?

13 Is it possible to assign the same interrupt for two peripherals of the same machine?

14 What is the purpose of the input/output address? ☐

15 For what purpose are low-memory addresses used? ☐

16 Is an EISA bus compatible with an ISA bus? ☐

17 Is an MCA bus compatible with an ISA bus? ☐

18 Which are the most common bus standards that are used at present? ☐

19 What is the width of the VLB bus? ☐

20 State one of the advantages of PCI. ☐

21 In which circumstances can a transceiver be integrated into a network interface card? ☐

22 Which type of connector is used for networks that are connected using twisted pair cables? ☐

23 What is the purpose of a bootable PROM? ☐

24 State three factors that allow you to enhance the performance of network interface cards.

## Data encoding

25 Which signaling technique uses a single frequency to encode data?

26 What is the difference between data and a signal?

27 Which encoding technique uses frequency to convert digital data into an analog signal?

28 What are the two types of digital encoding?

29 Which encoding method that converts 1 Bit into a transition between 2 voltages, is used in Ethernet networks?

30 What type of network uses Manchester Differential encoding?

31 What is the encoding efficiency of Manchester Differential encoding?

32 Which encoding technique is used in FDDI networks?

33 What is the operational frequency of 10 Mbps Ethernet card?

34 What term is used to refer to the weakening of a digitally encoded signal?

35 What term is used to refer to the technique of decomposing a signal into different frequencies so as to be able to transmit several communication channels simultaneously?

36 What are DTE and DCE?

37 What is the purpose of a Modem?

38 What device allows you to digitize a voice signal?

## Networking transmission media

39 Which type of cable allows you to emit and receive simultaneously?

40 Which type of cable allows only alternate emission and reception?

41 Which type of cable allows only unidirectional transmission?

*Data transmission physical layer*

42 Which type of signal is implemented in broadband signaling?

43 What are the two most commonly used types of twisted pair cable?

44 Which type of twisted pair cable is used particularly in Token Ring networks?

45 Which type of connector is used with shielded twisted pair cables?

46 Which type of twisted pair allows transmission speeds of up to 100 Mbps on Ethernet networks?

47 In which type of network is UTP category 3 used?

48 What is the maximum length that can be used currently for a cat.3 UTP cable?

49 With which types of cable are RJ-11, RJ-14 and RJ-45 used?

50 To which phenomenon does Near End Cross Talk (NEXT) refer?

51 Which reference numbers are used to identify a thick coaxial cable in an Ethernet network?

52 What does RG-58 C/U signify?

_____
_____

53 What term is used to refer to a network cable that is fire resistant and suitable for installation in confined spaces?

_____

54 What material is used for the outer jacket of a standard RG-58 cable?

_____

55 What is the maximum length of a thin coaxial cable segment?

_____

56 What is the difference between a monomode and a multimode fiber?

_____
_____

57 What is the maximum length of an RG-8 cable?

_____

58 What is the maximum length of a fiber optics cable segment?

_____

59 What material is used for the central conductor of a coaxial cable?

_____

60 What happens if the central conductor of a coaxial cable comes into contact with the braided outer conductor?

_____

61 How can thick coaxial cables or fiber optic cables be used in an Ethernet network?

62 What is the purpose of the outer aluminum jacket of an STP cable?

63 Which type of twisted pair allows transmission speeds of up to 500 Mbps?

64 Which cable material allows data to be transmitted using luminous signals?

65 Which cable material is insensitive to electromagnetic interference?

66 Which cable material allows highly confidential data transmission?

# Results

Check your answers on pages 122 to 128. Count one point for each correct answer.

Number of points [ /66 ]

For this chapter you need to have scored at least 50 out of 66.

Look at the list of key points that follows. Pick out the ones with which you have had difficulty and work through them again in this chapter before moving on to the next.

# Key points of the chapter

☐ Characteristics of network peripheral devices.
☐ Data encoding.
☐ Networking transmission media.

*Data transmission physical layer*

## Solutions

### Characteristics of network peripheral devices

1 What is the purpose of a network interface card?

*It provides an interface between the computer and the rest of the network.*

2 On which layer of the OSI model does the driver of the network interface card operate?

*On the data link layer.*

3 Is the data transmitted between the different elements of the computer in series or in parallel?

*The data is transmitted via the bus in parallel.*

4 Which are the three most important pieces of information that you need to know in order to configure a network interface card? Give an example of each.

*The IRQ, the input/output address and the type of connector. For example, IRQ: 10, I/O address: 300, Connector type RJ-45.*

5 How many bytes are contained in a MAC address?

*6 bytes.*

6 What is the purpose of the two most significant bits of the physical address?

*The I/G bit identifies either an individual address (identifying a unique card, I=0), or a group address (G=1). U/L indicates if the address is a universal (IEEE) address (U=0), or if the address has been redefined (local, L=1).*

7 Which IRQ is used by the first serial port?

*IRQ 4.*

8 Which IRQ is used by the first parallel port?

*IRQ 7.*

9 In which circumstances is IRQ 11 available?

*When no peripheral device is using it (such as an SCSI host for example).*

10 My system has two IDE hard disks. Is IRQ 15 available?

*IRQ 15 will be available if the second IDE channel does not use it. However, in this case it is unlikely that IRQ 15 would be available.*

11 Which IRQ must be specified for a network interface card of a server?

*The lowest possible reference; if possible IRQ 3.*

12 If two requests arrive simultaneously from two peripherals, one on IRQ 5 and the other on IRQ 4, which of them will have priority?

*The one that uses IRQ 4.*

13 Is it possible to assign the same interrupt for two peripherals of the same machine?

*No.*

14 What is the purpose of the input/output address?

*The I/O address is used to transfer all data that is input to, or output from, the machine.*

15 For what purpose are low-memory addresses used?

*They are used as cache memory buffers for data that is being transferred.*

16 Is an EISA bus compatible with an ISA bus?

*Yes.*

17 Is an MCA bus compatible with an ISA bus?

*No.*

18 Which are the most common bus standards that are used at present?

*ISA and PCI.*

19 What is the width of the VLB bus?

*32 bits.*

20 State one of the advantages of PCI.

*Plug and Play feature.*

21 In which circumstances can a transceiver be integrated into a network interface card?

*When you use twisted pair or thin coaxial cabling.*

22 Which type of connector is used for networks that are connected using twisted pair cables?

*RJ-45.*

23 What is the purpose of a bootable PROM?

*It allows a computer, which does not have a local disk, to startup the network automatically.*

24 State three factors that allow you to enhance the performance of network interface cards.

*The bus width, operation in Bus Master mode and the use of a DMA channel.*

### Data encoding

25 Which signaling technique uses a single frequency to encode data?

*Digital or baseband signaling.*

26 What is the difference between data and a signal?

*Data is raw information, whereas a signal is data that has been specially prepared so that it can be transmitted via a transmission medium.*

27 Which encoding technique uses frequency to convert digital data into an analog signal?

*Frequency modulation.*

28 What are the two types of digital encoding?

*Online encoding and complete encoding.*

29 Which encoding method that converts 1 Bit into a transition between 2 voltages, is used in Ethernet networks?

*Manchester.*

30 What type of network uses Manchester Differential encoding?

*Token Ring.*

31 What is the encoding efficiency of Manchester Differential encoding?

*50%.*

32 Which encoding technique is used in FDDI networks?

*NRZ-1.*

33 What is the operational frequency of 10Mbps Ethernet card?

*20 Mhz.*

34 What term is used to refer to the weakening of a digitally encoded signal?

*Signal attenuation or linear attenuation.*

35 What term is used to refer to the technique of decomposing a signal into different frequencies so as to be able to transmit several communication channels simultaneously?

*Frequency division multiplexing (FDM).*

36 What are DTE and DCE?

*Data Terminal Equipment and Data Communications Equipment.*

37 What is the purpose of a Modem?

*A Modem is a ModulatorDemodulator that allows you to transmit digital data in the form of an analog signal. Its main purpose is to extend the distance over which transmissions can be made.*

38 Which device allows you to digitize a voice signal?

*A CODEC.*

### Networking transmission media

39 Which type of cable allows you to emit and receive simultaneously?

*Twisted pair cable.*

40 Which type of cable allows only alternate emission and reception?

*Coaxial cable (for digital signaling).*

41 Which type of cable allows only unidirectional transmission?

*Fiber optic cable.*

42 Which type of signal is implemented in broadband signaling?

*An analog signal.*

43 What are the two most commonly used types of twisted pair cable?

*UTP and STP.*

44 Which type of twisted pair cable is used particularly in Token Ring networks?

*STP.*

45 Which type of connector is used with shielded twisted pair cables?

*A shielded connector RJ-45.*

46 Which type of twisted pair allows transmission speeds of up to 100 Mbps on Ethernet networks?

*UTP category 5.*

47 In which type of network is UTP category 3 used?

*In 10 Mbps Ethernet networks.*

48 What is the maximum length that can be used currently for a cat.3 UTP cable?

*Approximately 100 meters.*

49 With which types of cable are RJ-11, RJ-14 and RJ-45 used?

*They are used with twisted pair cables composed of 2, 3 and 4 pairs respectively.*

50 To which phenomenon does Near End Cross Talk (NEXT) refer?

*It refers to the interference that is caused by adjacent pairs in a twisted pair cable.*

51 Which reference numbers are used to identify a thick coaxial cable in an Ethernet network?

*RG-8 and RG-11.*

52 What does RG-58 C U signify?

*This is a strict military Ethernet specification for a thin coaxial cable.*

53 Which term is used to refer to a network cable that is fire resistant and suitable for installation in confined spaces?

*A plenum cable.*

54 Which material is used for the outer jacket of a standard RG-58 cable?

*PVC.*

55 What is the maximum length of a thin coaxial cable segment?

*185 meters.*

56 What is the difference between a monomode and a multimode fiber?

*A monomode fiber has a smaller core diameter and allows the transmission of only one luminous signal at once.*

57 What is the maximum length of an RG-8 cable?

*500 meters.*

58 What is the maximum length of a fiber optics cable segment?

*2 kilometers.*

59 Which material is used for the central conductor of a coaxial cable?

*Copper.*

60 What happens if the central conductor of a coaxial cable comes into contact with the braided outer conductor?

*A short circuit occurs.*

61 How can thick coaxial cables or fiber optic cables be used in an Ethernet network?

*Thick coaxial cables or fiber optic cables can be used to interconnect LANs.*

62 What is the purpose of the outer aluminum jacket of an STP cable?

*Its purpose is to reduce electromagnetic interference coming from the environment.*

63 Which type of twisted pair allows transmission speeds of up to 500 Mbps?

*STP.*

64 Which cable material allows data to be transmitted using luminous signals?

*Fiber.*

65 Which cable material is insensitive to electromagnetic interference?

*Fiber.*

66 Which cable material allows highly confidential data transmission?

*Fiber.*

## Prerequisites for this chapter

☒ Knowledge of the configuration options of a network interface card.

## Objectives

When you have completed this chapter you will be able to:
☒ Describe the different types of network interface card.
☒ Choose appropriate configuration options.
☒ Define the NDIS and ODI specifications
☒ Install the network interface card drivers in different environments.
☒ Describe the testing tools for a network interface card, which are supplied by the manufacturer.
☒ Detect a configuration problem
☒ Configure the network protocol stack.

# Summary

A. Types of configuration . . . . . . . . . 131
   1. Hardware . . . . . . . . . . . . . . . . . . . 131
   2. Software . . . . . . . . . . . . . . . . . . . 131

B. Configuration options for the network interface card . . . . . . . . . . . . . . 132
   1. IRQ . . . . . . . . . . . . . . . . . . . . . . 132
   2. Input/output address . . . . . . . . . . . . 132
   3. Types of connector . . . . . . . . . . . . . 132
   4. Other options . . . . . . . . . . . . . . . . 133
   5. Physical address . . . . . . . . . . . . . . 133

C. NDIS and ODI . . . . . . . . . . . . . 134

D. Installing a network interface card driver . . . . . . . . . . . . . . . . . . 136
   1. Resolving hardware conflicts . . . . . . . . 136
   2. Adding a new network interface card . . . . 142

E. Network protocol stack . . . . . . . . 146

This chapter will describe the installation, configuration and test of a network interface card in its operating environment.

## A. Types of configuration

Before you install the driver, you must be sure that you know the exact parameters of the peripheral device: you must configure it at a hardware level concerning its input/output address, the interrupt it will use and possibly other parameters.

### 1. Hardware

According to the network interface card concerned, you may have to configure the card manually, using switches or jumpers, or automatically using software supplied by the manufacturer.

Recent Plug and Play cards configure themselves and can even detect the type of network connector used (for example SMC 8432 PCI).

### 2. Software

The utility supplied by the manufacturer selects values that will not conflict with the other peripheral dives that are installed.

In addition, it is always useful to carry out preliminary tests of the card using this tool. This allows you to check that it functions correctly before installing the driver.

## B. Configuration options for the network interface card

As mentioned earlier in this book, a network interface card is, above all, a peripheral device of the computer. Consequently, a certain number of parameters must be set to ensure that it will function correctly.

### 1. IRQ

Every peripheral device is connected to the CPU via a dedicated line, known as an interrupt request line. When the peripheral device needs the CPU, it sends it a signal on this line.

As we saw in the previous chapter, most of the IRQs are already used. Therefore, you must choose one of the IRQs that is not being used. The following IRQs are often available: 3, 5, 10, 11 and 15.

☞ *Always remember to allocate low IRQs to servers that are heavily used.*

### 2. Input/output address

This address range is one of the pieces of information you have to set up. Use an address range between 280 and 340.

### 3. Types of connector

The third essential option is the type of connector. This ensures that the card will use the right connector when it has several output options.

For example, Ethernet 10 cards are often equipped with RJ45, BNC and AUI connectors.

☞ *Always check that the right connector is used. Cards that are equipped with the Autoselect feature are supposed to be able to detect the connector type. However, they sometimes have difficulty in detecting the right piece of hardware.*

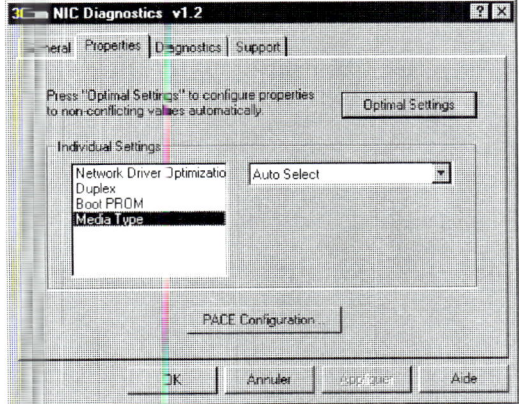

### 4. Other options

Other options can include the DMA channel and the base memory address. Nowadays, the tools that are supplied by the card manufacturer determine this information automatically.

For Token Ring networks, you may need to choose the transmission speed used. This can be 4 or 16 Mbps. You must ensure that all Token Ring cards function at the same speed, or else the whole network may be disrupted.

### 5. Physical address

At the lowest level, every network interface card is identified by a physical address. This address is known as the MAC (Media Access Control). This is an Ethernet address or a Token Ring address according to the case.

The IEEE predefines this physical address. In some types of network, you can redefine this address (for example with ARCNet).

## C. NDIS and ODI

NDIS (Network Device Interface Specification) and ODI (Open Datalink Interface) were created to allow several network interface cards to be associated with a given protocol (for example IPX or IP). They also allow you to link a single network interface card with several protocols.

The type of specification that you choose will depend on the network operating system that you use. For example, Novell and Apple developed ODI, and Microsoft and 3COM developed NDIS.

NDIS defines a communication interface between the MAC sublayer and the network adapter.

### NDIS specification levels

NDIS defines a number of different specification levels:
- NDIS 2 defines a driver specification in real mode.
- NDIS 3 describes component operation in extended mode. In extended mode, each peripheral device can be managed using an access context that allows non-exclusivity (in contrast to real mode that does not).
- NDIS 4 introduces the Plug and Play feature. This is for drivers that are used by Windows NT.

For example, when you access the properties of a network interface card on Windows 95, you can choose the type of driver used.

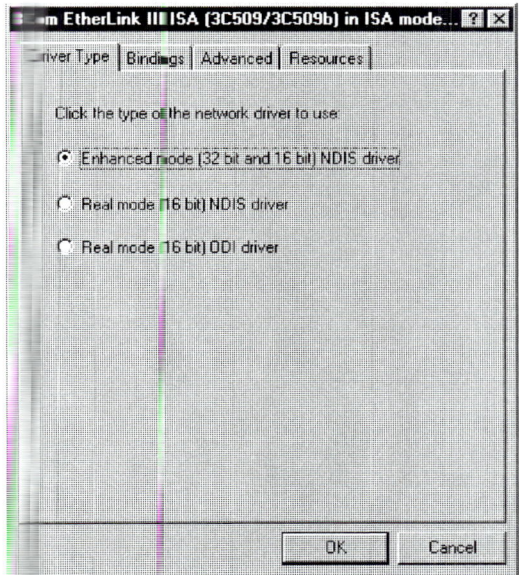

## D. Installing a network interface card driver

Once you know the options available for a network interface card, and you have read conscientiously the documentation supplied by the manufacturer, you can start installing the network interface card. The first step is to insert the network interface card into an available expansion slot of your computer. Then, you must set up your operating system so that it will control your network interface card.

This second step is described below.

### 1. Resolving hardware conflicts

#### a. The floppy disk that is supplied by the manufacturer

All network interface cards are delivered with a floppy disk for installation. This floppy disk contains the drivers for the different operating systems and the different specifications (including ODI and NDIS).

For each new network interface card, you must know if the driver that is to be used, is the standard driver that is supplied with your operating system. If this is the case then the card will be detected automatically. Otherwise, you must use the driver supplied by the card manufacturer.

The floppy disk supplied by the manufacturer has several purposes:
– To provide a driver that is suitable for the operating system used.
– To auto-configure the card, and to write this configuration to the EEPROM of the card. Ideally, this should be done in its final operating environment. In this way, any conflicts with other peripherals that are already configured in the same environment can be detected and avoided.
– To test the card using elementary tests and by making data exchanges with other cards.

### b. Configuring the network interface card using the utility supplied by the manufacturer

When a network interface card is configured with parameters that have already been attributed to another peripheral, a configuration conflict occurs. This can result in system malfunctions.

Therefore, you must ensure that the network interface card functions properly along with all the peripherals that were installed previously. You must also be sure that you choose configuration parameters that are not yet being used: IRQ, input/output address and type of connector.

There are a number of utilities that allow you to auto-configure the network interface card so that it will not cause any system conflicts.

Here is an example of such a utility:

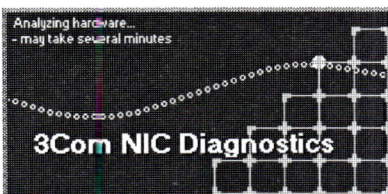

The following screen appears when you start up this test utility:

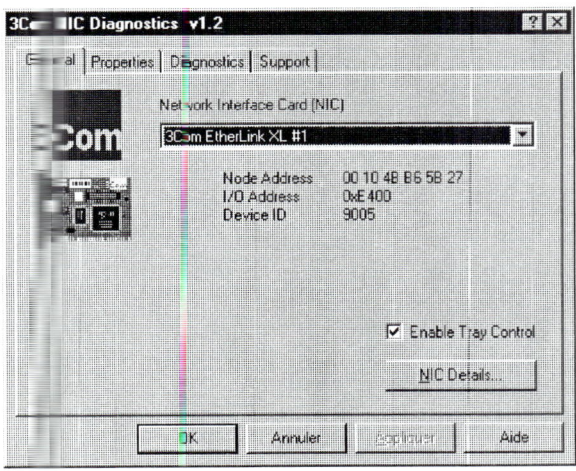

You can then auto-configure the card, or run diagnostic tests to examine its operation:
- Local loop tests (staying within the network).

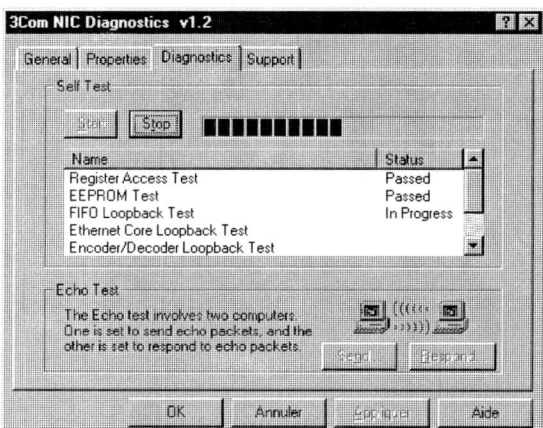

- External testing of the physical transmission medium, by listening to other machines (one server emits frames, which are captured by a listening server; these are known as the *Echo server* and the *Responder* respectively).

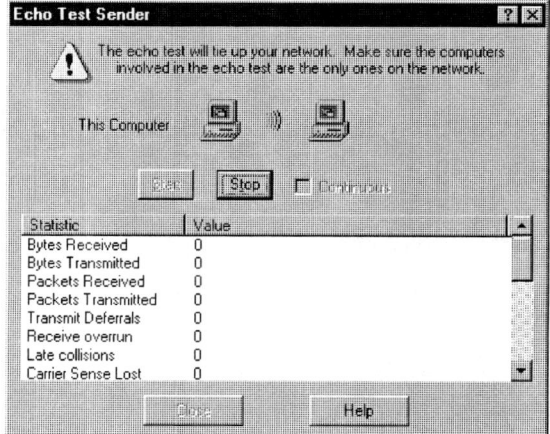

If any problems remain unsolved, you can use the on-line documentation that is supplied with the manufacturer's software. You can also use the manufacturer's BBS or the Internet to download the very latest version of the driver.

### c. Detecting a configuration problem using the operating system

There are a number of ways of identifying conflicts. For example, on Windows 95 or Windows NT, if a parameter has already been used, an **asterisk** appears before it.

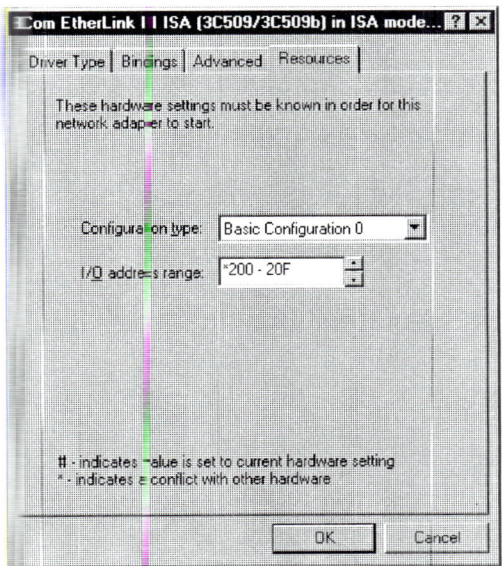

In addition, when you start up the operating system, a message may appear to indicate a configuration problem.

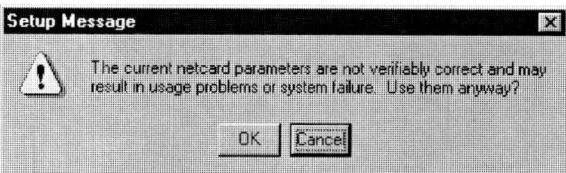

Specific tools are available, according to the operating system you use. For example, Windows NT offers Windows NT Diagnostics. This utility provides a general view of the parameters that have been attributed to the different system peripheral devices.

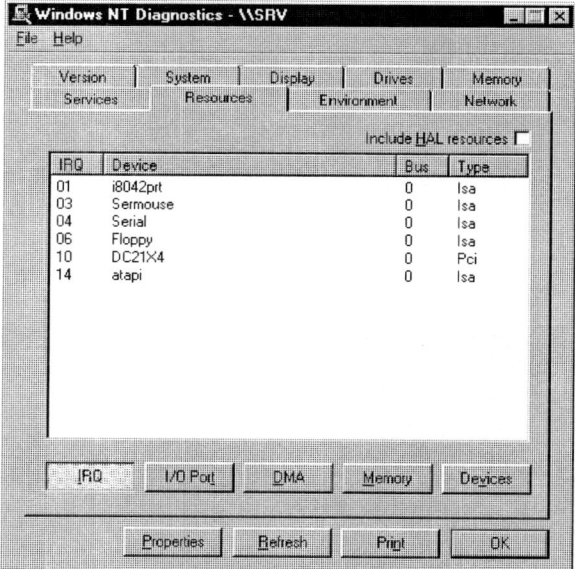

On Windows 95, there is a very useful tool that provides a general view of the peripheral devices, and indicates whether or not they are correctly configured. You can access this tool by clicking the **Control Panel - System** icon.

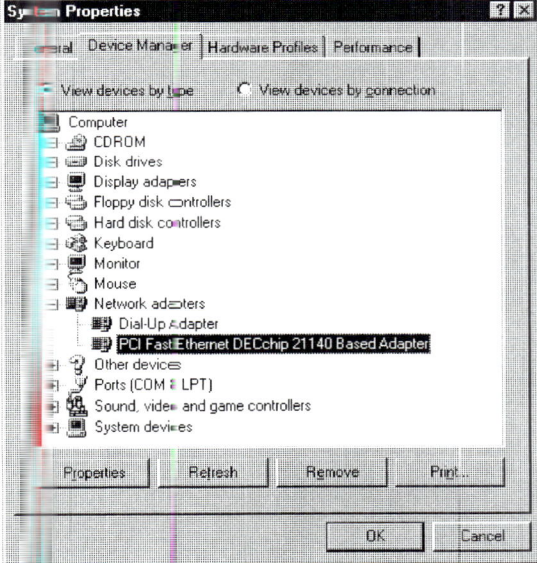

The following screen clearly shows that the network interface is badly configured as it uses the input/output address of another peripheral device:

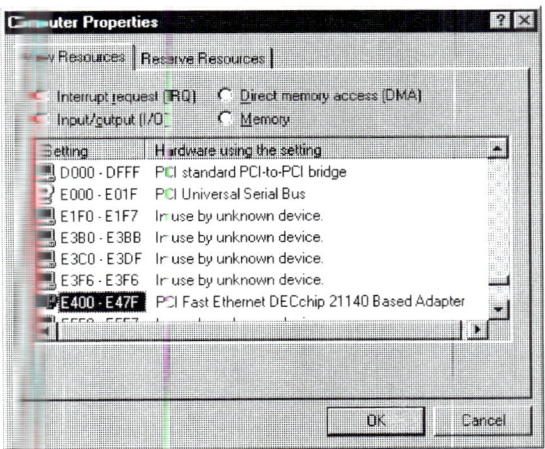

## 2. Adding a new network interface card

This section describes how to install a network interface card on Windows 95 and on Windows NT.

### a. On Windows 95

In **My Computer** click the **Network** icon.

☞ *You can also right-click the Network Neighborhood and then select Properties from the shortcut menu that appears.*

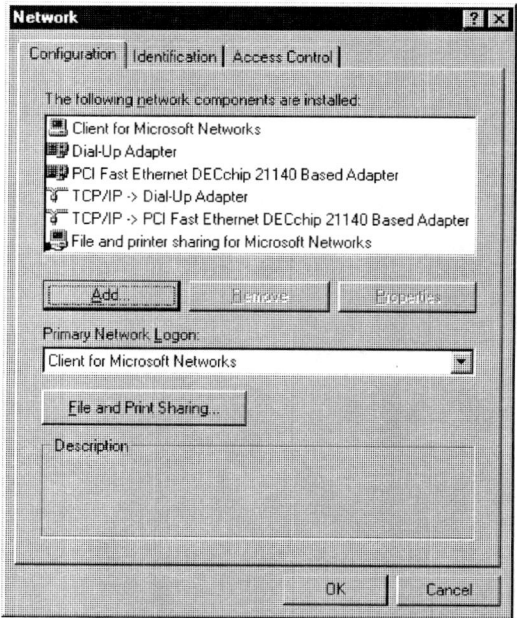

Click the **Add** button to obtain the following screen, which allows you to choose the component to be installed (a network interface card in this case):

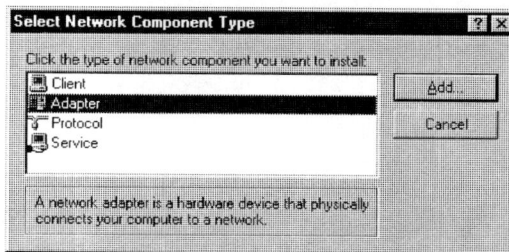

You must then be careful to specify the correct type of network interface card.

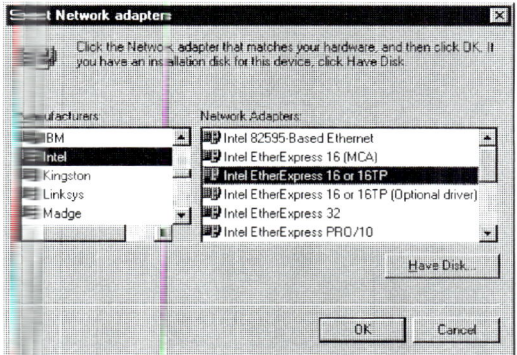

☞ It must be noted that, in general, the installation programs are able to detect the first network interface card without too much trouble.

Finally you must verify that the configuration that was seen by the operating system is the same as that which is actually configured in the EEPROM of the network interface card.

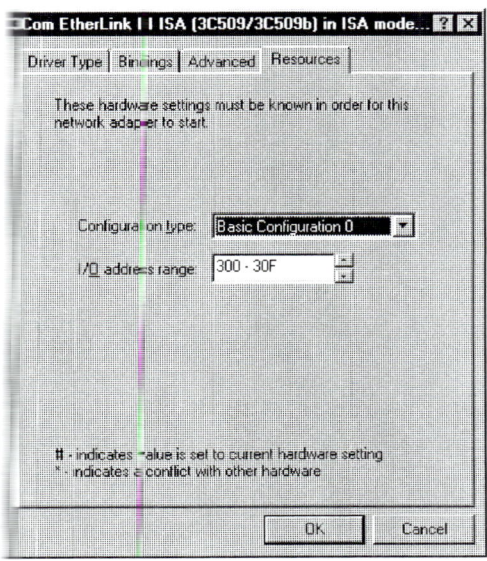

☞ *In general, you do not need to configure the EEPROM of the card. Nor do you need to concern yourself with the configuration that is actually used. On the other hand, if a problem occurs, knowing the exact configuration of the card greatly helps you to solve the problem.*

**b. On Windows NT**

In **My Computer** or **Control Panel**, click the **Network** icon and select the **Adapters** tab:

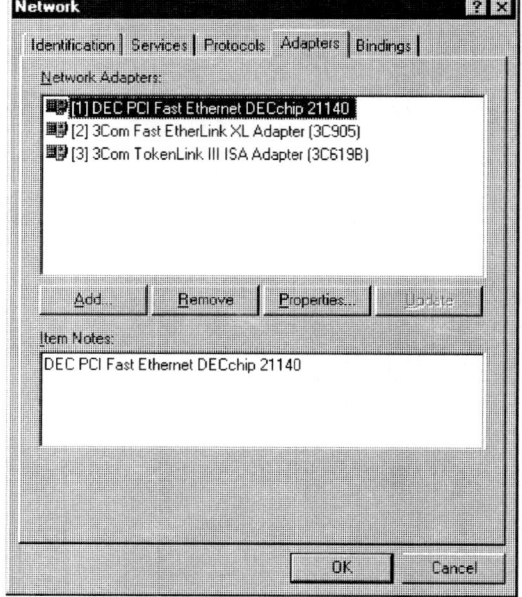

Click the **Add** button and then select the network interface card that you wish to install:

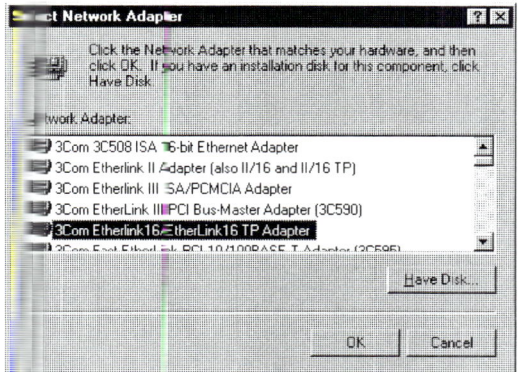

Finally, you must check that the card is correctly configured.

☞ Although Windows NT is usually able to detect the right type of card, it often has difficulties in determining if the card is configured properly. Consequently, this must be checked by the network administrator.

## E. Network protocol stack

A computer can be equipped with several network interface cards. These network interface cards can have several protocols, which can run several services. The term protocol stack is used to refer to this set of protocols and the bindings between the different levels.

At any given level, a layer can work with other layers that are immediately adjacent to it. When you configure the network model that you are using, you can optimize your configuration by favoring one binding with respect to another.

The following example shows how to **Move Up** or **Move Down** one binding with respect to another on an NT Server machine. In this case, we are favoring one network interface card with respect to another:

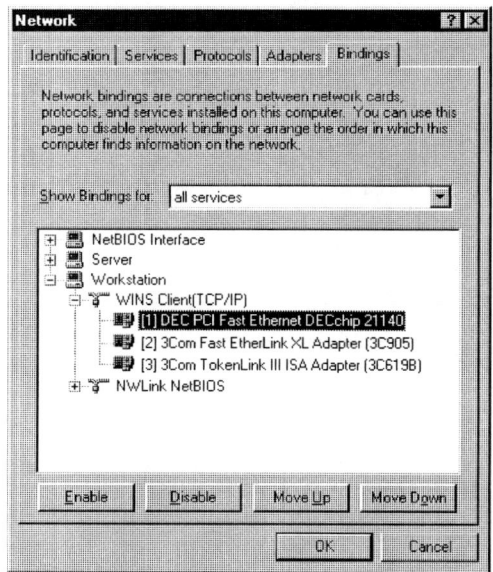

When several protocols are used, you can also favor one network interface card with respect to another, for a given protocol. In addition you can favor one service with respect to another, for a given protocol.

## Exercises

To be absolutely sure that you have assimilated this chapter, work through the corresponding exercises. These are set out from page 385.

☒ Network planning.

## Assessing your skills

Try the following questions if you think you know this chapter well enough.

### Configuring a network interface card

1 Which interrupt would you choose for the network interface card of an application server running SQL Server on Windows NT, if you have the choice between: the IRQ of the second serial port, the IRQ of the second parallel port or IRQ 10? ☐

2 Which range of input/output addresses is normally used for network interface cards and other supplementary peripheral devices? ☐

3 Which type of connection is used with a BNC? ☐

4 Which three types of connector are most commonly used with Ethernet? ☐

5 Which configuration option is particularly important on a Token Ring card? ☐

6 Which speeds do Token Ring networks currently support?

7 What identifies a network interface card at the lowest level?

8 What is the relationship between MAC and Apple?

9 Which organization is responsible for attributing part of the physical addresses that are used in networks?

10 Which specification must be used for a network interface card driver that must be installed on Windows NT 4?

11 Which organizations were responsible for the ODI specification?

### Installing and testing a network interface card

12 What are the three useful items that are included on the floppy disk of the network interface card manufacturer?

13 Which tests are available on the manufacturer's floppy disk?

14 What is an Echo Server?

☐

___

15 Which means are available to solve a problem with a network interface card?

☐

___

16 Which means are available to optimize the functioning of a network on a Windows NT machine, according to the different services used?

☐

___

## Solving configuration problems

17 How can you detect if a conflict exists in the configuration of a network interface card on Windows NT, when you examine the properties of the card?

☐

___

18 Which graphical tool on Windows 95 allows you to determine whether or not a peripheral is correctly configured?

☐

___

19 Which tool on Windows NT allows you to determine the precise parameters that are attributed to the different peripheral devices used?

☐

___

20 Which are the different types of network component that you can install on Windows 95?

☐

## Results

Check your answers on pages 151 to 153. Count one point for each correct answer.

Number of points ⬜ /20

For this chapter you need to have scored at least 15 out of 20.

Look at the list of key points that follows. Pick out the ones with which you have had difficulty and work through them again in this chapter before moving on to the next.

## Key points of the chapter

☐ Configuring a network interface card.
☐ Installing and testing a network interface card.
☐ Solving configuration problems.

## Solutions

### Configuring a network interface card

1 Which interrupt would you choose for the network interface card of an application server running SQL Server on Windows NT, if you have the choice between: the IRQ of the second serial port, the IRQ of the second parallel port or IRQ 10?

*The lowest IRQ. In this case it would be the IRQ that is associated with the second serial port (IRQ 3).*

2 Which range of input/output addresses is normally used for network interface cards and other supplementary peripheral devices?

*From 280 to 340.*

3 Which type of connection is used with a BNC?

*A thin coaxial connection (Ethernet 10).*

4 Which three types of connector are most commonly used with Ethernet?

*RJ45, AUI and BNC.*

5 Which configuration option is particularly important on a Token Ring card?

*Transmission speed.*

6 Which speeds do Token Ring networks currently support?

*4 or 16 Mbps.*

7 What identifies a network interface card at the lowest level?

*The physical address (MAC), which is coded onto 6 bytes.*

8 What is the relationship between MAC and Apple?

*There is no relationship between them as MAC signifies Media Access Control.*

9 Which organization is responsible for attributing part of the physical addresses that are used in networks?

*The IEEE.*

10 Which specification must be used for a network interface card driver that must be installed on Windows NT 4?

*The NDIS 4 specification.*

11 Which organizations were responsible for the ODI specification?

*Novell and Apple.*

### Installing and testing a network interface card

12 What are the three useful items that are included on the floppy disk of the network interface card manufacturer?

*The drivers associated with the different operating systems, the test tools and the auto-configure tools for the card.*

13 Which tests are available on the manufacturer's floppy disk?

*There are local looping tests, internal tests of the card components, and tests that exchange packets with another card via the network.*

14 What is an Echo Server?

*When you want to test the input/output functioning of a network interface card, you can configure the network interface card of one machine as an emitter and the network interface card of another machine in the network as a responder. The second machine, the Responder, then listens for the frames coming from the first machine, the Echo Server.*

15 Which means are available to solve a problem with a network interface card?

*The online help, access to the manufacturer's BBS and, of course, access to the Internet.*

16 Which means are available to optimize the functioning of a network on a Windows NT machine, according to the different services used?

*You can define a binding order associated with a specific service, under the **Bindings** tab of the **Network Properties** on a Windows NT computer.*

## Solving configuration problems

17 How can you detect if a conflict exists in the configuration of a network interface card on Windows NT, when you examine the properties of the card?

*An asterisk indicates a conflict problem.*

18 Which graphical tool on Windows 95 allows you to determine whether or not a peripheral is correctly configured?

*The Device Manager, which is accessible from the System icon of the Control Panel.*

19 Which tool on Windows NT allows you to determine the precise parameters that are attributed to the different peripheral devices used?

*Windows NT Diagnostics.*

20 Which are the different types of network component that you can install on Windows 95?

*Client, Card, Protocol and Service.*

## Prerequisites for this chapter

- [x] Knowledge of the different types of physical media.

## Objectives

When you have completed this chapter you will be able to:
- [x] Describe the different topologies: bus, ring, star and hybrid.
- [x] Distinguish between point-to-point and multi-point topologies.
- [x] Distinguish between physical topologies and logical topologies.
- [x] Choose a network topology according to the application.
- [x] Explain the different communication modes.
- [x] Define the principal methods of accessing the media: contention, token passing and polling.
- [x] Explain the different switching methods.
- [x] Describe the network interconnection components: repeaters, bridges, routers and gateways.
- [x] Choose the interconnection component according to the application.

# Network and interconnection architecture

# Summary

- **A. Topologies** . . . . . . . . . . . . . . . 157
  1. Basic architecture . . . . . . . . . . . . . 157
  2. The different topologies . . . . . . . . . . 158

- **B. Choosing a network topology** . . . . . 163
  1. Bus topology . . . . . . . . . . . . . . . 163
  2. Star topology . . . . . . . . . . . . . . . 163
  3. Ring topology . . . . . . . . . . . . . . . 163

- **C. Communications management** . . . . 164
  1. Communication modes . . . . . . . . . . . 164
  2. Types of transmission . . . . . . . . . . . 165
  3. Transmission media access methods . . . . . 166
  4. Switching techniques . . . . . . . . . . . 170

- **D. Interconnecting networks** . . . . . . . 172
  1. Introduction . . . . . . . . . . . . . . . 172
  2. Repeaters . . . . . . . . . . . . . . . . 173
  3. Bridges . . . . . . . . . . . . . . . . . 174
  4. Routers . . . . . . . . . . . . . . . . . 178
  5. Switches . . . . . . . . . . . . . . . . . 181
  6. Gateways . . . . . . . . . . . . . . . . 183

- **E. Choice of connection hardware** . . . 183
  1. Repeaters . . . . . . . . . . . . . . . . 183
  2. Bridges . . . . . . . . . . . . . . . . . 184
  3. Routers . . . . . . . . . . . . . . . . . 184
  4. Bridge-routers . . . . . . . . . . . . . . 185
  5. Gateways . . . . . . . . . . . . . . . . 185
  6. Switches . . . . . . . . . . . . . . . . . 185

First, this chapter will examine the different network topologies. Then we will study the principal access methods that allow you to manage shared physical media. Finally we will examine network extension solutions, by defining the concepts of broadcast domains and collision domains.

## A. Topologies

### 1. Basic architecture

A network topology defines the relative configuration of the different pieces of network equipment.

Distinction is made between **physical topology** (with respect to the layout of the network) and **logical topology** (which defines how information circulates at the lowest level).

> ☞ It is very important to distinguish clearly between these two aspects. For example, from a logical viewpoint a MAU hub could be seen as a Token Ring, whilst physically it is has a star configuration.

Among these topologies, those using **point-to-point connections** (one to one links) must be clearly distinguished from those using **multipoint connections** (n to n links).

There are four main types of topology: **bus**, **star**, **ring** and **tree**.

## 2. The different topologies

### a. Bus

The bus topology uses a linear medium in the form of a cable onto which nodes are connected (workstations, interconnection equipment, peripherals and so on). This is a multipoint configuration. The cable is the unique hardware element that provides the network, and only the nodes generate signals.

A central point is not necessary with bus topologies and a minimal number of cables are used. The main disadvantage of this type of topology is that only one cable is used which limits the types of workstations that can exchange information on the network.

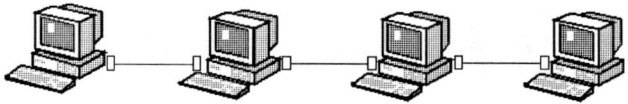

Examples of point-to-point protocols are UUCP (*Unix to Unix CoPy*), PPP (*Point-to-Point Protocol*) and SLIP (*Serial Line IP*). These protocols allow you to interconnect servers, which are equipped with terminals. The terminals can access other servers via the point-to-point connectors between servers.

### b. Star

Star topology is based on active hardware items. **Active** hardware item are able to regenerate signals (they integrate repeater functions).

These central points are called **hubs**. You can create a hierarchical structure by setting up a limited number of levels.

☞ There are also **passive** hubs whose purpose is merely to interconnect the cables physically. The Ethernet twisted-pair hub interconnects the input to a port with all the outputs of all the other ports. Some hubs are called **intelligent** as they include a switching function.

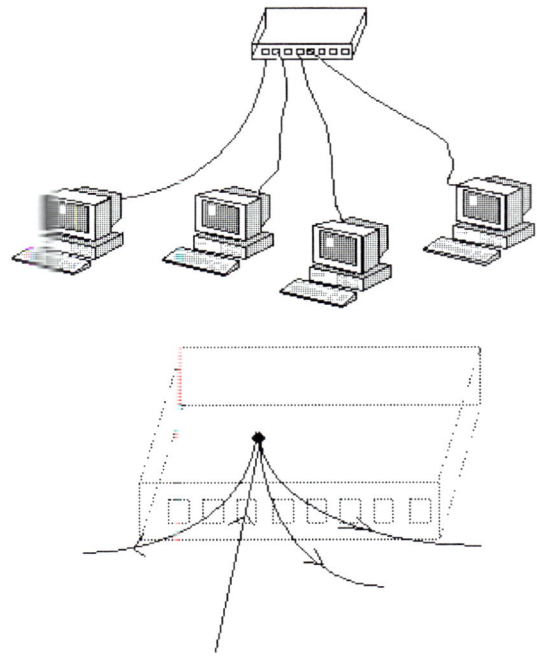

☞ Twisted-pair Ethernet is an example of a logical star topology.

### c. Ring

Ring topology is based on a closed loop in the form of a ring, with point to point connections between peripherals. All communication frames pass via each node. In addition, each node is an active item and acts as a repeater. Ring topology hubs (or MAUs, Multistation Access Units) are passive items. Using a set of electromagnetic relays, they allow you to insert workstations into the network very easily.

☞ *Nowadays, there are also active hubs that can be used with ring topologies.*

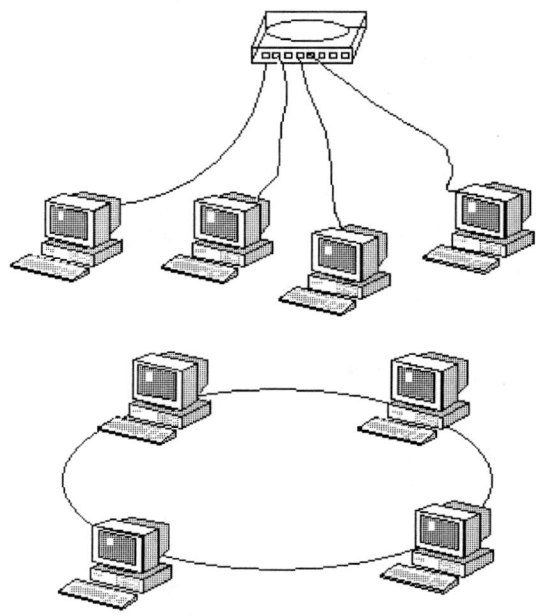

The diagram below illustrates the logical ring principle in terms of the connection hardware used.

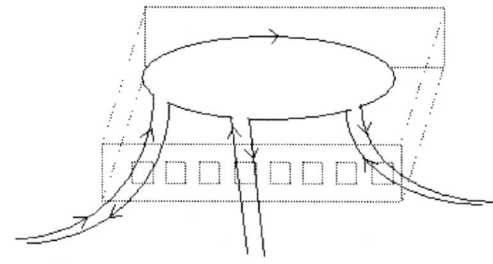

☞ *Token Ring, FDDI, CDDI and 802.5 are examples of logical ring topology.*

### d. Tree

With tree topology, the machines are connected together in a hierarchical tree. This configuration is realized using stackable hubs. This connection must be a cross connection. You can implement this mechanically by installing a button on a port of the hub. Alternatively, you can install a cross cable for this connection.

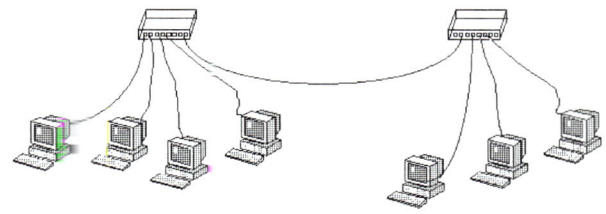

☞ With **twisted-pair Ethernet**, you can interconnect up to four hub levels.

### e. Topology variations

### Mesh

We will discuss mesh networks in the section dealing with mixed topologies. An example of a mesh topology is the Internet (**World Wide Web**).

A **hybrid network** is created when two sites that use different topologies communicate via a point-to-point connection (using modems for example).

## Star bus

An Ethernet hub is a bus onto which workstations can connect. You can connect hubs together using a coaxial cable backbone. This configuration is called a star bus topology.

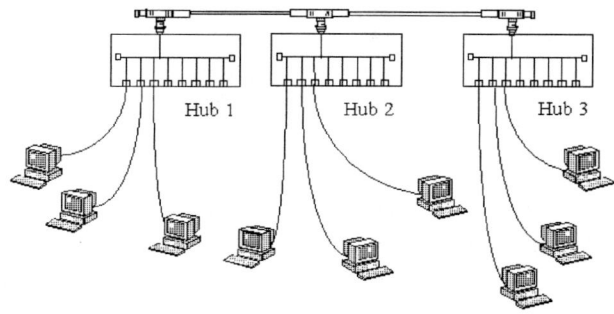

## Star ring

A star ring topology is created when you connect several rings together (cf. chapter 6 - section B - 5).

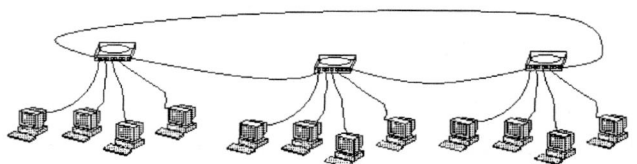

## B. Choosing a network topology

This section will discuss which topologies are most suitable for Token Ring and Ethernet networks, in different situations.

### 1. Bus topology

A bus topology is most suitable in the following cases:
– for small networks,
– when a low budget solution is sought,
– when the network cabling is fixed,
– for networks that will not be greatly extended.

### 2. Star topology

A star topology is most suitable in the following cases:
– for networks that need to be flexible and easy to reconfigure (by adding and removing workstations in the topology),
– when you want rapidly to diagnose any network malfunctioning,
– for networks containing large numbers of nodes,
– for networks that are liable to evolve rapidly.

### 3. Ring topology

A ring topology is most suitable in the following cases:
– when response times must be met, even if the network is heavily loaded,
– when a high-speed network is required,
– when the network configuration is reasonably stable and unlikely to evolve to any great extent.

## C. Communications management

### 1. Communication modes

There are three communication modes that are defined according to the direction of data flow on the communications medium that is used: **simplex** indicates communication in one direction only; **half-duplex** indicates alternate communication in both directions; and **full-duplex** indicates simultaneous communication in both directions.

#### a. Simplex

In simplex mode, you can have one emitter and n receivers. Information can be transmitted in one direction only.

Simplex medium hardware is generally inexpensive.

☞ *A radio program is an example of simplex communication.*

☞ *Most fibers are simplex. This means that information is transmitted in only one direction and different hardware items are required at either end. To be able to emit and receive, you must use either multimode fibers or two separate fibers.*

#### b. Half-duplex

In this mode, each interface is an emitter and a receiver. However, only one interface can emit at once. Communication is therefore **bi-directional** but **alternate**.

☞ *CB radio communication is an example of half-duplex communication.*

☞ *An example of a half-duplex physical medium is a coaxial cable, which can be used for digital baseband signaling.*

### c. Full-duplex

In this mode, you can **transmit simultaneously from both ends of the medium**. This is generally the most expensive solution.

☞ *Telephone switching is an example of full-duplex communication.*

☞ *An example of a full-duplex physical medium is the twisted pair. You can connect two network cards to a switch using a twisted pair cable. To implement full-duplex communication you must use two pairs: one for emission and the other for reception.*

## 2. Types of transmission

The type of transmission refers to the way in which the receiver synchronizes transmitted data so that it can be read. There are two transmission types: **synchronous** and **asynchronous**.

### a. Synchronous transmission

Synchronous transmission is characterized by a continuous flow of exchanged information that is exchanged at regular intervals.

### b. Asynchronous transmission

Asynchronous transmission is used when you need to manage the occasional transmission of information on an event driven basis.

### c. Comparison of the two transmission types

The following table summarizes the characteristics of these two modes:

|  | Synchronous | Asynchronous |
|---|---|---|
| Advantages | more efficient<br><br>high speed<br><br>better error detection | simple<br><br>inexpensive |
| Disadvantages | emission and reception circuits are more complex and more expensive | frame formatting and error detection requires the use of 20 to 30% of the transmitted information<br><br>The parity bit detects only one error<br><br>low speed |

## 3. Transmission media access methods

### a. Introduction

With a point-to-point channel, an emitter can transmit freely. On the other hand, in the case of a shared transmission medium, data transmission must be managed specifically.

### b. Access methods

Access methods depend on the network architecture, or more precisely, on the **logical topology**. According to the case concerned, the signal will either be transmitted on the media and will reach each network card, or it will pass from machine to machine and be repeated by each machine.

An access method defines the rules for each hardware item, for the transmission of the information and the freeing of the shared channel. There are three types of access methods: **contention**, **polling** and **token passing**.

## Contention

With contention methods, each machine listens to the channel (carrier sense) in order to check that no other signal is being emitted that may disturb the emission. The machine then emits information when the carrier is free. There is no centralized management of the channel. Even though two machines listen to the channel in this way, they can still emit simultaneously. The effect of this varies according to the transmission medium used: in the case of a coaxial cable, this will lead to a transmission overload, whereas in the case of a twisted-pair medium, data will be emitted on one pair and received simultaneously on the other. In either case, a **collision** is said to have occurred. The essential aspect of this method is that an emitting machine is able to detect if its frame has collided with another frame or not.

☞ Collision detection is possible provided that a certain number of conditions are met. For example, with **Ethernet**, a frame must not be smaller than 64 bytes. This ensures that the emitting machine is able to detect a collision before it has sent the last byte of its frame.

☞ As a general rule, a data bit of an Ethernet 10 Mbps frame is represented by a signal that extends across 23 meters. This means that the smallest Ethernet frame (64 bytes) can extend over more than 10 kms!

When a collision occurs, the first machine that detects it extends its transmission with a special signal called a JAM. The purpose of the JAM is to ensure that all emitting machines are informed that a collision has taken place.

In this case, a different waiting time is defined, at random, for each machine that was emitting at the time of the collision. This ensures that the machines concerned will not try again to reuse the channel at the same time.

The two most common contention protocols are CSMA/CD and CSMA/CA.

CSMA indicates that the carrier (Carrier Sense) is listened to on a shared medium (Multiple Access). The two protocols are distinguished by the fact that one involves Collision Detection and the other involves Collision Avoidance.

The second method (CA) is in fact a variation on the first method (CD), which is described above. With CA, instead of trying to send data and risking a collision (after listening to the medium), the machine sends a preliminary frame to warn the other stations that it is about to send its data frame on the channel.

☞ *CSMA/CD is an Ethernet implementation, whilst Macintosh LocalTalk networks have adopted the CSMA/CA method.*

### Advantages and disadvantages

The main advantage of the contention method is its **simplicity**. However this method is **not deterministic** as the access time on the channel cannot be known in advance. Also, **no priority management** is possible. This can be a problem for peripherals that require quick access to a shared medium.

## Polling

With polling, one of the hardware items is designated as the channel access administrator. This item, the master item, asks each of the other machines in the network if they wish to emit information. The machines are asked in a predetermined order. In general, the master is a hub and the other machines are the nodes in the star.

### Advantages and disadvantages

The main advantage with polling is that access to the channel is controlled centrally. In addition, the access time and the volume of data that is handled on the channel is fixed and known in advance.

However, this method uses part of the network's bandwidth in order to send warnings and acknowledgements.

☞ *An example of polling is the DPAM (Demand Priority Access Method). This is governed by the 100VG AnyLan specification.*

## Token passing

With the token passing method, the frames are transmitted from machine to machine. Each machine acts as a repeater. Initially, a small frame, called a token, is repeated from machine to machine. If one of the machines wishes to emit information it keeps the token for a fixed time before passing it on.

In fact, the token acts as an authorization message that grants control of the channel to the machine that possesses it. The machine that holds the token can emit its data frame, which will then be repeated by each machine all around the ring. The recipient of the frame makes a copy of it when it passes by (provided that the frame does not contain errors and that the destination machine has enough room in its reception buffer). The destination machine marks the frame in order to inform the emitter whether or not the frame has been read. Once the frame has been all around the ring, the emitter withdraws its frame and then retransmits the token to the next machine.

### Advantages and disadvantages

Token passing is a deterministic solution that provides a means of managing the channel. Maximum effective transmission speeds are much higher than with Ethernet, which is subject to collisions.

☞ *There are a number of token passing standards. These apply to ring topologies (IEEE 802.5, Token Ring and FDDI) and also to bus topologies (IEEE 802.4).*

### Token passing versus contention

Contention is more suitable for lightly loaded networks on which very few collisions occur.

☞ *It is considered that the collision rate must not exceed 11%.*

In contrast to contention, token passing requires the implementation of a channel management mechanism. However, token passing can greatly improve the performance of a heavily loaded network.

## 4. Switching techniques

### a. Circuit switching

This type of switching allows you to **set up a temporary physical link for the whole duration of the communication**.

☞ *This technique is used in Telephone Switching Networks, for example.*

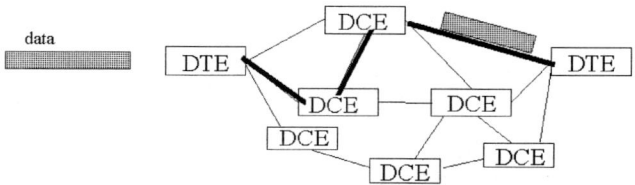

### b. Message switching

With this technique, **it is not necessary to set up a dedicated link between the two machines** that are communicating. When one machine sends a message, it adds the destination address to the packet. The message is then sent in one block, from node to node. Each node receives the whole message, stores it temporarily and then transmits it to the next node. This technique is known as **store and forward**.

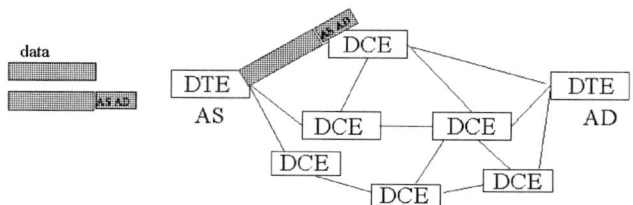

### c. Packet switching

Packet switching tries to combine the advantages of circuit switching and message switching. There are two methods of packet switching: using datagrams and using virtual circuits. Both methods involve decomposing the message into packets, and marking each packet with the source address and the destination address.

## Datagram

With this method, each datagram follows its own route (in the same way as messages do in message switching). Consequently, not only must datagrams contain the destination address, but they must also be numbered in their correct sequence. This allows the datagrams to be re-assembled at the destination in order to reconstruct the original message. This is necessary because each of the datagrams follows its own route which implies that they can arrive at destination in any order.

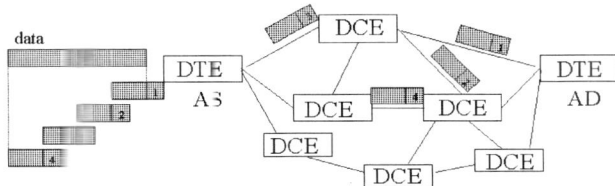

## Virtual circuit

With virtual circuits (VC), logical connections are set up between the emitter and the receiver. A logical connection is set up at the start of the exchange, in order to fix all the parameters that are required for the communication. These parameters include choice of the route, packet size, necessary acknowledgements, transmission control and error management. Virtual circuits also involve the allocation of bandwidth.

☞ *This technique was defined by the X.25 standard.*

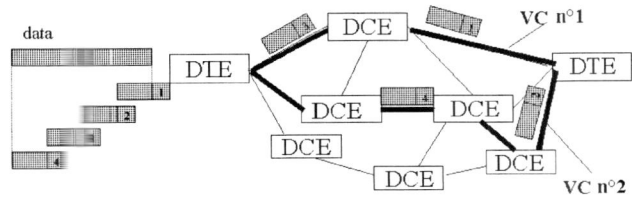

## D. Interconnecting networks

### 1. Introduction

Each of the topologies has its limits in terms of the maximum segment length and the number of machines per segment etc. Because of this, it became necessary to increase the number of machines per network or simply to connect networks together. It was necessary to connect together, both networks of the same type (topology, access method) and networks of different types. In addition, the development and diversification of media used has led to major developments being made in the field of interconnection hardware.

On an Ethernet network, collision domains define the maximum extent of a frame that would flood a physical network. These frames arrive at network peripherals, which do not necessarily accept them. The collision domain then, defines that part of the multipoint medium, which is flooded by the physical signal that corresponds to the frame.

On an Ethernet network, if data frames are above a certain length, they can inundate part of the network. The part of a multipoint medium that is inundated by a physical signal in this way is called a **collision domain**. It is possible to specify the maximum length of a data frame as that length which will cause data inundation to occur.

 With Ethernet, you can use a bridge to divide an existing network into two collision domains. This technique often allows you to decongest the network.

A second type of domain, called a **broadcast domain**, has been defined to identify those parts of a network that a broadcast frame will cover (a broadcast frame is a data frame that has its MAC address set to the broadcast address FF.FF.FF.FF.FF.FF). Some services work exclusively with broadcasts and it is often useful to reduce broadcast domains using routers.

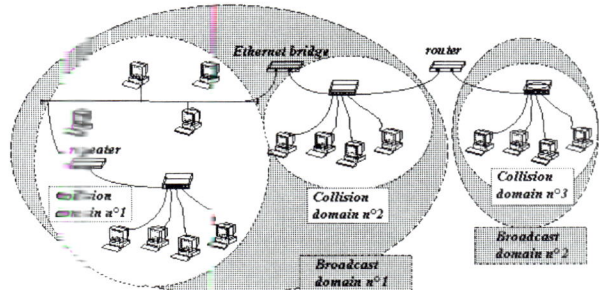

Finally this chapter will examine the cases that lead to segmenting a network, or to joining networks together or to connect to other extended LANs. The characteristics of the different items of interconnection equipment will be discussed: repeaters, bridges, routers, gateways and switches (Ethernet and Token Ring).

## 2. Repeaters

A repeater acts on the physical layer of the OSI model. It reconditions the data it receives and then retransmits it. The purpose of the repeater is to increase the distance over which data can be transmitted. As digital signals are subject to high attenuation, data is transmitted in the form of analog signals. This means that the router must convert the analog signal into data, and then retransform the data into an analog signal for retransmission.

☞ During transmission, square signals tend to lose amplitude and become triangular.

A repeater generally acts on one physical medium, although it can be used to interconnect heterogeneous media.

**Examples:** 10base2/10base5 or 10base5/10baseFL **repeaters.**

The repeater has no knowledge of the semantics of the fields that are used to make up the MAC layer frame. It merely transforms the signal into elementary bits. Consequently, a router cannot distinguish between a valid frame and an invalid one. However, a repeater must be able to detect a collision so that it can transmit the frame on the other side.

As the repeater works on level 1, it cannot interconnect media that operate at different speeds. In addition, it is not advisable to use repeaters on busy networks. As the MAC layer manages access methods, the repeater cannot be used if the segments concerned use different access methods.

### 3. Bridges

#### a. The role of the bridge

Bridges act on the MAC, data link layer. You can use them to connect together two or more different physical media, provided that the same MAC address formats are used on both sides. Bridges can also interconnect networks that run at different speeds as they have a **store and forward** operating mode. However, packets will be lost if the internal buffers of the bridge become full. You can use bridges to extend a network that has reached its maximum extension using repeaters (Ethernet 543 rule). The functionalities of a bridge can be integrated entirely into an independent hardware item.

### b. Types of bridge

A bridge that connects together two extended LANs is called a **local bridge**, whereas the term **remote bridge** is used when two networks are connected together via modems and a serial line.

### c. Filtering action of a bridge

The bridge has a filtering action on the data that it transfers. By observing the MAC source address of the packet, a bridge can learn that the emitter is situated on one side rather than the other (bridge learning). Some bridges can be programmed so that they will filter data according to the values of certain fields in the Ethernet packet. In this way, a bridge can be used to segment an overloaded network.

In addition, a bridge can **detect an invalid frame** (for example, a frame that is too short or too long, or a frame that has an erroneous CRC).

### d. Bridge learning

Bridges are able to learn, progressively, the source addresses of the peripherals that emit packets (some peripherals, such as printers, never appear in bridge tables). Each source address is associated with a lifespan. When his lifespan expires, the corresponding mapping is deleted from the bridge tables.

### e. Addressing bridges

As the bridge has access to physical addresses, it can decide not to let a frame through when it knows that the destination is not located on the other side.

However, the bridge will let the frame through if it does not know where the destination is located. Similarly, bridges also let multicast or broadcast packets through.

You do not need to address bridges. In fact, bridge interface addresses never appear in packets, except for service packets that are transmitted between two bridges.

### f. Coherence of the access method

A bridge is able to avoid collisions by delaying the transfer of frames to the other segment.

Using its buffers, the bridge is able to memorize a packet and re-emit it only when the network on the other side is ready to receive the information (this is implemented using CSMA/CD for Ethernet, or by awaiting tokens for Token Ring).

### g. Loop management

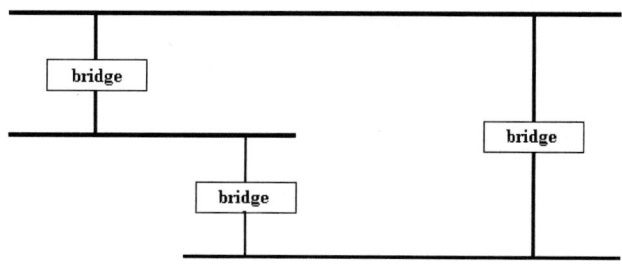

The generalized use of bridges to interconnect networks has led to network configurations becoming more and more complex. In view of this situation, hardware manufacturers have developed loop detection algorithms. For Ethernet this is called the Spanning Tree Algorithm (IEEE 802.1D). In certain configurations, a loop can generate a continuous circulation of frames that inundate the network (if it is not detected by the bridges). The bridge can carry out loop detection itself. It does this by emitting a frame from one of its ports and listening for the frame on the other port. When a loop has been detected, the problem can be solved by momentarily deactivating one of the ports that is included in the loop.

☞ *The MAC address 01.80.C2.00.00.00 has been assigned to allow bridges to communicate with each other.*

A **cost** is generally associated with each port of a bridge. In general, this cost is inversely proportional to the network transmission rate and is coded on 32 bits (1 to 65535). The recommended value is 1000 divided by the network transfer rate in Mbit/s.

For example: 10 for FDDI (100 Mbit/s), 100 for Ethernet 10 Mbit/s.

### h. Interconnecting networks

The most common use of the bridge is to segment a network on which too many collisions occur, in order to create two distinct collision domains. Notably, bridges are used in this way, for overloaded Ethernet networks.

In general, a bridge can interconnect two networks, only if they have the same access method. Consequently, there are **Ethernet bridges** and **Token Ring bridges**. However, some bridges have a **frame translation** feature, which allows them to interconnect networks having topologies that manage different access methods. It must be noted that the difficulty also stems from the fact that Ethernet uses the **Spanning Tree** algorithm to detect loops, whilst Token Ring uses the **Source Routing** algorithm.

### i. Bridge capacities

A bridge has two main characteristics:

**Filtering capacity**

> The filtering capacity corresponds to the number of packets per port that the bridge can process in order to decide if the packet must be transmitted or not to the other side.

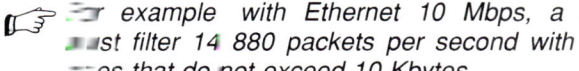
> For example with Ethernet 10 Mbps, a bridge must filter 14 880 packets per second with buffer sizes that do not exceed 10 Kbytes.

**Throughput capacity**

> The filtering capacity corresponds to the number of packets that the bridge is able to transfer to the other segment in one second.

## 4. Routers

### a. Principles

A router is a piece of interconnection hardware, which has access to all the information of layers 1, 2 and 3. In particular, routers have access to logical addresses, which are independent of access methods and physical topology. The router must modify the physical layer when it changes from one medium to another. It must modify the MAC layer to specify the new MAC addresses for itself, and for the next intermediary peripheral, which may be another router. It must also modify the MAC layer to take the new access method into account.

The logical addresses provide the router with a logical view of the inter-network. This means that the router knows the different routes that are possible to reach the destination machine. The router must know all existing logical networks. This information is stored in a table.

Routing may be either static or dynamic. With **static routing**, this data is written to the routing table once and for all. With **dynamic routing** this data can be updated regularly using information provided by other routers (the routers keep each other informed of any internet work topology modifications).

☞ *In some cases, all routing tables may be predefined and fixed for security reasons.*

A routing table contains the following information:
- The complete set of known network addresses.
- The means of connecting to other networks (the logical address of the next peripheral that will allow the data to reach the destination network in which the host is located).
- The different routes between routers.
- The costs associated with the transmission of the data.

A router can also act as a firewall by filtering certain logical addresses.

Routing is possible only if the **protocols** that are used are **routable protocols**. To be routable, a protocol must manage a logical address that is composed of a network number and a number of the host within the network.

☞ *IP and IPX are routable protocols. NetBEUI is not a routable protocol.*

By definition, a router cannot transfer a broadcast.

Almost all modern routers are multi-protocol (IP, IPX and DECnet). In addition they manage different types of routing protocols such as RIP (Routing Information Protocol), BGP (Border Gateway Protocol), EGP (Exterior Gateway Protocol), OSPF (Open Shortest Path First), IS-IS and ES-IS (Intermediary System and End System).

A router can be configured using a terminal connected to a DB25 port of the router. Alternatively it can be configured via the network (for example, via TCP/IP TELNET).

### b. Exploring different paths

Routing algorithms can be **single path** or **multipath**. The later type allows transmission loads to be spread over several paths.

In addition, a distinction is made between **flat** routing algorithms and **hierarchical** routing algorithms. Using the latter type of algorithm means that the router does not need to learn all the logical networks that are possible.

In all cases, a router must choose the best possible route, according to the different criteria. The number of HOPS corresponds to the number of routers that must be crossed between the different networks. The TICKS parameter corresponds to the time required to cross networks. The criteria that are used to choose the best path include cost of the line, network loading, transmission speed and reliability of the links that must be crossed.

### c. Types of router

## Static routers

With static routers, the network administrator initializes the routing table manually (via telnet for example). The possible paths are predefined and the intermediary routers make no routing decisions.

## Dynamic routers

With dynamic routers, the first route (from the first router) is often configured manually. Each intermediary router then chooses the best path when it transfers the data.

### d. Choosing a distance

## Distance vector algorithms

Each router constructs its own routing table. It does this by combining information from the tables of adjacent routers.

A drawback to this type of algorithm is that it requires a lot of data to be transferred between routers. By default, complete routing tables are transmitted every 30 seconds. In addition, convergence time is relatively long.

**Example: RIP is managed by IP and IPX.**

## Link-state algorithms

With link-state algorithms, a global broadcast is made initially, followed by modifications as and when they occur. Using this method, routing tables are maintained up-to-date permanently.

### *Examples:*

Open Shortest Path First is managed by IP (this implements hierarchical routing).
*Netware Link State Protocol* is managed by IPX.
IS-IS and ES-IS are managed by OSI.

## 5. Switches

Switches appeared in 1990 for Ethernet and in 1994 for Token Ring. These devices combine the functionalities of bridges and those of intelligent hubs. They are generally based on RISC (Reduced Instruction Set Component) architectures.

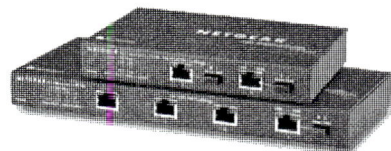

Ethernet switches provide segments that run at 10 Mbps per port for Ethernet and 16 Mbps per port for Token Ring. Each port can be connected to a machine or to a hub. When the switch forwards a frame from a port, it sets up a virtual circuit (VC) that corresponds to the MAC source address and the MAC destination address for the specified ports. A switch can memorize a certain number of MAC addresses per port (for example 1000 entries per port). The subsequent frames are switched directly to the destination using the VC that was set up.

Switch functionality is similar to that of the bridge, except that switching can take place in parallel on the full set of ports. This can be done because of the switch capacity (the capacity of the connector bus on Ethernet, or of the FDDI ring on Token Ring).

A switch can contain from 4 to 25 ports.

☞ Some recent network interface cards such as the 3COM 3C509B, allow full-duplex communication with the switch.

There are several different types of switching method.

With **cut-through switching** (or *switching on the fly*) frames are processed simultaneously, without any intermediate storage. The advantage of this method is that the switch needs very little buffer memory and transfer speeds are high. However, invalid frames and collisions are let through.

With **store and forward** switching, the frame is stored, analyzed and then forwarded to its destination. The advantage of this technique is that invalid frames are eliminated.

With Ethernet, a switch allows you to divide the network into as many segments as it has ports. This means that if you connect one machine per port, you will obtain an Ethernet network without collisions. In practice, switches are configured with one hub per port.

It is also useful to use switches that are equipped with 1 port at 100 Mbps, and N ports at 10 Mbps, to use the 100 Mbps link to interconnect two LANs.

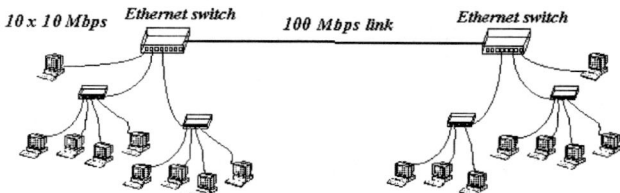

## 6. Gateways

Gateways act on layers 3 to 7. These devices interpret medium and high level layers, notably by formatting data. A gateway is generally a dedicated machine.

For example, the Gateway Service for NetWare on NT Server allows NT clients to access the resources of a Novell server, just as if the resources were those of the NT server. The client has no visibility of the Netware server. All that is seen are resources on the Microsoft server, which are in fact redirected Novell resources.

The NT server interprets medium level layers (for example NetBEUI to IPX/SPX) and high level layers (Server Message Block to Netware Core Protocol). The NT server becomes a Novell client on behalf of the Microsoft client.

# E. Choice of connection hardware

In order to simplify the choice between the different interconnection hardware items described above, we will summarize the characteristics of each of them. In this way, we can indicate the cases in which one item must be chosen rather than another.

## 1. Repeaters

Repeaters act on the physical layer of the OSI model. They allow you to extend the maximum length of a segment. This is done by amplifying the signal. In addition they allow you to interconnect different transmission media.

Repeaters cannot work at the semantic level of the data frame contents. However, they are capable of detecting collisions and transmitting them on the other side.

As they work on level 1, repeaters cannot interconnect media that run at different speeds.

It not advisable to use repeaters with heavily loaded networks.

As access methods are managed at the MAC level, repeaters cannot be used with segments that operate with different access methods.

## 2. Bridges

Bridges allow you to interconnect networks that have the same data link layer (the same MAC address format and the same access method). This enables the bridge to carry out a filtering action, based on physical addresses. This technique allows the bridge to decongest an overloaded network.

☞ *Some bridges have a frame translation feature that enables them to interconnect Ethernet networks and Token Ring networks.*

Bridges let multicast and broadcast messages through, along with frames for which the destination address is unknown. They operate on the MAC layer and works with MAC addresses. They can manage only one path, unless a special algorithm is used to detect loops (spanning tree algorithm or source routing algorithm).

## 3. Routers

Most routers do not let broadcasts through (although some of them do offer an option that does).

They are able to choose the best possible logical address path.

They do not let packets through that have unknown destination addresses.

A router can work only with a routable protocol, unless it offers bridge functionality (in which case it is called a bridge-router, or "brouter").

### 4. Bridge-routers

Bridge-routers offer the main features of bridges as well as those of routers. They can forward selected routable protocols and they can also transfer non-routable protocols, thanks to their bridge feature.

They provide a simpler and less expensive approach than that of using a mixed topology that integrates bridges and routers.

### 5. Gateways

Gateways act as interpreters of medium and high level layers. For example, they translate character tables, international characteristics and even protocols. Gateways allow you to avoid installing specific network components on each client machine. They offer universal access whilst minimizing network heterogeneity.

### 6. Switches

Switches act as multiple-connection bridges. They offer a centralized architecture for the interconnection of LANs. Situated at the heart of the topology, they are ideally placed to monitor network utilization.

A switch is a quick way of providing an Ethernet backbone. A bridge can be used to set up distinct collision domains on each of its ports.

If twisted-pair cables are installed between the switch and the network computers, communication can take place with the network interface cards directly in full-duplex. This technique allows you to double the overall transmission capacity of the network.

☞ *With a 10BaseT implementation, direct connection to the hub allows you to run at speeds of 20 Mbps.*

You can also use switches to interconnect two LANs using a 100 Mbps link.

# Exercises

To be absolutely sure that you have assimilated this chapter, work through the corresponding exercises. These are set out from page 388.

☒ Extended networks.

# Assessing your skills

Try the following questions if you think you know this chapter well enough.

### Network topologies

1 What is the term that is used to indicate the design or the organization of a network?

2 Which are the three principal topologies on which most networks are based?

3 Which type of topology is a passive topology?

4 Which component allows you to extend a network?

5 What is the name of the component that is placed at the end of a bus topology in order to absorb signals so that they do not reflect back up the bus?

6 What is the name of the topology variation that is composed of a bus topology, which links together star topologies?

7 What is the name of the component that centralizes cable connections? ☐

8 Which topology requires the least cabling? ☐

9 Which topology has a deterministic functionality? ☐

10 Which physical topology is the easiest to repair? ☐

11 In which topology would a broken segment result in a breakdown of the whole network? ☐

12 Which physical topology favors monitoring and centralized management? ☐

13 Which topology is an active topology? ☐

14 Which topology is the most suitable for small networks? ☐

15 Which topology is the least expensive? ☐

16 Which topology is the most suitable when future network development and reconfiguration is planned? ☐

17 With which topology do response times remain unaffected, even when the network is highly loaded? ❏

## Communications management

18 In Ethernet, which physical medium is used in half-duplex? ❏

19 Which physical medium can operate in full-duplex? ❏

20 Which physical medium allows only simplex communication? ❏

21 What is the main purpose of the access method for a physical medium? ❏

22 With CSMA/CD contention protocol, what happens when the number of exchanged packets increases? ❏

23 Which method manages network access by asking each node in turn if it wishes to emit? ❏

24 What is a Token Ring token? ❏

25 Which access method involves listening to the physical medium before sending data? ❏

26 Which are the three most commonly used access methods? ❏

**Essentials**                                            Chapter 5 - Page 189

27 Which access method allows a network machine to decide when to emit data? ☐

28 Which contention access method reserves the transmission channel before transmitting data? ☐

29 How can a collision be detected on a twisted pair medium? ☐

30 What is the minimum length of an Ethernet frame? ☐

31 What action does a network machine take, when it detects a collision on the network? ☐

32 Which access method do LocalTalk networks use? ☐

33 What is the main advantage of the contention access method? ☐

34 What is the principal quality of token passing? ☐

35 Which access method does 100VG Any LAN use? ☐

36 Which access method uses an (active) ring topology? ☐

*Network and interconnection architecture*

37 Which item grants control of a channel to a network machine that wishes to transmit data?

38 Which network machine withdraws a frame from a ring?

39 With token passing, is the frame modified by its recipient?

40 Which access method is used in IEEE 802.5?

41 Which access method is used in IEEE 802.4?

42 Which access method is used in IEEE 802.3?

43 For a heavily loaded network, which method is preferable: contention or token passing? Which is preferable for a lightly loaded network?

44 What is the maximum collision rate that is acceptable on Ethernet networks?

45 Which switching technique implements a permanent path for the duration of the communication?

46 Which switching method is used for telephone communications?

47 Which switching method sends the whole message without setting up a dedicated path between emitter and receiver?

48 From which types of switching method is packet switching derived?

49 Which type of switching divides the initial message into smaller elements, each of which have their own paths that are not defined at the outset?

50 Which type of switching uses virtual circuits to transmit small parts of the message?

51 Which switching method is used by X.25?

## Interconnection hardware

52 Which concept identifies that part of a network that a physical signal can cover without interpreting signals?

53 Is the broadcast domain contained within the collision domain?

54 Which interconnection component operates on the physical layer level of the OSI model?

55 Which term is used to describe square signals that lose amplitude and assume triangular forms? ☐

56 Which interconnection component interprets signals, transforms them into elementary bits and has no knowledge of the semantics of the fields of a frame? ☐

57 Which interconnection component acts at data link level? ☐

58 Which interconnection component acts as a filter and works with logical addresses? ☐

59 Which type of interconnection component learns the addresses of the emitters? ☐

60 Which component can be used to isolate two collision domains? ☐

61 Which component can be used to isolate two broadcast domains? ☐

62 Which component allows a packet through even though it does not know where the destination address is located? ☐

63 Which type of component lets through multicast and broadcast packets? ☐

64 Which algorithm is used to detect loops in an Ethernet network with bridges? Which algorithm is used to detect loops in a Token Ring network?

65 Which interconnection component manages multiple paths as a standard feature?

66 Which component can be used to reduce collisions on an Ethernet network, by physically separating the interconnected segments?

67 Which component can be used to interconnect networks that implement different access methods?

68 Which component accesses OSI model layers 1, 2 and 3?

69 Give two examples of routable protocols.

70 Does a router let broadcasts through by default?

71 Which type of protocol provides access to the configuration menu of the router?

72 What are the two types of routing?

73 Give two examples of dynamic routing protocols with IP and IPX. ☐

74 Which component allows you to segment an Ethernet network using a centralized architecture whilst providing the functionality of an intelligent hub? ☐

75 Which component allows you to activate the full-duplex functionality that is present on some network interface cards, by connecting with them via twisted pairs? ☐

76 What is the purpose of a gateway? ☐

77 Give an example of a gateway that operates in an NT Server environment and that can be used to interconnect Novell and Microsoft networks. ☐

78 Which low-level component allows you to extend a segment beyond that normally allowed? ☐

79 If an Ethernet network is heavily loaded, is it advisable to use a repeater to add extra machines? ☐

80 Which interconnection component provides a cost-effective solution offering the advantages of the bridge and the router, without their drawbacks? ☐

81 Which component allows you to avoid installing network components on each client machine by offering universal access that minimizes network heterogeneity?

82 Which component is described by the following definition: it acts as a multi-connection bridge; it allows you to introduce a centralized architecture to interconnect with other LANs; it is situated at the heart of the topology and provides an ideal means of monitoring network utilization?

# Network and interconnection architecture

## Results

Check your answers on pages 197 to 205. Count one point for each correct answer.

Number of points ☐ /82

For this chapter you need to have scored at least 62 out of 82.

Look at the list of key points that follows. Pick out the ones with which you have had difficulty and work through them again in this chapter before moving on to the next.

## Key points of the chapter

☐ Network topologies.
☐ Communications management.
☐ Interconnection hardware.

## Solutions

### Network topologies

1 What is the term that is used to indicate the design or the organization of a network?

*The topology.*

2 Which are the three principal topologies on which most networks are based?

*Bus, ring and star topologies.*

3 Which type of topology is a passive topology?

*Bus.*

4 Which component allows you to extend a network?

*Repeater.*

5 What is the name of the component that is placed at the end of a bus topology in order to absorb signals so that they do not reflect back up the bus?

*Terminator.*

6 What is the name of the topology variation that is composed of a bus topology, which links together star topologies?

*Star bus.*

7 What is the name of the component that centralizes cable connections?

*Hub.*

8 Which topology requires the least cabling?

*Bus.*

9 Which topology has a deterministic functionality?

*Ring.*

10 Which physical topology is the easiest to repair?

*Physical star topology.*

11 In which topology would a broken segment result in a breakdown of the whole network?

*Bus.*

12 Which physical topology favors monitoring and centralized management?

*Star topology.*

13 Which topology is an active topology?

*Ring.*

14 Which topology is the most suitable for small networks?

*Bus.*

15 Which topology is the least expensive?

*Bus.*

16 Which topology is the most suitable when future network development and reconfiguration is planned?

*Star.*

17 With which topology do response times remain unaffected, even when the network is highly loaded?

*Ring.*

## Communications management

18 In Ethernet, which physical medium is used in half-duplex?

*Coaxial cables for digital signaling.*

19 Which physical medium can operate in full-duplex?

*Twisted pair.*

20 Which physical medium allows only simplex communication?

*Optical fiber.*

21 What is the main purpose of the access method for a physical medium?

*It allows you to manage simultaneous access to the physical medium.*

22 With CSMA/CD contention protocol, what happens when the number of exchanged packets increases?

*The number of collisions increases.*

23 Which method manages network access by asking each node in turn if it wishes to emit?

*Polling.*

24 What is a Token Ring token?

*A small frame.*

25 Which access method involves listening to the physical medium before sending data?

*CSMA/CA.*

26 Which are the three most commonly used access methods?

*Contention, token passing and polling.*

27 Which access method allows a network machine to decide when to emit data?

*CSMA.*

28 Which contention access method reserves the transmission channel before transmitting data?

*CSMA/CA.*

29 How can be detected a collision on a twisted pair medium?

*When a signal is detected on the reception pair whilst the card is still emitting.*

30 What is the minimum length of an Ethernet frame?

*64 bytes.*

31 What action does a network machine take, when it detects a collision on the network?

*It sends a signal to notify the other machines that a collision has occurred.*

32 Which access method do LocalTalk networks use?

*CSMA/CA*

33 What is the main advantage of the contention access method?

*Simplicity.*

34 What is the principal quality of token passing?

*It is a deterministic method.*

35 Which access method does 100VG Any LAN use?

*Demand Priority Access Method (this is a polling method).*

36 Which access method uses an (active) ring topology?

*Token passing.*

37 Which item grants control of a channel to a network machine that wishes to transmit data?

*The token.*

38 Which network machine withdraws a frame from a ring?

*In general, the frame is withdrawn by the machine that emitted it.*

39 With token passing, is the frame modified by its recipient?

*Yes, the recipient modifies the frame to inform the emitter that the frame has been received.*

40 Which access method is used in IEEE 802.5?

*Token passing.*

41 Which access method is used in IEEE 802.4?

*Token passing.*

42 Which access method is used in IEEE 802.3?

*Contention.*

43 For a heavily loaded network, which method is preferable: contention or token passing? Which is preferable for a lightly loaded network?

*Token passing is preferable for a heavily loaded network and contention is preferable for a lightly loaded network.*

# Essentials
## Chapter 5 - Page 201

44 What is the maximum collision rate that is acceptable on Ethernet networks?

*11%*

45 Which switching technique implements a permenant path for the duration of the communication?

*Circuit switching.*

46 Which switching method is used for telephone communications?

*Circuit switching.*

47 Which switching method sends the whole message without setting up a dedicated path between emitter and receiver?

*Message switching.*

48 From which types of switching method is packet switching derived?

*From circuit switching and message switching.*

49 Which type of switching divides the initial message into smaller elements, each of which have their own paths that are not defined at the onset?

*Datagram switching.*

50 Which type of switching uses virtual circuits to transmit small parts of the message?

*Virtual circuit switching.*

51 Which switching method is used by X.25?

*Virtual circuit switching.*

### Interconnection hardware

52 Which concept identifies that part of a network that a physical signal can cover without interpreting signals?

*Collision domain.*

53 Is the broadcast domain contained within the collision domain?

*No, the broadcast domain includes the collisions domain.*

**Network and interconnection architecture**

54 Which interconnection component operates on the physical layer level of the OSI model?

*The repeater.*

55 Which term is used to describe square signals that lose amplitude and assume triangular forms?

*Attenuation.*

56 Which interconnection component interprets signals, transforms them into elementary bits and has no knowledge of the semantics of the fields of a frame?

*The repeater.*

57 Which interconnection component acts at data link level?

*The bridge.*

58 Which interconnection component acts as a filter and works with logical addresses?

*The router.*

59 Which type of interconnection component learns the addresses of the emitters?

*The bridge.*

60 Which component can be used to isolate two collision domains?

*The bridge.*

61 Which component can be used to isolate two broadcast domains?

*The router.*

62 Which component allows a packet through even though it does not know where the destination address is located?

*The bridge.*

63 Which type of component lets through multicast and broadcast packets?

*The bridge.*

64 Which algorithm is used to detect loops in an Ethernet network with bridges? Which algorithm is used to detect loops in a Token Ring network?

*Spanning Tree. Source Routing.*

65 Which interconnection component manages multiple paths as a standard feature?

*The router (bridges require explicit management of multiple paths).*

66 Which component can be used to reduce collisions on an Ethernet network, by physically separating the interconnected segments?

*The bridge.*

67 Which component can be used to interconnect networks that implement different access methods?

*The router. However, certain bridges offer frame translation functionalities that allow them to connect an Ethernet network with a Token Ring network.*

68 Which component accesses OSI model layers 1, 2 and 3?

*The router.*

69 Give two examples of routable protocols.

*IP and IPX.*

70 Does a router let broadcasts through by default?

*No. A router will allow a broadcast through only if it includes a bridge function and if this function has been activated.*

71 Which type of protocol provides access to the configuration menu of the router?

*Telnet*

72 What are the two types of routing?

*Static and dynamic.*

73 Give two examples of dynamic routing protocols with IP and IPX.

*RIP applies to both. In addition, Open Shortest Path First and Netware Link State Protocol are managed by IPX.*

74 Which component allows you to segment an Ethernet network using a centralized architecture whilst providing the functionality of an intelligent hub?

*The Ethernet switch.*

75 Which component allows you to activate the full-duplex functionality that is present on some network interface cards, by connecting with them via twisted pairs?

*The switch.*

76 What is the purpose of a gateway?

*A gateway translates medium and high level layers (usually including the presentation layer). A gateway is generally a software component*

77 Give an example of a gateway that operates in an NT Server environment and that can be used to interconnect Novell and Microsoft networks.

*Gateway Service for NetWare.*

78 Which low-level component allows you to extend a segment beyond that normally allowed?

*Repeater.*

79 If an Ethernet network is heavily loaded, is it advisable to use a repeater to add extra machines?

*No. The number of collisions will increase, which may cause the network to break down.*

80 Which interconnection component provides a cost-effective solution offering the advantages of the bridge and the router, without their drawbacks?

*The bridge-router, or brouter.*

81 Which component allows you to avoid installing network components on each client machine by offering universal access that minimizes network heterogeneity?

*Gateway*

82 Which component is described by the following definition: it acts as a multi-connection bridge; it allows you to introduce a centralized architecture to interconnect with other LANs; it is situated at the heart of the topology and provides an ideal means of monitoring network utilization?

*Switch*

# Prerequisites for this chapter

☒ Knowledge of physical media, topologies, access methods and types of encoding.

# Objectives

When you have completed this chapter you will be able to:
☒ Describe the different IEEE standards.
☒ Explain how the IEEE 802.3 and IEEE 802.5 standards function.
☒ Describe the functioning of AppleTalk, ArcNet, FDDI and ATM.

# Summary

A. Characteristics of the physical layer . 209
   1. Introduction . . . . . . . . . . . . . . . 209
   2. Specifications . . . . . . . . . . . . . . 209
   3. Null-modem cable . . . . . . . . . . . . 211

B. IEEE protocols . . . . . . . . . . . . . 212
   1. IEEE 802.1 . . . . . . . . . . . . . . . . 212
   2. IEEE 802.2 or LLC (Logical Link Control) . . . . 213
   3. IEEE 802.3 . . . . . . . . . . . . . . . . 214
   4. IEEE 802.4 . . . . . . . . . . . . . . . . 220
   5. IEEE 802.5/Token ring . . . . . . . . . . 221
   6. IEEE 802.6 . . . . . . . . . . . . . . . . 224
   7. IEEE 802.7 . . . . . . . . . . . . . . . . 225
   8. IEEE 802.8 . . . . . . . . . . . . . . . . 225
   9. IEEE 802.9 . . . . . . . . . . . . . . . . 225
   10. IEEE 802.10 . . . . . . . . . . . . . . . 225

11. IEEE 802.11 . . . . . . . . . . . . . . . . . . . 225
12. IEEE 802.12 . . . . . . . . . . . . . . . . . . . 225

## C. AppleTalk . . . . . . . . . . . . . . . . . . . 227
1. Overview . . . . . . . . . . . . . . . . . . . . 227
2. LocalTalk . . . . . . . . . . . . . . . . . . . . 227
3. Topology and cabling . . . . . . . . . . . . 227
4. Logical addressing . . . . . . . . . . . . . . 228

## D. ARCnet (Attached Resource Computer Network) . . . . . . . . . . . . . . . . . 229

## E. FDDI . . . . . . . . . . . . . . . . . . . . 231

## F. ATM (Asynchronous Transfer Mode from the ATM Forum) . . . . . . . . . . . 233
1. Overview . . . . . . . . . . . . . . . . . . . . 233
2. Relaying cells . . . . . . . . . . . . . . . . . 233
3. Traffic control . . . . . . . . . . . . . . . . . 234
4. Types of service offered . . . . . . . . . . 234
5. Topology . . . . . . . . . . . . . . . . . . . . 235
6. ATM transmission speeds . . . . . . . . . 235

## G. Summary of the capacities of the different physical layers used . . . 235

# Essentials     Chapter 6 - Page 209

This chapter will examine the physical layer. It will begin by describing the RS232 standard, followed by the IEEE 802.3 and 802.5 standards. Finally, it will cover the LocalTalk, ARCNet, FDDI and ATM protocols.

## A. Characteristics of the physical layer

### 1. Introduction

This is the first layer of the OSI model. The most commonly used physical layer standard is RS232, which was developed by the EIA (Electronic Industries Association).

Initially, this specification concerned data exchange between a terminal and a modem. Today, it describes the connection between a computer and a printer, or between two computers.

### 2. Specifications

Four aspects are defined: mechanical characteristics of the interface, electrical signals, the functions of each electrical signal and the procedures used for certain applications.

#### a. Mechanical characteristics

An example of the mechanical characteristics of this standard is that the cable length must not exceed 15 meters. DB-25 connectors are generally used, with 24 pins and one signal per pin.

#### b. Electrical signals

For digital signals, a voltage of -3v defines the logic 1 and a voltage of +3v defines the logic 0. Transmission speeds must not exceed 20 kbps.

*Lower layer protocols*

### c. Functional specifications

There are four categories of functional specification: data, earth, system timer and checking. Concerning the data category, full-duplex communication is provided by one wire for each direction.

### d. Procedures

The procedures define the signal sequences and the corresponding actions of the DTE and the DCE machines. Each signal acts in reaction to another.

For example, suppose there are two DTE computers, which exchange information via modems (DCE's).

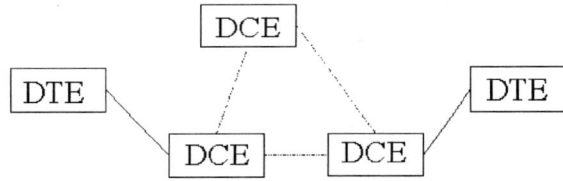

Two signals are validated when the peripherals (DTE and DCE) are switched on. The local computer asks the local modem for permission to transmit. In order to grant this permission the local modem asks for validation from the remote modem. When the two modems are in agreement, the local computer can begin to transmit data. The remote modem receives the data from the local modem and retransmits it onto the reception pin of the distant computer.

The same procedure can be implemented in the other direction simultaneously (full-duplex communication).

### 3. Null-modem cable

If two computers are directly connected via an RS232 cable, there is no DCE. To take this configuration into account, the two DTEs are made to believe that they are communicating via modems by crossing certain lines in the connection. For example, with 25-pin connectors, the following connections are often made:

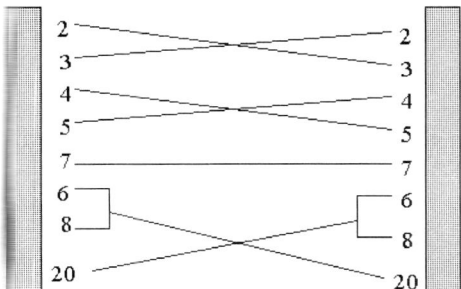

## B. IEEE protocols

The development of standards has played an important role in the knowledge and the use of networks.

In February 1980, the *Institute of Electrical and Electronic Engineers* started their development of a set of network standards. The '802' committees were set up ('80' for the year of 1980, and '2' for the month of February).

In 1985, the 802 committees published the following standards:

| | IEEE 802.2 (LLC) | | |
|---|---|---|---|
| DATA LINK | | | |
| | IEEE 802.3 CSMA/CD | IEEE 802.4 Token Bus | IEEE 802.5 Token Ring |
| PHYSICAL | | | |

Other standards followed, allowing the *opening* of a certain number of systems. These standards concern both security and network administration. They also cover aspects of training for the installation of fiber optics.

### 1. IEEE 802.1

This standard provides an introduction to the 802 standards. It describes the overall relationships between all the other 802 standards. It covers the problems relating to systems management and network interconnection.

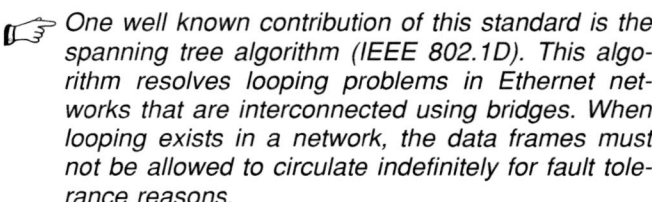 *One well known contribution of this standard is the spanning tree algorithm (IEEE 802.1D). This algorithm resolves looping problems in Ethernet networks that are interconnected using bridges. When looping exists in a network, the data frames must not be allowed to circulate indefinitely for fault tolerance reasons.*

## 2. IEEE 802.2 or LLC (Logical Link Control)

### a. LLC principles

Logical link control defines standard services that are independent of topology and media access methods. They cover point-to-point, or multipoint links that are implemented using cables or wireless media, in half-duplex or full-duplex, on packet switching or circuit networks.

LLC can ensure end-to-end transmission integrity between two machines.

☞ *The High Level Data Link Control (HDLC) protocol was created in 1979. This was an intermediary step towards LLC.*

### b. Types of service

The LLC protocols offer **three types of service**:

#### Connectionless service (type 1):

This is the simplest and least reliable service. It is also the most commonly used, as most sets of protocol use a reliable transport (OSI layer 4).

#### Connection oriented service (type 2):

A logical connection is set up between the emitter and the receiver.

#### Acknowledged connectionless service (type 3):

Each frame is acknowledged individually, but there is no logical connection between the two machines.

## 3. IEEE 802.3

### a. Overview

The 802.3 standard uses the services of the LLC layer. Although there are slight differences between Ethernet and 802.3, there is frequently no distinction made between these two standards. Both of these standards are based on the CSMA/CD (listening to the carrier on a shared medium with collision detection).

 *75% of LANs use Ethernet.*

### b. Physical layer standards

The 802.3 standards offer a number of physical layer options that take into account different topologies, media, types of signal and transmission speeds.

The 802.3 standards have names that correspond to the following format:

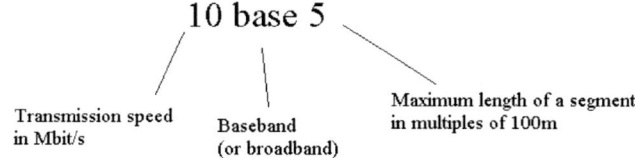

10base2 corresponds to an Ethernet network with a thin coaxial cable (10 Mbps, digital signaling with maximum segment lengths of 200 meters; in practice, a maximum length of 185 meters is used).

10baseT corresponds to Ethernet with twisted pairs (the T stands for Twisted pair).

100baseT corresponds to twisted pair Ethernet with transmission speeds of 100 Mbps (category 5).

10baseFL corresponds to a fiber optics implementation.

Digital signaling is used with the Manchester encoding method (network interface cards run at 20 Mhz). A frame has a minimum length of 64 bytes and a maximum length of 1518 bytes.

Performance deteriorates markedly when more than 40% of the bandwidth is used. This is because the number of collisions increases rapidly when this level of usage is exceeded, and a lot of frames have to be retransmitted. However, an effective maximum transmission rate of 6 Mbps is obtained.

### c. IEEE 10 Mbps standards

#### 10base2

This standard is referred to as **thin-net** or **cheap-net**. System designers also refer to it as thin Ethernet. Implementation in thin coaxial media provides a less costly solution than thick coaxial solutions.

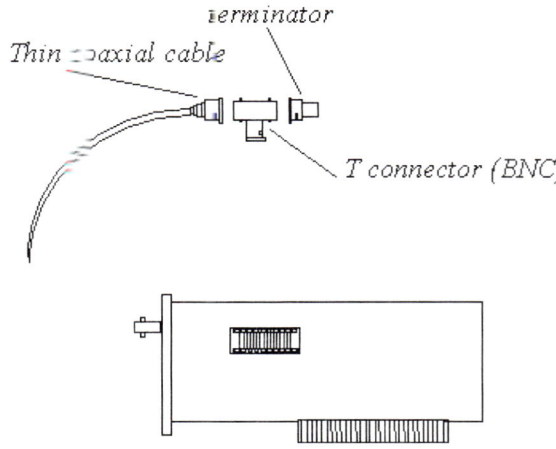

Bus topology is used and segment lengths must not exceed 185 meters (in order to avoid high attenuation factors). BNC (British Naval Connectors) are used. The maximum distance between T's is 0.5 meters. A maximum of 30 machines can be connected per segment. The network must not extend beyond 925 meters (including a maximum of 5 segments and 4 repeaters). A terminator must be placed at each end of the bus. With 10base2, the transceiver, which allows signals to circulate, is integrated into the network interface card.

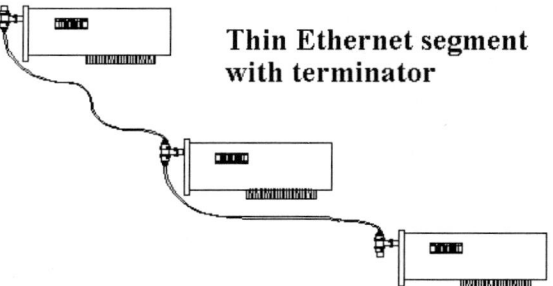

Thin Ethernet segment with terminator

## 10base5

10base5 Ethernet networks use thick coaxial cables. These networks are also known as **thick-net**, **thick-wire Ethernet** and **thick Ethernet**, because of their rigidity and the space they occupy. The CSMA/CD access method functions as with 10base2 using a bus topology. Segments have a maximum length of 500 meters. This means that 10base5 networks can extend over distances of up to 2500 meters.

☞ *Ethernet configurations are subject to a rule that is called the 5-4-3 rule. This rule allows you up to interconnect 5 segments using 4 repeaters, and only 3 of the segments can have workstations connected to them. This means that the maximum extent of Ethernet networks is 925 meters for thin Ethernet and 2500 meters for thick Ethernet.*

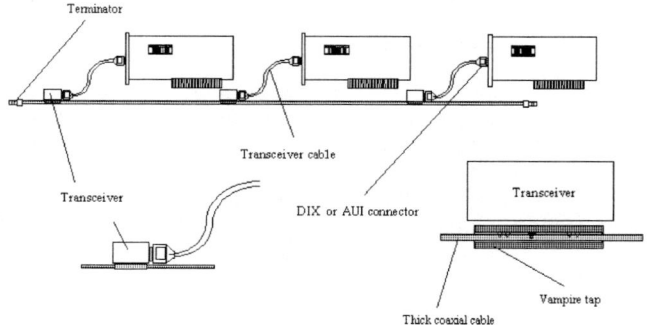

With 10base5, an external **transceiver** is used that can be located at a distance of up to 50 meters from the network interface card. The cable that links the transceiver to the AUI (Access Unit Interface) connector, or to the DIX (Digital Intel Xerox) connector, of the network interface card is called the **transceiver cable**. The minimum distance between two transceivers is 2.5 meters, and there must not be more than 100 transceivers per segment.

☞ *The external transceiver is often connected to the thick cable using a vampire tap. AUI/RJ-45 adaptors are also used. These connectors have integrated transceivers, which allows you to connect the network interface card in 10baseT configurations using an AUI connector.*

## 10baseT

Ethernet networks configured with a star topology use twisted pair cables. The machines are connected together using a hub, and the length of the cable that connects the machine to the hub must not exceed 100 meters. RJ-45 connectors are used, both on the network interface cards and on the hubs. Stackable hubs can be used to extend the network, in which case a tree topology is implemented. Alternatively, the hubs can be interconnected using a bus (this can be implemented using a thin coaxial, a thick coaxial or optical fiber cables). Category 3, unshielded twisted pair (UTP) cables are most commonly used. The higher quality category 5 allows transmission speeds of up to 100 Mbps (100baseT).

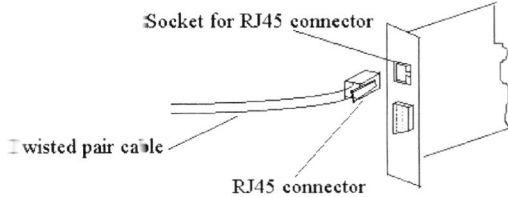

## Ethernet and fiber optics (FOIRL)

Fiber optics are implemented on Ethernet networks using FOIRL (Fiber Optics Inter Repeater Link).

### Fiber links

Fiber optics are used to interconnect two LANs that are relatively close together (situated at one or two kilometers (around a mile) from each other). The interconnection can be made using a repeater, a bridge or even an active optical star (with collision management).

☞ *As the optical fiber is a simplex medium, you must use two fibers (one for emission and the other for reception).*

☞ *In order to be compatible with FDDI (Fiber Distributed Data Interface), it is advisable to use multimode optical fibers, 62.5/125 mm, with ST type connectors.*

### Ethernet fiber optics standards

The use of the fiber optics for low throughput transmission, has given rise to Ethernet solutions with segment lengths of up to two kilometers. In addition you can use fiber optics cables to interconnect remote LANs, using mixed repeaters (fiber/coaxial for example).

At the end of 1993, standards were defined concerning Ethernet and fiber optics. These standards are called **10BaseF**. They define three types of segment: 10BaseFL or Fiber Link, 10BaseFB or Fiber Backbone and 10BaseFP or Fiber Passive.

### 10BaseFL

This standard replaces the FOIRL standard. It defines a point-to-point segment that can extend across distances of up to 2 kms, provided that only 10BaseFL equipment is used. If FOIRL equipment is used, the segment length cannot exceed 1 km.
A 10BaseFL segment can connect two computers, two repeaters, or a computer to the port of a repeater.

**10BaseFB**

This standard defines a fiber optics solution as the **backbone** in a star topology. This implementation specifies a synchronous signal that allows you to exceed the number of repeaters that are normally allowed with Ethernet. 10BaseFB is not used to link computers together. Its sole purpose is to provide a backbone to interconnect 10BaseFB optics star topologies. Each segment can be up to 2 kms long. In addition, the 10BaseFB standard allows **remote fault diagnostics**.

**10BaseFP**

This set of specifications defines a passive star, linking several computers together without using repeaters. A 10BaseFP segment must not be longer than 500 m. A passive 10BaseFP star can interconnect up to 33 computers.
10BaseFP uses ST, or SMA 905, connectors.

 Hardware that is equipped with AUI connectors can use a fiber optics transceiver to connect to a 10BaseFP network.

**d. IEEE 100 Mbps standards**

A number of applications require bandwidths in excess of 10 Mbps, for example:
- CAD
- CAM
- Multimedia applications
- Client-server applications that involve the consultation of voluminous databases.

First we will examine the characteristics of Fast Ethernet. Later on in this chapter we will describe the 100VG AnyLan standard.

**Fast Ethernet**

Since 1994, Fast Ethernet has provided a very good alternative to Ethernet. This is for the following reasons:

It offers a bandwidth that is ten times greater than that of 10BaseT, for less than twice the price.

It accommodates existing installations without requiring them to be totally replaced. For example, you can integrate Fast Ethernet switching in an existing 10BaseT Ethernet network.

Finally, it allows you to reuse existing cabling, provided that it is category 5 cabling. As with 10BaseT, Fast Ethernet implements star topology and CSMA/CD (Carrier Sense Multiple Access/Collision Detection).

### 100BaseT4

100BaseT4 uses four unshielded twisted pair (UTP) cables of category 3, 4 or 5. The connectors are also compatible with 10BaseT; 100BaseT4 simply uses two extra pairs. 100BaseT4 implements 8B/6T type encoding. This uses three of the four pairs for transmission in both directions, whilst the fourth pair is used for collision detection.

### 100BaseTX

This is the most commonly used of the Fast Ethernet standards. It uses, two unshielded twisted pairs (UTP) of category 5, or two shielded twisted pairs (STP) of category 1. 100BaseTX connectors are compatible with 10BaseT connectors. It uses 4B/5T and MLT3 (3-Level Multiline Transmission) type encoding.

### 100BaseFX

100BaseFX specifies a fiber optics implementation (using two fibers).

## 4. IEEE 802.4

This norm defines a MAC sublayer with token passing on a bus topology.

## 5. IEEE 802.5/Token ring

### a. Network configuration

The 802.5 standard defines a token passing method on a ring topology. Different bandwidth combinations are possible: 4 Mbps, 16 Mbps and 100 Mbps according to the cabling used: UTP, STP or multimode fiber.

The computers are configured physically, in a star topology using MAU (Multistation Access Unit). The logical topology is a point-to-point ring configuration, in which each machine acts as a repeater.

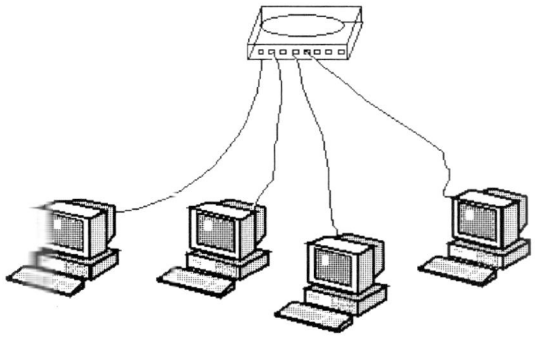

Interconnecting the MAUs can expand the principal ring. This is done by connecting together MAUs using the Ring In ports and the Ring Out ports of these devices. The frames move from RI to RO:

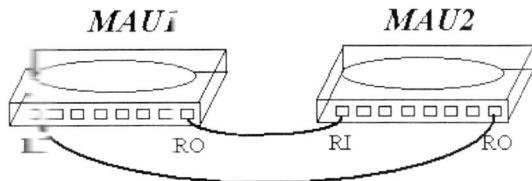

☞ According to the MAUs that are used, the signal may or may not be repeated. Token ring MAC addressing is based on a specific format. This format depends on the topology and on the source routing algorithm that is implemented by the bridges.

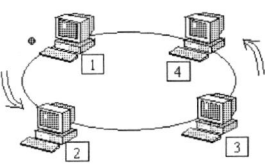
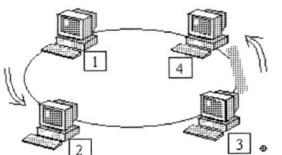

As the token passes around the ring, it is repeated from machine to machine

Station 3 wishes to send a frame. It keeps the token and sends its frame.

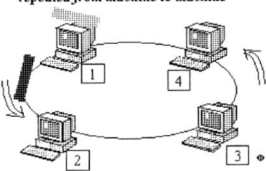
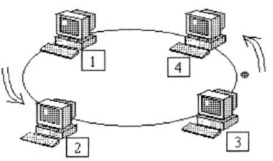

The frame is repeated from station to station until it reaches its destination, station 1, which makes a copy of it if possible. The frame is then marked to indicate to the emitter whether or not the data has been correctly received.

The frame returns to its emitter, wich notices that the data reached its destination. The token is put back into circulation and the process restarts.

In addition, a machine can reserve the next token with a certain level of **priority**. In this way, the regenerated token can be reused only by a machine that has a high enough priority (this priority must be at least that of the token). If no priority is specified, the token can be used by any of the machines.

☞ The 16 Mbps implementation operates in the same way as with FDDI: the token is reemitted immediately after the frame.

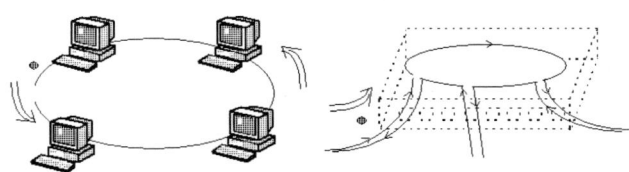

A form of fault tolerance is integrated into the MAUs, which are configured to detect a fault in a machine. When this happens, the machine is automatically disconnected.

The Token Ring implemented in UTP can include up to 260 machines with transmission speeds of 4 Mbps. The maximum length of connections linking the machines to the MAU is 45 meters. With STP, 136 machines can be included in the ring with transmission speeds of 16 Mbps. In this case, the maximum length of connections linking the machines to the MAU is 100 meters.

The media used is either two (type 1) shielded twisted pair cables or fiber optics cables. DB-9 connectors are used for the network interface cards, and male/female connectors are used for the MAU.

Manchester differential encoding is used.

The maximum distance between two MAUs is 45 meters for UTP, 200 meters for STP and 1 km for fiber optics.

In Token Ring, the maximum length of the principal ring, varies according to the number of MAUs, the number of repeaters and the number of premises that are crossed. The various manufacturers supply graphs that indicate the time required to transmit a frame, according to the maximum length of the ring.

 *The minimum frame length is 21 bytes. The maximum frame length depends on the transmission speed: this is 4493 bytes for speeds of 4 Mbps and 18000 bytes for speeds of 16 Mbps.*

### b. Automatic reconfiguration of the ring

An important aspect of Token Ring is the management of the ring by a specific machine. This is the machine that has been switched on for the longest, with the highest MAC address. This machine is called the **active monitor**. Its role is to ensure the following functions:

Token loss detection. A token can be lost if a machine disappears abruptly from the network.

Deletion of frames that have already completed a circuit of the ring. Frames may remain in circulation in this way if the machine that emitted the token disappears abruptly from the network.

Detection of errors in the priority mechanism. For example, a token must not be regenerated consecutively with the same priority, except for the lowest priority level.

☞ *Every seven seconds, approximately, the active monitor checks that the network is functioning correctly. It does this by sending a token to its immediate neighbor. Each machine repeats the token and memorizes the address of the active monitor along with that of the machine that is immediately before it in the ring. When the active monitor gets the token back, the test is considered as having been successful.*

It must be noted that a problem can also originate from the active monitor itself, for example, if the active monitor is stopped abruptly. In order to provide for this eventuality, if a machine has not heard from the machine immediately before it in the ring for seven seconds, it sends a message onto the network. This message contains the following information: the machine's own network address, the network address of the machine immediately before it in the ring (from which it has not heard), and the type of problem detected. This process allows identification of the parts of the network that are causing problems. During this process, each Token Ring network interface card disconnects itself from the network and carries out self-tests to determine whether or not it was at the origin of the problem. If a card detects no problem, it reintegrates itself into the network automatically. Otherwise, the network administrator must reconfigure the card manually so that it functions in the network again.

## 6. IEEE 802.6

This standard originated in Australia with the QSPX (Queued packet and Synchronous exchange) specification. The IEEE used QSPX as a basis for the DQDB (Distributed Queue Dual Bus) specification. This standard concerns a double fiber optic bus (emission and reception) that can transmit data such as voice and video, on MAN networks. This method is based on queue management with equitable (deterministic) access to the transmission medium. The bandwidth is allocated dynamically according to the needs of each exchange. According to the physical layer that is implemented, transmission speeds can vary from 45 Mbps to 139 Mbps.

## 7. IEEE 802.7

The 802.7 subcommittee is concerned with wideband technology. It produces installation and maintenance documents on wideband networks.

## 8. IEEE 802.8

This working group is concerned with **fiber optics** technology. It examines the use of fiber optics as an alternative to the other networking media. The standards developed cover fiber optics installation and the training of installation personnel.

## 9. IEEE 802.9

The 802.9 subcommittee is concerned with the integration of voice and data. The standards produced concern the interfaces for office multimedia peripherals. The objective is to use the 802.2 standard for this purpose, with unshielded twisted pair media.

## 10. IEEE 802.10

This working group is concerned with network security. This includes reliability of data exchange, network management and data encrypting, whilst adhering as closely as possible to the OSI model.

## 11. IEEE 802.11

802.11 describes a standard for wireless networks.

## 12. IEEE 802.12

The 100VG AnyLan standard concerns telephone quality (VG stands for Voice Grade). The IEEE approved this standard in June 1995. However, the IEEE did not wish to show any preference between 100BaseT and 100VG AnyLan. 100VG AnyLan is a specification for a LAN running at 100 Mbps. AnyLan specifies the same frames as for 802.3 or 802.5, but with a different access method.

**Lower layer protocols**

This method is called the Demand Priority Access Method. As the name indicates, it is based on priority requesting. It operates on a star topology with up to three cascading levels. The method is based on the use of intelligent hubs, which examine each port to find out which machine wishes to emit. When such a machine is identified, an amount of time is allotted for it to send its data.

The maximum distance between two nodes is 100 meters for category 3 twisted pair media, and 150 meters for category 5 twisted-pair media. With fiber optics multimode media, the maximum length of a segment is 2000 meters.

5B/6T type encoding is used on four or two pairs.

This is a deterministic protocol that allows isochronous transmission (voice or video). Provided that there are no collisions to manage, the real transmission speed is 96 Mbps.

## C. AppleTalk

### 1. Overview

AppleTalk is a complete communications environment for Apple networks. It is included in Macintosh computers and covers the seven layers of the OSI model. AppleTalk was introduced in 1983 to connect together a small group of Apple computers.

### 2. LocalTalk

You can use different lower layers from AppleTalk Phase 2 such as Ethernet (EtherTalk) or Token Ring (TokenTalk). However, LocalTalk is a solution that was implemented specifically for Macintosh networks.

☞ *A LocalTalk interface is included in all Macintosh peripherals (workstations, printers and so on).*

This development towards other types of physical layer has resulted in higher transmission speeds and the simplification of network interconnection.

Although this provides a limited solution, it is very easy to implement. The CSMA/CA (Collision Avoidance) access method is used. This method ensures that data is not transmitted from a machine until all the other network machines are awaiting the emission.

### 3. Topology and cabling

AppleTalk is a proprietary network architecture, and has therefore not been standardized. It was designed for small groups, with a maximum of 32 peripherals. Nowadays however, it allows up to 254 peripherals to be interconnected using UTP media.

The transmission speed is 230.4 Kbps on bus or tree topologies using STP. Recent developments have increased the extent of these networks to 1500 meters, according to the configuration used.

RJ-11 type connectors are used, and **biphase FM-0** type encoding is applied.

## 4. Logical addressing

Logical AppleTalk addresses are composed of 24 bits. The network or **zone** number is coded on 16 bits and the number of the node is coded on 8 bits (hence the restricted number of peripherals). In this last byte, values between 1 and 127 are reserved for clients, and values between 128 and 254 are reserved for servers. The value 255 is reserved for broadcasts, and a value of 0 means that the address is not specified. This address allocation is completely dynamic. When a node becomes active, it seeks the first free address. It does this empirically by sending an inquiry packet.

## D. ARCnet (Attached Resource Computer Network)

ARCnet was introduced by the Datapoint Corporation in 1977, and was commercialized in 1983.

☞ *ARCnet is defined by the ANSI 87.1 standard. This must not be confused with Token Bus, which is defined by the IEEE 802.4 standard.*

ARCnet offers a simple, flexible and inexpensive architecture for relatively small networks (up to 255 nodes in theory). It uses star, bus, or tree, physical topologies.

☞ *ARCnet networks are still very common in the USA.*

ARCnet supports transmission speeds of up to 2.5 Mbps, whilst ARCnet plus, a new specification, offers transmission speeds of up to 20 Mbps.

☞ *TCNS (Thomas Conrad Network Systems) is a further version of ARCnet. It offers transmission speeds of up to 100 Mbps and is less expensive than FDDI.*

ARCnet uses the **token passing** (logical ring) access method, with coaxial (RG-62 at 93 Ohms), twisted pair (UTP) or fiber optics cables. As a logical ring topology is used, each machine knows the address of the next machine in the ring, in order to ensure that token is passed correctly.

☞ *An ARCnet card includes configurable switches, which work with the network interface card. These switches identify the number of the node. It is often useful to number the nodes in such a way as to minimize the path that must be followed by the frame in order to reach the next machine.*

☞ *You can combine physical layers by using heterogeneous repeaters (coaxial - UTP or coaxial - fiber).*

Frames are composed of a maximum of 512 bytes.

Maximum segment lengths vary from 30.5 meters when a passive hub is used, to 610 meters in active hub configurations.

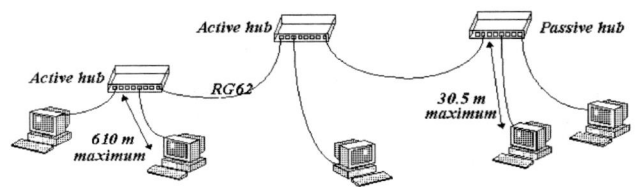

Although ARCnet is a proprietary architecture, it offers a number of advantages: its physical star topology, and the filters that are implemented on the hubs, provide the network with a high level of reliability.

## E. FDDI

FDDI (Fiber Distributed Data Interface) was developed in 1982, by former employees of the Sperry Corporation. It was submitted to the ANSI and then standardized by the ISO.

FDDI specifies a high-speed (100 Mbps) double token ring network. It is implemented using standardized monomode and multimode fiber optics cables. The FDDI card is installed in the computer and connected directly to the FDDI hub. This connection is either a single connection (MIC Media Attachment Connector type S) or a double connection (MIC types A and B). With a double connection, the type A MIC is associated with the entry point to the primary ring, as well as with the exit point from the secondary ring, whilst the type B MIC is associated with the exit point from the primary ring, as well as with the entry point to the secondary ring.

Similarly, different types of FDDI hub are available, according to the required fault tolerance: there are hubs with double connectors (MIC types A and B) and there are hubs with single connectors (MIC type S). In addition, there are hubs with null connectors (MIC type M) that are used for the final connections at the extremities of an FDDI tree topology.

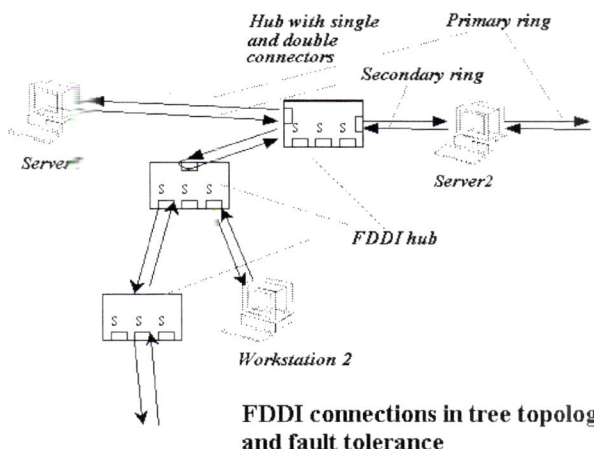

**FDDI connections in tree topology and fault tolerance**

FDDI is dimensioned for MANs. However it can be used also as a backbone to interconnect LANs. Its services are used by LLC and its technology is similar to that of 802.5.

With FDDI, the token passing method has been improved. The token is released immediately after the data frame has been emitted. This means that the frames are repeated from machine to machine and the token is always the last frame in the sequence. In this way, a machine can grab the token, and then emit its own information straight after the other data frames.

With FDDI, there are two rings on which two separate tokens circulate in opposite directions. This architecture allows the looping to be restarted automatically in case of a breakdown. In this way, high fault tolerance is provided.

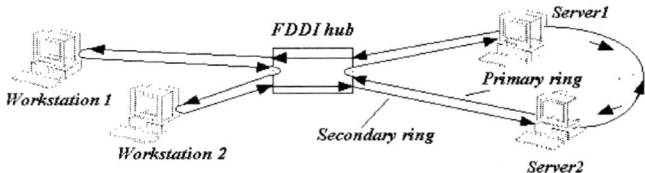

Thus, an FDDI network can contain 500 machines for a ring perimeter of 100 km. If each machine takes part in the fault tolerance mechanism, network breakdown leads to a relooping that implements a total ring of almost 200 Km long that includes 1000 machines.

Each machine acts as a repeater, which is necessary every 2 kms.

After one complete ring circuit, a frame can have one of several status values. These values tell the emitter whether or not the frame was received correctly. The **unchanged** state indicates that the destination machine has not seen the frame. In all other cases, the recipient machine modifies the frame status so as to indicate, either that the frame has been copied or that the frame has been refused (a frame can be refused either because of a CRC error, or if the destination machine does not have enough space in its reception buffer to accommodate the frame).

NRZI - 4B / 5T type encoding is used.

☞ *FDDIII provides a solution that can function in synchronous mode.*

## F. ATM (Asynchronous Transfer Mode from the ATM Forum)

### 1. Overview

ATM was created as a result of combining telephone and computing technologies. It is an evolved form of packet switching that offers transmission speeds between 25 Mbit/s to 622 Mbits/s, or more. It is used for WANs, and as a backbone between networks. It has the peculiarity of switching at physical level using telephone system style addressing. ATM provides a means of computerizing three different forms of network traffic: **voice, video** and **data**.

### 2. Relaying cells

ATM is a form of **cell relay**. An ATM cell is a short, fixed-length frame of 53 bytes: 5 bytes are used for the header and 48 bytes are used for the data. An ATM link is made up of a train of cells (made up of ATM wagons). When an application wishes to communicate on ATM, it fills in available cells according to its needs (available cells are those cells that are not being used already). A virtual channel identifier (VCI) is stored in the cell header. This number identifies the cell within the multiplexer as being a part of an ATM communications channel. In this way, instead of working with addresses that identify each node, ATM defines the path that must be followed in order to reach the required destination. In addition, on an ATM network, each machine can emit data continuously, even if most of the cells remain unoccupied.

## 3. Traffic control

With this method, it must be ensured that no application can monopolize the available bandwidth. Thus, average and instantaneous transmission levels are defined, and each application must restrict its data emissions to these authorized levels.

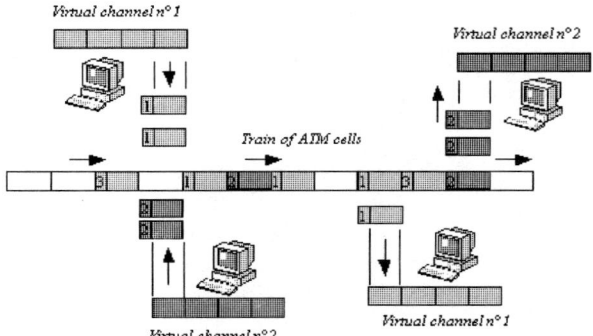

In this way, the ATM protocol provides dynamic allocation of the bandwidth using time division multiplexing and space division multiplexing. Thus, it is possible to route cells in a switch onto different logical paths. A communications channel is identified by a VPI (Virtual Path Identifier) and a VCI (Virtual Channel Identifier). The VPI identifies a possible path, whilst the VCI identifies a channel within this path.

## 4. Types of service offered

ATM defines several levels of service:
- Circuit emulation with constant transmission rate.
- Audio and video with variable transmission rate.
- Connection oriented service for data transmission.
- Connectionless service for data transmission.

## 5. Topology

ATM protocols cover approximately, layer 1 to 3 of the OSI model.

ATM is a high-speed network that is implemented using fiber optics or category 5 twisted pair media. It is based on a point-to-point switching network topology, in which each machine is connected to a switch, and each switch can be connected to other switches.

## 6. ATM transmission speeds

A range of transmission speeds have been defined for ATM:

| | |
|---|---|
| T1 | 1.544 Mbps on a telephone network |
| T3 | 44.736 Mbps on a telephone network |
| ATM-25 | 25 Mbps on twisted pair media |
| SONET OC-1 | 51 Mbps on fiber optics media |
| SONET OC-3 | 155 Mbps on fiber optics media |
| SONET OC-12 | 622 Mbps on fiber optics media |
| SONET OC-48 | 2.4 Gbps on fiber optics media |

# G. Summary of the capacities of the different physical layers used

This chapter has covered the physical layers that are most commonly used. The following table indicates the number of nodes that are allowed per segment according to the physical network concerned. Of course, the use of network components such as routers, allow you to make interconnections that extend these values indefinitely

| | Ethernet | | | Token Ring | | ARCNet | FDDI | Apple Talk |
|---|---|---|---|---|---|---|---|---|
| | 10base2 | **10base5** | 10BaseT | UTP type 3 | STP | | | |

| Max num. nodes per segment | 30 | 100 | 1024 | 72 | 260 | 255 | 1000 | 254 |
|---|---|---|---|---|---|---|---|---|

# Exercises

To be absolutely sure that you have assimilated this chapter, work through the corresponding exercises. These are set out from page 391.

☒ LANs.

# Assessing your skills

Try the following questions if you think you know this chapter well enough.

## IEEE standards

1 On which layer is the RS232 standard based?

2 Which intermediate components are used in data exchanges involving signals that are defined by the RS232 standard?

3 What is the role of the NullModem?

4 Which organization is responsible for the 802.x standards?

5 Which working group was responsible for a loop detection algorithm for Ethernet networks?

6 Which are the two sublayers that decompose layer 2 of the OSI model?

7 With which sublayer is the 802.2 project associated?

8 Which IEEE standard is defined by 802.4?

9 Which standard defines an implementation for MAN type networks?

13 Which standard implements the Polling access method?

14 What is the signification of AnyLAN in 100VG AnyLAN?

## IEEE 802.3

15 What is the signification of 10Base5?

16 What is the signification of 10BaseT?

17 Which encoding method is used with Ethernet networks?

18 Which standard defines cheapnet?

19 What is the maximum extent of a 10Base2 network?

20 Which access method is used with 100BaseT?

21 Which cabling is used when the transceiver is integrated into the Ethernet network interface card?

22 In which environment is a vampire tap used?

23 Which type of twisted pair cable is most commonly used with Ethernet?

24 Which type of physical medium can be used to interconnect two Ethernet10 LANs, which are situated 1 kilometer (0.6 miles) apart?

**Essentials**  Chapter 6 - Page 239

25  What is meant by 10BaseF? ❏

26  What is meant by Fast Ethernet? ❏

27  Which physical media can be used with Fast Ethernet? ❏

### IEEE 802.5

28  Which IEEE standard is defined by 802.5? ❏

29  What are the two transmission speeds that are commonly used with Token Ring? ❏

30  Which cabling is generally used with 802.5? ❏

31  What is a MAU? ❏

32  How do you extend an 802.5 ring? ❏

33  Which algorithm is used in Token Ring to neutralize a physical loop? ❏

*Lower layer protocols*

34 Which mechanism allows you to allocate different priority levels to different peripherals? ☐

35 How can a MAU be used to ensure a certain level of fault tolerance? ☐

36 What type of encoding is used on Token Ring networks? ☐

37 Which types of connector are used to connect a network machine to a MAU? ☐

38 What does the term 'active monitor' signify with Token Ring? ☐

39 What happens when a machine does not receive a frame for more than 7 consecutive seconds in a Token Ring network? ☐

## AppleTalk

40 What is the name of the lowest layer that is implemented on proprietary Apple networks ? ☐

41 Which physical layers are available on Apple networks for Ethernet and Token Ring ? ☐

42 Which access method is used on Apple networks ? ☐

43 Why might it be preferable to avoid collisions rather than detecting them ? ☐

44 Was AppleTalk designed to implement large networks? ☐

45 How many bytes are used in AppleTalk addressing ? ☐

46 How are addresses allocated in an AppleTalk network ? ☐

## ARCnet

47 Which topologies are suitable for ARCnet networks ? ☐

48 In theory, what is the maximum number of nodes that an ARCnet network can accomodate ? ❏

49 Which transmission speeds are offered by ARCnet networks ? ❏

50 How is concurrent access managed on the physical medium ? ❏

51 Which type of coaxial cable is used in an ARCnet network? ❏

## FDDI

52 Which topology is used with FDDI? ❏

53 Which type of physical medium is used with FDDI? ❏

54 What is the purpose of a double connector on an FDDI hub? ❏

55 How was the token passing method improved with FDDI? ❏

## ATM

56 Which types of data can be transported using ATM? ❏

57 What is the length of an ATM packet? ❏

58 Which information is stored in the ATM header? ❏

59 On which layers of the OSI model does ATM operate? ❏

60 Which physical media are used with ATM? ❏

61 Which transmission speed is associated with a T1 line? ❏

62 Which transmission speed is associated with a T3 line? ❏

63 Which physical medium is used with SONET? ❏

64 Which physical medium is used with T3? ❏

## Results

Check your answers on pages 245 to 252. Count one point for each correct answer.

Number of points ☐ /64

For this chapter you need to have scored at least 48 out of 64.

Look at the list of key points that follows. Pick out the ones with which you have had difficulty and work through them again in this chapter before moving on to the next.

## Key points of the chapter

- ☐ IEEE standards.
- ☐ IEEE 802.3.
- ☐ IEEE 802.5.
- ☐ AppleTalk.
- ☐ ARCnet.
- ☐ FDDI.
- ☐ ATM.

# Solutions

## IEEE standards

1 On which layer is the RS232 standard based?

*The physical layer.*

2 Which intermediate components are used in data exchanges involving signals that are defined by the RS232 standard?

*Data Terminal Equipment (DTE) and Data Communications Equipment (DCE).*

3 What is the role of the NullModem?

*A NullModem allows you to interconnect two computers by crossing connections between data emission and data reception. A complete NullModem manages all the signals, looping certain signals back onto themselves.*

4 Which organization is responsible for the 802.x standards?

*Institute of Electrical and Electronic Engineers (IEEE).*

5 Which working group was responsible for a loop detection algorithm for Ethernet networks?

*IEEE 802.1 was responsible for the Spanning Tree Algorithm (802.1D).*

6 Which are the two sublayers that decompose layer 2 of the OSI model?

*The LLC (Logical Link Control) sublayer, and the MAC (Media Access Control) sublayer.*

7 With which sublayer is the 802.2 project associated?

*The LLC (Logical Link Control) sublayer.*

8 Which IEEE standard is defined by 802.4?

*Token passing on a physical bus topology.*

9 Which standard defines an implementation for MAN type networks?

*IEEE 802.6.*

10 Which IEEE working group examines the use of fiber optics?

*IEEE 802.8*

11 Which IEEE working group defined 100VG AnyLAN?

*IEEE 802.12*

12 Which IEEE working group examines the application of wireless networking technologies?

*IEEE 802.11*

13 Which standard implements the Polling access method?

*100VG AnyLAN, with the Demand Priority Access Method.*

14 What is the signification of AnyLAN in 100VG AnyLAN?

*AnyLAN signifies that 802.3 and 802.5 frames can be used with this access method.*

### IEEE 802.3

15 What is the signification of 10Base5?

*10 Mbps, with digital signaling, on a thick coaxial medium, with maximum segment lengths of 500 meters, without repeaters.*

16 What is the signification of 10BaseT?

*100 Mbps, with digital signaling, on a twisted pair medium, with maximum segment lengths of 100 meters.*

17 Which encoding method is used with Ethernet networks?

*Manchester encoding.*

18 Which standard defines cheapnet?

*Ethernet on thin coaxial, running at 10 Mbps with digital signaling on a bus topology.*

19 What is the maximum extent of a 10Base2 network?

*The 5-4-3 rule defines the use of 5 segments, and 4 repeaters, with a maximum of 3 occupied segments. As the maximum length of a thin coaxial segment is 185 meters, the maximum extent of a 10Base2 network is 5x185 = 925 meters.*

20 Which access method is used with 100BaseT?

*CSMA/CD*

21 Which cabling is used when the transceiver is integrated into the Ethernet network interface card?

*Thin coaxial or twisted pair cabling.*

22 In which environment is a vampire tap used?

*In an Ethernet 10Base5 network.*

23 Which type of twisted pair cable is most commonly used with Ethernet?

*UTP: in category 5 (100 Mbps), in category 3 (10 Mbps).*

24 Which type of physical medium can be used to interconnect two Ethernet LANs, which are situated 1 kilometer (0.6 miles) apart?

*Fiber optics.*

25 What is meant by 10BaseF?

*This refers to Ethernet standards that have been adapted to suit fiber optics.*

26 What is meant by Fast Ethernet?

*This is 100BaseT or IEEE 802.3u.*

27 Which physical media can be used with Fast Ethernet?

*Fiber optics or twisted pair.*

## IEEE 802.5

28 Which IEEE standard is defined by 802.5?

*Token passing on a ring topology.*

29 What are the two transmission speeds that are commonly used with Token Ring?

*4 and 16 Mbps.*

30 Which cabling is generally used with 802.5?

*Shielded twisted pair (STP).*

31 What is a MAU?

*A Multistation Access Unit is a hub that is used in Token Ring Networks (MAU also signifies Media Access Unit, which is an Ethernet transceiver).*

32 How do you extend an 802.5 ring?

*Each MAU is equipped with two extension ports called Ring In (RI) and Ring Out (RO). These ports allow you to interconnect two MAUs.*

33 Which algorithm is used in Token Ring to neutralize a physical loop?

*Source routing.*

34 Which mechanism allows you to allocate different priority levels to different peripherals?

*The priority concept that is associated with emitted tokens: by this means, a peripheral is allowed to use a token only if the priority of the peripheral is greater than or equal to that of the token.*

35 How can a MAU be used to ensure a certain level of fault tolerance?

*A MAU will automatically disconnect a network machine that is no longer functioning. In this way, the network is able to circulate information permanently.*

36 What type of encoding is used on Token Ring networks?

*Manchester differential encoding.*

37 Which types of connector are used to connect a network machine to a MAU?

*On the network interface card of the machine, nine-pin connectors (DB-9) are used, whereas on the MAUs, male/female connectors are generally used.*

38 What does the term 'active monitor' signify with Token Ring?

*An active monitor is a peripheral that is designated to manage all problems that occur on a Token Ring network. These problems include loss of tokens, frames that loop for more than one circuit of the ring and detection of errors in the priorities mechanism.*

39 What happens when a machine does not receive a frame for more than 7 consecutive seconds in a Token Ring network?

*The machine sends a special signal to the next machine in the ring to warn of the problem. This is done so that the machine that is causing the problem is quickly identified and excluded from the network.*

## AppleTalk

40 What is the name of the lowest layer that is implemented on proprietary Apple networks?

*LocalTalk.*

41 Which physical layers are available on Apple networks for Ethernet and Token Ring?

*EtherTalk and TokenTalk.*

42 Which access method is used on Apple networks?

*CSMA/CA.*

43 Why might it be preferable to avoid collisions rather than detecting them?

*Implementation of CSMA/CD is less ordered as each peripheral tries to transmit data directly. In contrast, with CSMA/CA the peripheral must reserve the transmission channel before it can send data. In this way, data packet collisions are avoided.*

44 Was AppleTalk designed to implement large networks?

*Initially, AppleTalk allowed a maximum of 32 peripherals.*

45 How many bytes are used in AppleTalk addressing?

*3 bytes.*

46 How are addresses allocated in an AppleTalk network?

*Empirically. A new peripheral chooses an address and asks if another machine is using it already. If this is not the case, the address can be used.*

### ARCnet

47 Which topologies are suitable for ARCnet networks?

*Bus, star and tree.*

48 In theory, what is the maximum number of nodes that an ARCnet network can accomodate?

*255.*

49 Which transmission speeds are offered by ARCnet networks?

*2.5 Mbps and 20 Mbps.*

50 How is concurrent access managed on the physical medium?

*Using token passing.*

51 Which type of coaxial cable is used in an ARCnet network?

*An RG62 type cable at 93 Ohms.*

## FDDI

**52 Which topology is used with FDDI?**

Ring.

**53 Which type of physical medium is used with FDDI?**

Fiber optics.

**54 What is the purpose of a double connector on an FDDI hub?**

It allows a double ring to be implemented, thus providing a higher level of fault tolerance.

**55 How is the token passing method improved with FDDI?**

The token is reemitted immediately after the data frame. In this way, a machine can transmit several frames on the ring successively, without having to wait for the token to come back round the ring.

## ATM

**56 Which types of data can be transported using ATM?**

Data, voice and video (multimedia).

**57 What is the length of an ATM packet?**

With ATM, a data transfer packet is referred to as a cell. This is a fixed length structure of 53 bytes.

**58 Which information is stored in the ATM header?**

Each cell is identified as a part of a specific virtual communications channel. This identifier is stored in the header.

**59 On which layers of the OSI model does ATM operate?**

On layers 1, 2 and 3.

**60 Which physical media are used with ATM?**

Fiber optics or category 5, Unshielded Twisted Pair (UTP).

61 Which transmission speed is associated with a T1 line?

*1.544 Mbps.*

62 Which transmission speed is associated with a T3 line?

*Approximately 44 Mbps.*

63 Which physical medium is used with SONET?

*Fiber optics.*

64 Which physical medium is used with T3?

*Unshielded Twisted Pair (UTP).*

**Essentials**          **Chapter 7 - Page 253**

## Prerequisites for this chapter

☒ General knowledge of networking.

## Objectives

When you have completed this chapter you will be able to:

**TCP/IP**
- ☒ Describe the different TCP/IP standards.
- ☒ Compare the OSI model and the TCP/IP model.
- ☒ Define the features of IP, TCP and UDP.
- ☒ Identify IP address classes.
- ☒ Define the different classes of IP address.
- ☒ Describe the TCP/IP protocols that allow you to share information.

**Novell**
- ☒ Describe the Netware protocol stack.
- ☒ Explain the features of IPX and SPX.
- ☒ Describe the role of NCP.
- ☒ Explain the role of SAP.

**NetBIOS and NetBEUI**
- ☒ Describe the characteristics of NetBEUI.
- ☒ Implement a NetBIOS denomination
- ☒ Share information using SMB.

**DLC**
- ☒ Explain the cases in which DLC should be used.

**Medium and higher layer protocols**

# Summary

A. **TCP/IP and the Internet protocols** . . . 255
   1. Introduction . . . . . . . . . . . . . . . . . 255
   2. History . . . . . . . . . . . . . . . . . . . 256
   3. The Internet protocol suite and the OSI model . 257
   4. Other protocols . . . . . . . . . . . . . . . 260

B. **IP protocol** . . . . . . . . . . . . . . . . 263
   1. Introduction . . . . . . . . . . . . . . . . . 263
   2. IP addressing . . . . . . . . . . . . . . . . 263

C. **File sharing** . . . . . . . . . . . . . . . 266
   1. NFS (Network File System) . . . . . . . . . . 266
   2. FTP and TFTP . . . . . . . . . . . . . . . . . 267
   3. HTTP (Hyper Text Transfer Protocol) . . . . . 268
   4. SAMBA . . . . . . . . . . . . . . . . . . . . 269

D. **Netware and the OSI model** . . . . . . . 270
   1. Introduction . . . . . . . . . . . . . . . . . 270
   2. Netware and the OSI model . . . . . . . . . . 270
   3. IPX (Internetwork Packet eXchange) protocol . 271
   4. SPX (Sequenced Packet eXchange) protocol . 272
   5. NCP (Netware Core Protocol) . . . . . . . . . 272

E. **NetBEUI (NetBIOS Enhanced User Interface)** . . . . . . . . . . . . . . . . . 273
   1. Overview . . . . . . . . . . . . . . . . . . . 273
   2. Information Sharing and the SMB (Service Message Block) protocol . . . . . . 276

F. **DLC (Data Link Control)** . . . . . . . . 278
   1. The DLC protocol and the OSI model . . . . . 278
   2. Situations that require DLC . . . . . . . . . 279
   3. Configuring DLC . . . . . . . . . . . . . . . 280

# Medium and higher layer protocols

This chapter will examine the main protocols of the medium and higher layers.

It will examine the TCP/IP protocol family, along with the services associated. When we have examined the main TCP/IP protocols, we will define the different classes of IP address.

It will describe the IPX/SPX protocols that are associated with Novell and explain the gateway between these protocols and TCP/IP.

Finally, we will discuss the features of NetBEUI and DLC.

In passing, we will examine the different protocols that allow you to share information in these different environments; such as SMB, NCP, FTP, HTTP and NFS.

## A. TCP/IP and the Internet protocols

### 1. Introduction

TCP/IP was developed by the DoD (Department of Defense) of the USA. It covers around a hundred protocols and defines a model with four network layers. It appeared at the beginning of the 70s, ten years before the OSI model.

These are the most popular communication and application protocols that are used to interconnect heterogeneous systems, independently of the physical layer.

TCP (Transmission Control Protocol) is a transport protocol that ensures a reliable, connection oriented service for a stream of bytes.

In contrast to TCP, **UDP** (User Datagram Protocol) is a connectionless oriented transport protocol. UDP is very fast, but not very reliable.

☞ UDP is used on the Internet to transmit live sound to certain radio sites. The data concerned does not necessarily require perfect transmission.

IP (Internet Protocol) provides a connectionless oriented packet delivery system. It manages logical addresses, which decompose the identifier of each node, into a logical network number and a peripheral number, on 4 bytes (IP version 4).

☞ *The IP v.6 (or IP Next Generation) protocol is currently being developed. It will be compatible with IP v.4, but it will require all the TCP/IP protocols to be rewritten. The IP address will be extended to 16 bytes.*

One of the key factors that have made Internet protocols so popular is that the model is independent of the physical layers (layers 1 and 2).

## 2. History

The University of Stanford developed the TCP/IP architecture in 1970. This was financed by the DoD in the context of ARPANET (Advanced Research Projects Agency NETwork). The physical media was based essentially on packet switching.

The DARPA (Defense Advanced Research Project Agency) standardized the principal modules. In 1983 they made it obligatory for machines that were connected to ARPANET to use TCP/IP.

ARPANET evolved from a small, point-to-point, packet switching network on telephone lines, to an immense hybrid network: **the Internet**.

☞ *Today, the ARPANET is a part of the Internet, which is used by the DoD for research and development.*

The integration of Internet protocols into Unix BSD (Berkeley Software Distribution), and the free distribution of this operating system to universities, contributed greatly to the success of this protocol suite.

These protocols continue to evolve due to the actions of the *Internet Architecture Board* and to standardization documents such as the RFCs (Request For Comments), which are readily accessible.

☞ You can download an RFC from one of the many sites that accommodate them, for example http://www.rfc-editor.org/rfc.html.

## 3. The Internet protocol suite and the OSI model

It is important to remember that the TCP/IP model appeared 10 years before the OSI model. In fact the OSI model was inspired by certain TCP/IP protocols. However, it is interesting to examine the correspondence between the seven layers of the OSI model and the four layers of the Internet protocols:

*OSI Model*    *TCP/IP Model*

| OSI | TCP/IP | | | | |
|---|---|---|---|---|---|
| 5-6-7 | Application | Telnet | ftp | dns | snmp |
| | | Windows sockets | | | |
| 4 | Transport | TCP | | UDP | |
| 3 | Internet | | ICMP | | |
| | | ARP | IP | | |
| 1-2 | Network interface | Ethernet | Token Ring | others | |

### User application services

A certain number of services and applications are based on the stack of TCP/IP protocols.

#### Telnet

Telnet is a terminal emulation protocol. A session is set up between a workstation (Telnet client) and a remote machine (Telnet server). Commands are input on the client machine, and then they are transmitted to the Telnet server where they are executed. The echo of the remote process is redirected to the workstation, which receives the execution report for the command. To be able to use Telnet then, you must know which commands can be executed on the remote site.

**RIP** (*Routing Information Protocol*)

RIP is a dynamic routing protocol. One of its fundamental roles is to allow information exchange between routers. This is done in such a way, so as to provide each router with network details that allow the router to propose a better path (the criteria that is generally used is the number of routers that must be crossed).

☞ *Routed is an implementation of RIP on UNIX 4.2 BSD.*

**SMTP** (*Simple Mail Transfer Protocol*)

SMTP is a simple transfer protocol that is used for electronic mail. It is based on the UDP and IP protocols. It does not include a user interface.

**NFS** (*Network File System*)

NFS was developed by SUN around 1985. It is a distributed file system that can run in a heterogeneous environment (application layer). It allows users of different computers and operating systems, to access a remote file system without the need to know any new specific commands.

**DNS** (*Domain Name System*)

Rather than remembering the IP addresses of machines, it was found to be much simpler to work with names. At first, these names were aliases that were stored locally. Then, they were made available to all, using a centralized file (for example /etc/hosts on UNIX). Progressively, a hierarchical, distributed database was set up that associates each IP address with one or more names.

Today, the Internet uses such a database. At the root of this domain hierarchy, at a world level, there are 14 DNS servers. These servers are strategically placed. Each server knows the DNS servers that are situated on the next level up, which manage types of organization and country suffixes. In this way, DNS servers have been defined on the different levels of the domain hierarchy.

For example, *www.dev.microsoft.com* corresponds to a machine called www, in the subdomain dev (for development) of the Microsoft domain, of the com (commercial) type of organization.

There is nothing to prevent Microsoft from managing a DNS server in the microsoft.com domain, and another in the dev.microsoft.com subdomain.

### WINS (Windows Internet Naming Service)

WINS is an internetwork service of (NetBIOS) windows names. WINS must not be confused with the DNS of the Internet. WINS products are based on the (Microsoft) NetBIOS layer. They handle high-level identifiers called **NetBIOS names** (for example, the names of workstations). These names must be short (between 8 and 15 characters), and unique on a given internetwork.

The main drawback with these names is that they do not support a hierarchical structure. Internetwork functioning is possible because NetBIOS is situated above a routable protocol (IP).

 *NetBIOS was initially intended to run on LANs. In order to locate a specific machine, NetBIOS would send a broadcast packet to all the machines on the network. This allowed NetBIOS to find out the physical address that is associated with the name. The problem with this method is that, in general, routers do not transfer broadcasts.*

The objective of WINS is to **manage a centralized database on a WINS server that associates a NetBIOS name with its IP address**. This is a dynamic database. It is built up using the information contained in all the registration requests that are made for WINS client names. First, the WINS clients record their name and address on a server. Then, the other WINS clients question the server.

A client contacts its server by specifying the IP address of the server. The client can either register itself, or request the IP address corresponding to a name.

**DHCP** (*Dynamic Host Configuration Protocol*)

DHCP is an automatic configuration protocol for client TCP/IP options in a NetBIOS environment.

It enables you to assign the following items dynamically: an IP address, a subnetwork mask, an IP address of a DNS server, or even a default IP address of a gateway (this is an IP address of a router that allows you to access machines outside your LAN).

DHCP then, is very useful, especially for mobile machines, which must frequently change networks, and therefore network ID numbers.

**SNMP** (*Simple Network Management Protocol*)

SNMP is a simple network protocol that uses UDP. It allows you to administer hardware and software remotely. On one side, SNMP agents (SNMP compliant devices) store information and respond to SNMP requests. SNMP requesters may be application managers or platform administrators (for example, HPOV HP Open View on HPUX). SNMP agents collect large amounts of information from routers, switches, bridges and specific applications. They also display statistics and send orders for the remote management of peripheral devices.

Locally, SNMP agents operate on chosen layers of the OSI model. They store information on MIB (Management Information Base) databases.

## 4. Other protocols

### a. ICMP (Internet Control Message Protocol)

ICMP works with IP. It provides error and control information to TCP (IP itself does not operate in connection oriented mode and therefore cannot detect internetwork anomalies). ICMP is used by IP hosts, and by routers, in order to specify a certain number of important events.

These events include the following:

**Time Exceeded**

The timeout has expired. This message generally means that the maximum time required for the packet to reach the destination has been exceeded. It can also be sent if the packet has been lost (for example, if the message has crossed more than 16 routers and the TimeToLive countdown has reached zero).

**Destination Unreachable**

This message indicates that it was not possible to forward the packet to its destination.

**Source Quench**

This information is typically sent by a router to an emitter to tell it to reduce its transmission speed. For example, suppose that on one side of the router (the emission side) you have a 16 Mbit/s Token Ring network, and on the other side of the router (the destination side) you have a 10 Mbit/s Ethernet network. Frame sizes and transmission speeds are different on the two sides of the router. As the Ethernet network runs much slower, after a certain time, the reception buffer will overflow. When this happens IP will simply destroy the excess packets and inform the emitter that it must slow down its transmission rate.

**Redirect**

This message indicates that a better path can be used to reach the destination.

**Echo Request and Echo Reply**

These two messages allow you to test if a node can communicate with another node.

☞ *These messages constitute the PING (Packet InterNet Groper) command.*

### b. ARP (Address Restitution Protocol)

ARP allows you to determine the MAC address of a node. This is done by broadcasting an ARP request that contains the IP address of the node concerned. This technique allows you to send a frame to the right peripheral on a local IP network.

### c. RARP (Reverse ARP)

This protocol allows you to make a reverse resolution to that obtained with ARP. This protocol is useful in the case of a machine without a hard disk. It tells it the IP address of a machine for which it knows the MAC address.

## B. IP protocol

### 1. Introduction

IP provides a packet delivery service, connectionless and without guarantee. One of its major drawbacks is that it requires the implementation of an explicit addressing system. Each node in the network must be identified by an IP address. This address is made up of two parts: a logical network number and the host address within the logical network.

☞ *An analogy can be drawn with a postal address, where the logical network number corresponds to the name of a street and the host address corresponds to the number on the street.*

One useful aspect of IP is that it can be configured to obtain a certain type of service to suit your emission. For example you can specify **low delay** for an urgent packet, **high throughput** when you have a lot of data to transfer or **high reliability** for a packet that must not contain any error.

### 2. IP addressing

When TCP/IP is used, the administrator must define a static addressing scheme by allocating a logical (IP) address to each peripheral.

With IP version 4 an address is composed of four bytes. Each byte is separated by a decimal point, for example
132.143.57.2

The value of the first byte can be used to deduce the IP address class. Different IP address classes use different numbers of bytes for the network number and, consequently, for the host number within the network.

☞ *In practice, this is not always strictly true. For example, subnetting techniques can be used, whereby some of the host bits are used to designate a subnetwork. Conversely, supernetting techniques allow you to use some of the network bits to designate extra hosts.*

Three IP address classes have been defined to identify a host uniquely:

With **Class A**, 7 bits of the first byte are used for the network number, and the 24 bits of the three remaining bytes are used to identify the host. The first byte can have a value from 1 to 126 inclusive. A Class A network can contain up to 16 million hosts ($2^{24}-2$ combinations).

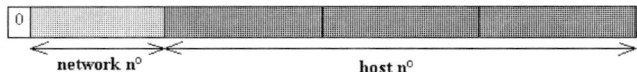

☞ *For example, 112.2.1.4 is a Class A address. '112' identifies the network and '2.1.4' identifies the host.*

With **Class B**, 14 bits are used for the network number, and 16 bits are used to identify the host. The first byte can have a value from 128 to 191 inclusive. A Class B network can contain 65 634 hosts ($2^{16}-2$ combinations). The mask by default is 255.255.0.0.

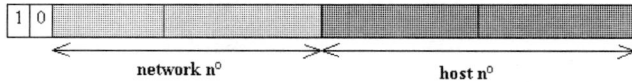

☞ *For example, 132.148.67.2 is a Class B address. '132.148' identifies the network and '67.2' identifies the host.*

With **Class C**, 21 bits are used for the network number, and 8 bits are used to identify the host. The first byte can have a value from 192 to 223 inclusive. A Class C network can contain 254 hosts.

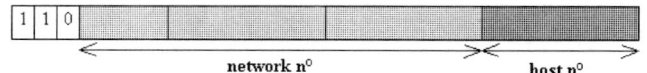

☞ *For example, 193.10.2.117 is a Class B address. '193.10.2' identifies the network and '117' identifies the host.*

In all cases, a **subnet mask** is used to specify how the IP address is split up into a network part and a host part. When expressed in binary notation, leading bits of the mask are marked as '1's and correspond to the network part. The other bits are marked as '0's.
For example 132.148.67.2
(10000100.10010100.01000011.00000010 in binary) is a class B address because it has 132 in the first byte.
The class B mask is 255.255.0.0
 (11111111.11111111.00000000 in binary).

Here are the different default masks for the different classes

255.0.0.0          for class A
255.255.0.0        for class B
255.255.255.0      for class C

Network numbers and host numbers cannot have values with all their bits set to '0' or to '1'. These values have special significations.

For example, an IP address with all its bits set to '1' is used for a broadcast.

**Example:** 132.148.255.255 identifies all the hosts in the network 132.148.

☞ *It must be noted that with certain Unix systems, you can configure a broadcast with all bits set to '0'. This is allowed for compatibility with other systems.*

**The number of the current network** is sometimes noted by setting all the host bits to '0'.

**Example:** 132.148.0.0 corresponds to the logical network number of 132.148.

A host in the current network is sometimes identified by setting all the network bits to '0'.

**Example:** 0.0.67.2 corresponds to the host 132.148.67.2 in the network 132.148.0.0.

Another example is the local loop address 127.0.0.1. This address designates the network interface card itself, without going out onto the network.

## C. File sharing

### 1. NFS (Network File System)

#### a. Description

NFS allows you to implement a distributed file system in a UNIX (TCP/IP) environment. It was developed by SUN in the 80s.

NFS was the first distributable file system to be fully operational and was an indispensable supplement to the SUN workstation environment. The popularity of SOLARIS, the SUN operating system, contributed largely to the success of NFS.

NFS is based on the RPC (Remote Procedure Call) and XDR (eXternal Data Representation) protocols. The implementation of these protocols is relatively simple.

Consequently, NFS was widely used in the UNIX operating systems, for example BSD 4.3 and SYSTEM V.3.

#### b. Other distributed file systems

Other distributed file systems were developed on UNIX, but NFS remains the best known.

RFS (Remote File Sharing) was created on System V.3 by ATT.

AFS (Andrew File System) was developed in the 80s, by Carnegie Melon University (CMU) and by IBM. This file system appeared at first, under the name of **DFS** on certain operating systems, such as those of Microsoft. An OSF version is normally available. This distributed file system incorporates the concepts of ACLs (Access Control Lists) and Logical Volumes.

## 2. FTP and TFTP

**FTP** (*File Transfer Protocol*)

FTP is based on a reliable transfer mode and uses the services of TCP. The big advantage of FTP is that it can be used between different operating systems based on heterogeneous file systems. After a connection has been set up (after name and password has been accepted) ftp clients see the directories of the users to whom the connections have been made on the ftp server (in addition to their own working directories).

☞ *On the Internet there are numerous ftp sites, from which anyone can download files (this is done using the anonymous ftp guest for whom there is no password).*

When you have connected to an ftp site in this way you can move files from one directory to another using special FTP commands (according to the user's permissions on each system).

☞ *Modern Internet browsers allow you to connect to ftp sites in graphic mode. In this way you can download files simply by clicking them, without knowing any particular command.*

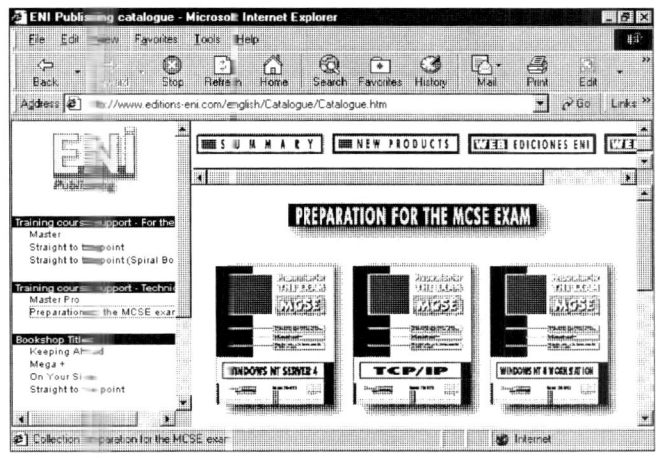

**TFTP** (*Trivial FTP*)

TFTP allows you to download information more rapidly. However, its integrity is not guaranteed. This lack of reliability is due to the fact that TFTP uses the UDP protocol instead of TCP.

### 3. HTTP (Hyper Text Transfer Protocol)

On a first level, **HTTP** is a file transfer protocol. On a second level, it uses the SGML (*Standard Generalized Markup Language*) system, which specifies a formatting language in the form of hyperlinks. Special codes, called *HTML tags*, indicate the signification of the HTML document to the browser (they indicate the header, body, links, images, animations and so on along with formatting instructions for each of these elements).

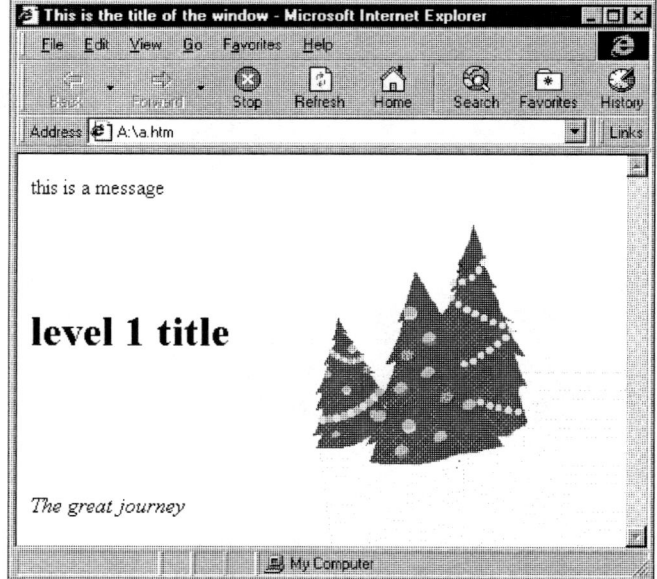

*Here are the contents of the a.htm file:*

```
<HTML>
<HEAD>
<TITLE> This is the title of the window
</TITLE>
</HEAD>
<BODY BGCOLOR="WHITE">
this is a message
<IMG ALIGN=RIGHT SRC = "Christmas trees.gif">
<H1>level 1 title </H1>
<H2>level 2 title </H2>
<A HREF="http://www.editions-eni.com">
<STRONG> <G> The great journey </I>
</STRONG></A>
</BODY>
</HTML>
```

HTTP is widely used and allows you to consult information.

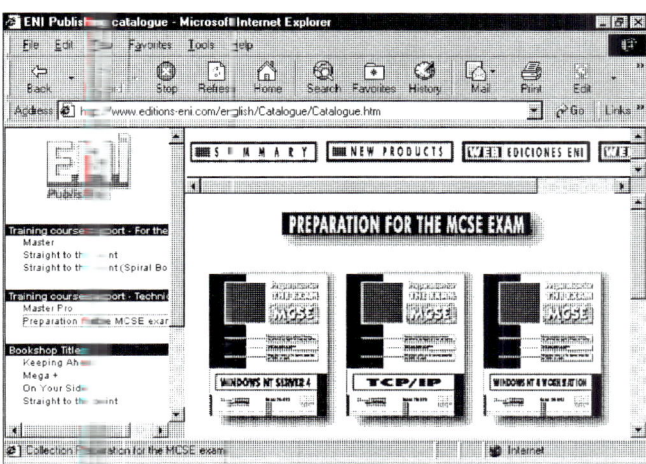

## 4. SAMBA

SAMBA is a version of the SMB server that is supplied with Unix. It allows a Unix server to share resources that are visible from the clients' network neighborhood. In addition, it can be used to transform a Unix server into an NT domain controller. This is done by sharing NETLOGIN, in order to download NT system scripts and policies.

## D. Netware and the OSI model

### 1. Introduction

Netware is a network operating system that was created by Novell. It appeared at the beginning of the 80s. Today, Novell offers Netware version 4.11. This is an extended network version that incorporates directory management in a distributed environment, called *Netware Directory Services* (NDS is compatible with the X.500 standard).

### 2. Netware and the OSI model

Originally, Netware was based on XNS (Xerox Network System). It supports the different physical layers as do Ethernet, ARCNet and Token Ring. A peculiarity of Netware is that it uses a network layer that is managed by the routable protocol IPX (Internetwork Packet eXchange). For the moment, all versions of Novell require this protocol to be installed before they can run (in addition to TCP/IP for Internet access).

☞ *Future versions of Novell will use only TCP/IP, as is already the case for Windows NT.*

The SPX (Sequenced Packet eXchange) protocol operates at transport layer level. It acts in a similar way to the TCP protocol and provides a reliable connection oriented service.

Another peculiarity of Novell is that it uses a **dedicated server** based on NCP (Netware Core Protocol). This protocol integrates software routines, called NLMs (Netware Loadable Modules). You can load and unload NLMs whenever you want, according to your needs.

| OSI Layer | Novell | |  |
|---|---|---|---|
| 7 - APPLICATION | Applications | | Netware Applications |
| 6 - PRESENTATION | NetBIOS Emulator | Shell Netware | Netware Core Protocol |
| 5 - SESSION | | | Netware STREAMS |
| 4 - TRANSPORT | IPX | SPX | Transport |
| 3 - NETWORK | | | |
| 2 - DATA LINK | Ethernet / Token Ring / ArcNet / Others | | ODI: Ethernet / Token Ring / ArcNet / Others |
| 1 - PHYSICAL | | | |

Unlike many other systems, the Novell server does not use virtual memory management. Because of this, the server cannot be used to execute client applications.

The session and presentation layers are implemented on the client machines in the form of a shell. Possible client machines include those running Windows, MacOS and even Unix.

Programs developed with the **NetBIOS** (Network Basic Input/Output System) API (Application Programming Interface) can run on Novell thanks to this emulation.

### 3. IPX (Internetwork Packet eXchange) protocol

IPX operates on the network and transport layers. As with IP, IPX is a connectionless oriented service that does not guarantee transfer reliability.

IPX is a **routable** protocol that identifies a host using a **logical address**. As with IP, IPX does not require a static addressing scheme. An **IPX address** is the concatenation of a 4-byte **external network number** and a 6-byte **MAC address** of the peripheral. IPX addresses are allocated automatically. In addition, the logical address is resolved into a physical address instantaneously, as the physical address is integrated into the IPX address.

On Netware, the external network number, which concerns peripherals, must not be confused with the **internal network number**, which concerns applications. The internal network number depends on the internal structure of Novell, which associates server applications with a node number and a network number. Thus, the Novell server acts as an internal router to switch the physical network (external network number) with the logical network (server applications). Thus, a Novell server has two network addresses, an internal address and an external address.

As with IP, all the nodes that are connected to the same physical network must have the same (external) network number. In addition, each IPX address must be unique in the internetwork. Similarly, the internal network numbers must be unique.

A peculiarity of IPX is that it can bypass the OSI model, by addressing the 5th layer of the destination machine, directly. It does not have to use SPX. In fact, IP+TCP corresponds to IPX+SPX, whilst IP+UDP is the equivalent of IPX alone.

### 4. SPX (Sequenced Packet eXchange) protocol

SPX is implemented on the transport layer of the OSI model. It is a connection-oriented protocol and ensures packet delivery. The best known implementations of SPX concern remote printing, remote consoles (RSPX), SNA gateways and the DOOM games on the network.

### 5. NCP (Netware Core Protocol)

The Novell protocol provides a distributed file system for Novell Clients.

On Microsoft systems, the NCP client is better known under the name of **Client for Novell Networks**, on Windows 95, or **Client Service for NetWare**, on Windows NT Workstation.

You can also install a NetWare server on a Windows NT machine, or even on a Windows 95 machine. On NT Server you can obtain the NCP server component that is called **File and Print Services for Netware**.

The services that are offered by the server are diffused in the form of SAP (Service Advertising Protocol) packets. This protocol provides regular announcements of services that are available on a given server: file services, print services, backup services, database management and so on.

# E. NetBEUI (NetBIOS Enhanced User Interface)

## 1. Overview

NetBIOS was introduced by IBM in 1985. It was optimized for use with small, extended LANs. It is simple to implement but it is not routable. It introduced the use of NetBIOS names that can be used to identify network machines without using logical addresses. Consequently, there is only one resolution of names into MAC addresses. In addition, this resolution is often managed by the machine itself, which sends a broadcast onto the network.

### a. The advantages of NetBIOS

NetBIOS is a simple protocol with low memory requirements. As a result, NetBIOS remains widely used (for example by Microsoft, IBM and Novell products).

The NetBIOS APIs (Application Programming Interfaces) were widely developed on the PC to provide independence from the underlying protocols used.

NetBIOS is available either directly, encapsulated in LCC (802.2) frames, or encapsulated in IPX or TCP/IP.

At present, Microsoft products run exclusively on NetBIOS. You can however, use any 3 or 4 layer from TCP/IP, IPX/SPX or NetBEUI.

## b. NetBIOS names

On a NetBIOS network, each machine must have a unique name made up of 15 characters or less.

NetBIOS names can contain any alphanumeric characters. They can also contain the following characters: ! @ # $ % ^ & ( ) _ ' { } . ~

☞ *You cannot use characters that may be interpreted as wildcards such as asterisks or question marks.*

It is not advisable to use spaces in NetBIOS names, although some applications are able to manage these. For example, the following command is authorized, provided that you protect parameters using double quotes:

```
Net view "\\THE SERVER"
```

## c. Implementing NetBIOS names

You must assign a name that identifies each machine. It is advisable to identify the machine with respect to its geographical location, to its operating system, to its role and possibly to the user who works with it.

For example, you can base your names on the following NetBIOS denominations:

Two characters to identify the **geographical location**, for example:

| | |
|---|---|
| EU | for Europe |
| AS | for Asia |
| CA | for Canada |

Five characters to identify the **operating system used**, for example:

| | |
|---|---|
| LMN22 | Lan Manager 2.2 |
| NW312 | Netware 3.12 |
| NTS40 | NT Server 4.0 |
| WFW31 | Windows for Workgroups 3.1 |
| WIN95 | Windows 95 |

Three characters to identify the hierarchy level within the organization:

| | |
|---|---|
| ENT | Enterprise |
| DIV | Division |
| DPT | Department |
| OFF | Office |

Finally, a 2-character machine code is used to provide a final identification level:
01 to 99

Thus, you can build complete names such as the following:
\\EULMNE2ENT07
\\CANTS0ENT01
\\ASWIN5DPT52

### d. Configuring the name of a computer

According to the operating system used, you must configure the NetBIOS name that you have defined. On Windows NT, once this has been done, you can access this name by selecting the **Identification** tab in the **Network** window

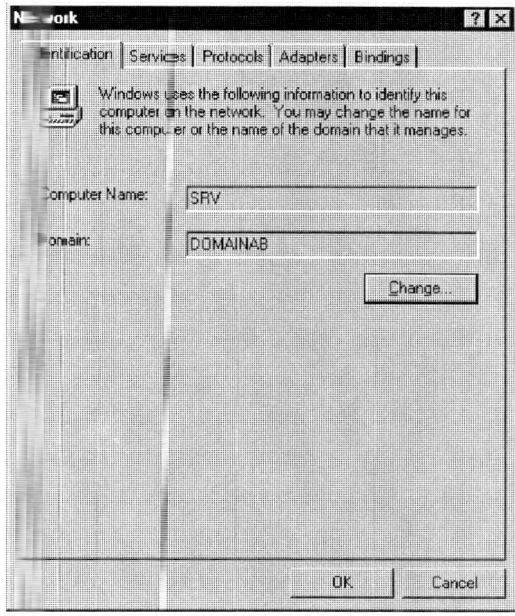

According to the underlying protocols that are used, you can even access the list of NetBIOS names that are registered on a server. These names correspond to services that are currently running:

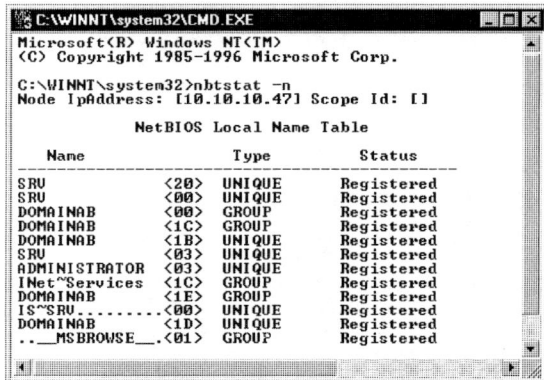

## 2. Information Sharing and the SMB (Server Message Block) protocol

The SMB protocol implements a distributed file system in a Microsoft or OS/2 environment.

SAMBA is a public domain version of this protocol that runs on UNIX servers.

With Microsoft products, on the server side, the SMB protocol appears under the name of **Server Service**, for Windows NT, Windows 95 and Windows for Workgroups.

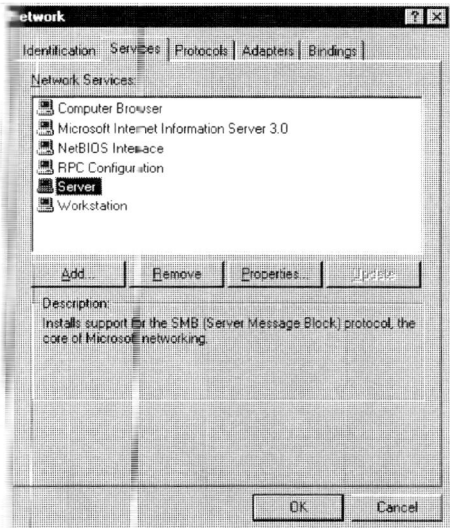

The client side of SMB is better known under the name of **Workstation Service** on Windows NT, or **Client for Microsoft Networks** on other Microsoft operating systems.

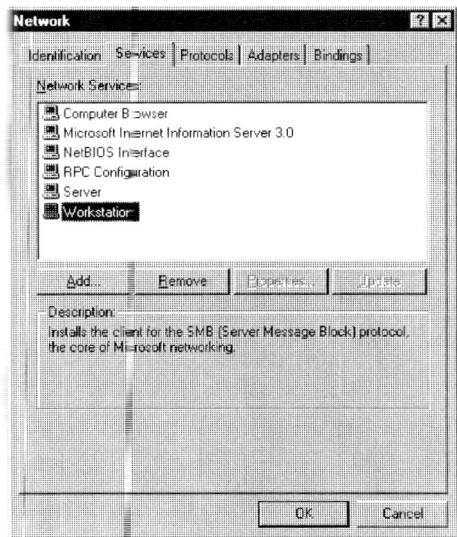

You can access the SMB resources using the **Network Neighborhood**. An interesting feature of this technique is that you can handle the resources in the same way you would handle local files and directories:

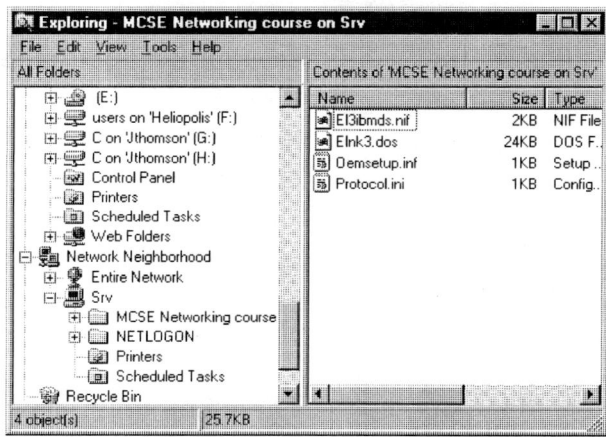

## F. DLC (Data Link Control)

### 1. The DLC protocol and the OSI model

Although DLC functions at the layer 2 (data link) level of the OSI model, it has been included in this chapter because DLC installation varies according to the physical layer concerned.

Each DLC interface network card has a unique DLC address. This address is better known under the name of **DLCI (DLC Identifier)**.

Unlike DLC, protocols such as TCP/IP use an extra logical address at the network layer level. Because of this, when DLC is used, logical addresses must be translated into DLC addresses (these are MAC addresses in fact). In a TCP/IP network, this resolution is carried out using the ARP (Address Resolution Protocol) protocol.

DLC is used primarily to connect to **IBM mainframes**. For example, Microsoft SNA Server for Windows NT uses the DLC protocol when it communicates using the Token Ring interface.

DLC is also used to connect directly to **network print peripherals** (such as HP JetDirect).

DLC allows Windows NT computers to connect to IBM Mainframes via a **3270 emulation**. In addition, you can access IBM AS/400 machines via a **5230 emulation**.

DLC runs with both Token Ring and Ethernet drivers. It can function with programs running on Windows NT, MS-DOS or even 16-bit Windows.

### 2. Situations that require DLC

There are a number of different situations that require the installation of this protocol.

You must install DLC in the following cases:
- To connect to SNA (Systems Network Architecture) gateways.
- To connect to network print peripherals such as HP JetDirect. The client computers that transmit their print jobs do not need to have DLC installed: only the print server that communicates directly with the printer needs to use DLC.
- To use remote startup services. On Windows NT, remote startup services require the installation of DLC on NT Server.

## 3. Configuring DLC

On Windows NT, for example, you have nothing to configure for this protocol.

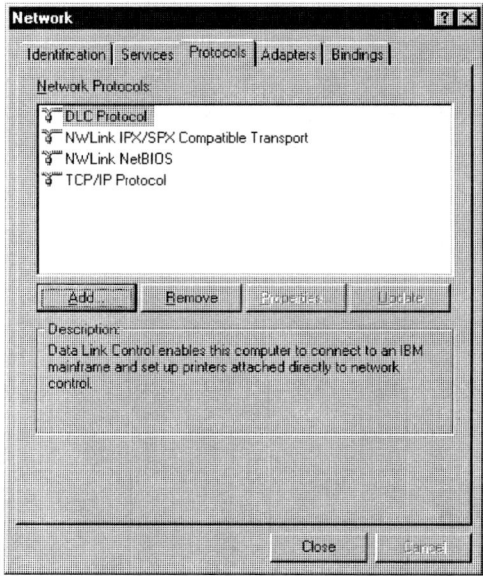

DLC is a non-routable protocol. However, a bridge can use the MAC addresses.

Once you have installed DLC, you can choose the printer port in order to configure your spool queue:

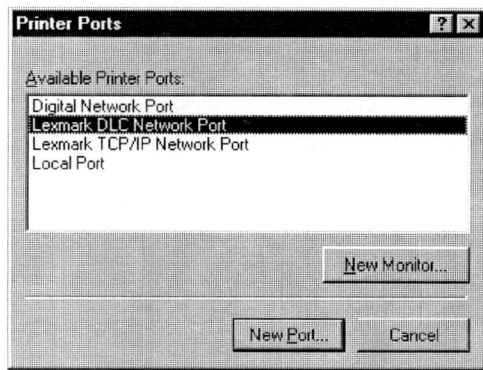

Essentials — Chapter 7 - Page 281

## Exercises

To be absolutely sure that you have assimilated this chapter, work through the corresponding exercises. These are set out from page 395.

☒ Standards and terminology.

## Assessing your skills

Try the following questions if you think you know this chapter well enough.

*TCP/IP*

1 Which are the layers that compose the TCP/IP model? ☐

2 Which transport layer protocol is connection oriented? ☐

3 Which Internet layer protocol is connectionless oriented? ☐

4 Which transport layer protocol favors speed? ☐

5 With IP version 4, how many bytes are used to identify a logical address? ☐

6 Which packet switching network was at the origin of the Internet? ☐

7 What is the name of the reference documents that are used for the TCP/IP standards? ☐

8 Which protocol allows you to access a Unix server via the network using terminal emulation? ☐

9 Which service allows you to resolve host names in IP addresses on TCP/IP? ☐

10 Which service allows you to resolve NetBIOS names in IP addresses? ☐

11 Which protocol allows the automatic configuration of IP parameters on clients that request it? ☐

12 Which protocol supports the remote control of certain components? ☐

13 What is the name of the information database that is accessible using a remote SNMP agent? ☐

14 Which protocol underlies ping? ☐

15 Which protocol allows you to resolve the address 00A00010CDF1 into 132.147.18.2? ☐

16 How many address classes allow you to identify uniquely, IP hosts in inter-networks? ☐

17 What is the class A mask by default? ☐

18 What is the class B mask by default? ☐

19 How many different networks can be used with class A? ☐

20 What is a local loop address? ☐

21 Which protocol is used especially for sharing files in a Unix workstation environment? ☐

22 Which protocols underlie NFS? ☐

23 Which protocol allows you to exchange files between TCP/IP machines on the Internet? ☐

24 Which file transfer protocol based on TCP/IP, favors speed or reliability? ☐

25 On which transport protocol is FTP based? ☐

26 Which client/server, file and application protocol is heavily used at present? ☐

27 Under which name is the Unix version of the SMB protocol better known? ☐

28 Which application allows a UNIX server to act as an NT domain controller? ☐

### Novell

29 In which type of structure is stored the distributed objects database that is managed by Novell 4.x? ☐

30 Which routable protocol underlies the initial Novell architecture? ☐

31 Which protocol ensures a connection oriented service in the protocol stack that is standard Netware supply? ☐

32 What is the peculiarity of a Novell Netware server? ☐

33 Which Novell protocol provides access to Novell files and spool queues? ☐

34 On how many bytes is an IPX address coded? ☐

35 Which routing protocol is supplied with IPX? ☐

36  Under which name is the Windows 95 NCP client known? ❏

37  Which protocol informs Novell clients of the presence of services on a Novell server? ❏

### NetBIOS and NetBEUI

38  Is NetBIOS routable? ❏

39  What are the advantages of NetBIOS? ❏

40  What is the maximum length of a NetBIOS name? ❏

41  How would you choose a NetBIOS denomination for a network that contains many machines? ❏

42  On an NT machine, how do you access the utility that enables you to change the name of a computer? ❏

43  Which name is more commonly used for the SMB server on a Windows 95 machine? ❏

44 Which name is more commonly used for the SMB client on a Windows 95 machine? ☐

45 Which name is more commonly used for the SMB server on a UNIX machine? ☐

46 Which name is more commonly used for the SMB client on a Windows NT machine? ☐

## DLC

47 Is DLC routable? ☐

48 On which OSI model layer does DLC operate? ☐

49 For which purposes is DLC particularly useful?

## Results

Check your answers on pages 288 to 292. Count one point for each correct answer.

Number of points [   /49  ]

For this chapter you need to have scored at least 37 out of 49.

Look at the list of key points that follows. Pick out the ones with which you have had difficulty and work through them again in this chapter before moving on to the next.

## Key points of the chapter

- ☐ TCP/IP.
- ☐ Novell.
- ☐ NetBIOS and NetBEUI.
- ☐ DLC.

# Solutions

## TCP/IP

1 Which are the layers that compose the TCP/IP model?

*TCP/IP has four layers: Application, Transport, Internet and Network interface.*

2 Which transport layer protocol is connection oriented?

*TCP.*

3 Which Internet layer protocol is connectionless?

*IP.*

4 Which transport layer protocol favors speed?

*UDP.*

5 With IP version 4, how many bytes are used to identify a logical address?

*4 bytes.*

6 Which packet switching network was at the origin of the Internet?

*ARPANET.*

7 What is the name of the reference documents that are used for the TCP/IP standards?

*RFC (Request For Comment).*

8 Which protocol allows you to access a Unix server via the network using terminal emulation?

*Telnet.*

9 Which service allows you to resolve host names in IP addresses on TCP/IP?

*DNS (Domain Name System).*

10 Which service allows you to resolve NetBIOS names in IP addresses?

*WINS (Windows Internet Name Service).*

11 Which protocol allows the automatic configuration of IP parameters on clients that request it?

*DHCP (Dynamic Host Configuration Protocol).*

12 Which protocol supports the remote control of certain components?

*SNMP (Simple Network Management Protocol).*

13 What is the name of the information database that is accessible using a remote SNMP agent?

*MIB (Management Information Database).*

14 Which protocol underlies ping?

*ICMP (Internet Control Message Protocol).*

15 Which protocol allows you to resolve the address 00A000100DF1 into 132.147.18.2?

*RARP (Reverse Address Resolution Protocol).*

16 How many address classes allow you to identify uniquely, IP hosts in internetworks?

*Three, classes A, B and C.*

17 What is the class A mask by default?

*255.0.0.0*

18 What is the class B mask by default?

*255.255.0.0*

19 How many different networks can be used with class A?

*126.*

20 What is a local loop address?

*This is the address 127.0.0.1, which is reserved for internal testing of the network interface card.*

21 Which protocol is used especially for sharing files in a Unix workstation environment?

*NFS (Network File System).*

22 Which protocols underlie NFS?

*RPC (Remote Procedure Call) and the XDR (eXternal Data Representation) presentation layer.*

23 Which protocol allows you to exchange files between TCP/IP machines on the Internet?

*FTP.*

24 Which file transfer protocol based on TCP/IP, favors speed to reliability?

*TFTP.*

25 On which transport protocol is FTP based?

*TCP.*

26 Which client/server, file and application protocol is heavily used at present?

*HTTP.*

27 Under which name is the Unix version of the SMB protocol better known?

*SAMBA.*

28 Which application allows a UNIX server to act as an NT domain controller?

*SAMBA.*

## Novell

29 In which type of structure is stored the distributed objects database that is managed by Novell 4.x?

*NDS (Netware Directory Service).*

30 Which routable protocol underlies the initial Novell architecture?

*IPX.*

31 Which protocol ensures a connection oriented service in the protocol stack that is standard Netware supply?

*SPX (Sequenced Packet eXchange) protocol.*

32 What is the peculiarity of a Novell Netware server?

*It is a dedicated server that does not use virtual memory.*

33 Which Novell protocol provides access to Novell files and spool queues?

*NCP (Netware Core Protocol).*

34 On how many bytes is an IPX address coded?

*4 for the IPX network number + 6 to identify the IPX host (the MAC address is used for this).*

35 Which routing protocol is supplied with IPX?

*RIP IPX (and also NLSP - Netware Link State Protocol).*

36 Under which name is the Windows 95 NCP client known?

*Client for Novell networks.*

37 Which protocol informs Novell clients of the presence of services on a Novell server?

*SAP (Service Advertisement Protocol).*

### NetBIOS and NetBEUI

38 Is NetBIOS routable?

*No, it does not include logical addresses, the names are resolved directly into MAC addresses.*

39 What are the advantages of NetBIOS?

*It is simple and economical in memory resources. NetBIOS APIs provide independence from the underlying protocol.*

40 What is the maximum length of a NetBIOS name?

*15 characters.*

41 How would you choose a NetBIOS denomination for a network that contains many machines?

*It is advisable to identify each machine with respect to its geographical location, to the operating system used, to the role of the machine and possibly to the user who works with the machine.*

42 On an NT machine, how do you access the utility that enables you to change the name of a computer?

*By selecting the **Identification** tab, from the **Network** icon in the **Control Panel**.*

43 Which name is more commonly used for the SMB server on a Windows 95 machine?

*Server Service.*

44 Which name is more commonly used for the SMB client on a Windows 95 machine?

*Client for Microsoft networks.*

45 Which name is more commonly used for the SMB server on a UNIX machine?

*SAMBA.*

46 Which name is more commonly used for the SMB client on a Windows NT machine?

*Workstation service.*

## DLC

47 Is DLC routable?

*No.*

48 On which OSI model layer does DLC operate?

*Layer 2.*

49 For which purposes is DLC particularly useful?

*To connect to an HP print peripheral or to an IBM mainframe.*

## Prerequisites for this chapter

☒ Knowledge of network topologies and switching methods.

## Objectives

When you have completed this chapter you will be able to:
☒ Define the characteristics of existing WAN connections.
☒ Describe the characteristics of ISDN.
☒ Describe the features of the SLIP protocol.
☒ Describe the features of the PPP protocol.
☒ Explain the functioning principle of X.25.
☒ Explain the principle of the Frame relay.
☒ Describe the features of ATM.

# Extended networks

## Summary

- A. Types of connection available . . . . 295
    1. Introduction . . . . . . . . . . . . . . . . . . . 295
    2. The switched telephone network . . . . . . . . 295
    3. Leased lines . . . . . . . . . . . . . . . . . . . 295

- B. ISDN (Integrated Services Digital Network) . . . . . . . . . . . . . . . . . 297
    1. Introduction . . . . . . . . . . . . . . . . . . . 297
    2. ISDN and the OSI model . . . . . . . . . . . 297
    3. Types of access . . . . . . . . . . . . . . . . . 298

- C. SLIP (Serial Line IP) . . . . . . . . . . . 300

- D. PPP (Point-to-Point Protocol) . . . . . . 302

- E. X.25 . . . . . . . . . . . . . . . . . . . . 303
    1. Terminology . . . . . . . . . . . . . . . . . . 304
    2. Example of X.25 access offered in Europe . . 304

- F. Frame relay . . . . . . . . . . . . . . . 305

- G. ATM (Asynchronous Transfer Mode) . . 306

After discussing the different possibilities of interconnection, this chapter will describe the specifications associated with extended networks, such as those for digital networks, frame relays, cell relays and packet switching.

## A. Types of connection available

### 1. Introduction

In order to interconnect remote sites, you can choose from a number of options: you can choose a solution based on a **point-to-point** connection, or you can choose a solution based on a **mulitipoint** architecture. The physical medium used may support **analog** or **digital** communications. The line may be **switched** or **leased, public** or **private**.

All these different elements combine together to define a certain number of interconnection options.

### 2. The switched telephone network

This is the means of communication that is the easiest to implement. It is also the most commonly used. It provides analog, switched, point-to-point connections. Transmission speeds are not very high, but they are fairly suitable for the transfer of small files and electronic mail.

### 3. Leased lines

#### a. Introduction

Unlike a switched line, a leased line allows you to make a point-to-point connection between two pre-defined numbers. Your telephone company sets up a permanent connection for the duration of the leasing term.

You cannot use a leased line to dial a telephone number, as you would on a switched telephone line.

☞ *For example, the ENI company uses a leased line so that its server is permanently available on the Internet.*

### b. Defined transmission speeds

According to your needs and your means, you can choose to lease at a specific transmission speed. You can choose a speed from 64 Kbps in Europe (56 Kbps in the USA) up to much higher speeds.

Here are the transmission speeds that are commonly used for digital point-to-point connections in the USA:

**T1**

> T1 provides a transmission equivalent to 24 channels of 64 Kbps, across two twisted pairs: one in emission and the other in reception. This results in a transmission speed of 1.544 Mbps.

**T2**

> T2 provides a transmission of 4 x T1: 96 x 64 Kbps, providing 6.312 Mbps.

**T3**

> T3 provides a transmission of 28 x T1: 672 x 64 Kbps, providing 44.736 Mbps.

**T4**

> T4 provides a transmission of 168 x T1: providing 274.176 Mbps.

In Europe, other transmission speeds are offered: E1, E2 and E3. These transmissions are also in the form of multiples of 64 Kbps, although the numbers of channels offered are slightly different.

# B. ISDN (Integrated Services Digital Network)

## 1. Introduction

ISDN is defined by a group of standards that was set up by the ITU-T to transform the existing analog Switched Telephone network into a world digital network.

☞ *In the UK, British Telecom provides ISDN access to its network.*

There is also a higher throughput version of ISDN called **Broadband ISDN**. This solution uses physical layers such as SONET (Synchronous Optical NETwork) and ATM (Asynchronous Transfer Mode).

The all-digital nature of this solution allows the transmission of a wide variety of data: voice, video and data. In addition a superior transmission quality is provided. This solution is suitable for the following types of application: file transfer, video-conferences, audio-conferences and fax.

## 2. ISDN and the OSI model

On a physical level, ISDN provides time division multiplexing between the different network items. At the data link level, the standards are defined by the ITU: I.450/Q.930 and I.451/Q.931.

ISDN acts like an information transmission service. The ISDN specifications are based on the **LAP-D** (Link Access Procedure, D channel) protocol, which manages the D channel. This protocol manages the connection. It starts up and shuts down the connection, and provides a full-duplex service.

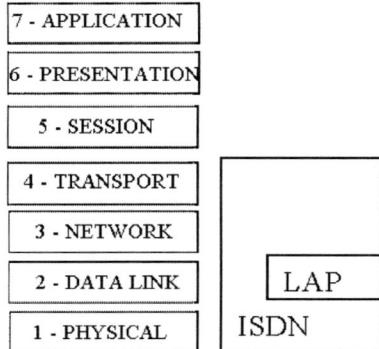

For an individual subscriber, the cost is generally far too high for the services offered. On the other hand, companies often use this to exchange data.

## 3. Types of access

For the user, **two types of access** have been defined concerning the basic speed required to transmit voice data: 64 Kbps.

☞ *Human voice varies between frequencies of 20 Hz and 1800 Hz. The telephone signal used can vary from 300 to 3400 Hz. A sample is taken in order to digitize the voice to 8000 Hz (125 s). After compression of 12 bits to 8 bits, the digitized throughput is 64 Kbps. MIC (Modulation by Impulse and Coding) type coding is used.*

Two channels are used to identify the types of access that are available:

The **B channel** can be used as a telephone link, as a fax link, or as a data link.

The **D channel** is used for dialing, setting up the communication, identifying the caller or for other services.

The first type of access, known as **basic rate access**, provides 2 B channels (64 Kbps) + 1 D channel (16 Kbps) for the signaling.

☞ The line management offered by protocols such as PPP allows you to combine two B channels to provide 128 Kbps.

☞ Thanks to ISDN compression, you can achieve transmission speeds of up to 400 Kbps.

☞ The S0 interface corresponds to RJ45 connection hardware with a T0 link.

Primary rate access provides 30 B channels at 64 Kbps and 1 D channel at 64 Kbps.

☞ The S2 interface is used to connect the computer to the PABX (Private Automatic Branch eXchange).

☞ In the USA and Japan primary rate access corresponds to 23 B channels and 1 D channel.

ISDN is a **switched service**. Consequently, the user is invoiced according to the communication time and the distance.

☞ It must be noted that, apart from standing charges for installation and leasing the line, the communication is invoiced as for a local connection. However, transmission speeds are twice those obtained using a standard modem.

Extended networks

## C. SLIP (Serial Line IP)

SLIP is an old protocol that is used for point-to-point connection to provide remote access to the Internet. It operates at the physical layer level of the OSI model. It is specifically based on IP.

As it is quite old, it has a number of drawbacks: it does not provide secure communications (authentication and data transfer), it does not offer a compression feature and it does not provide error checking.

☞ *The CSLIP version allows you to compress exchanged packets.*

All the SLIP connection parameters must be input manually, in particular the IP address. Consequently, in order to automate a SLIP connection, you must use a script, provided that the IP address is fixed.

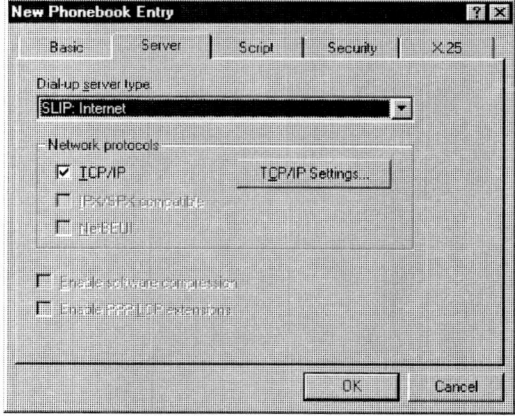

In order to set up the SLIP connection, you must know your own IP address and that of the destination machine (this is generally that of your Internet Access Provider). You must also know the other information concerning your TCP/IP configuration.

In spite of these major drawbacks, SLIP is a very popular protocol. This is largely due to the fact that many users do not necessarily need a secure connection and that most modems provide their own error checking.

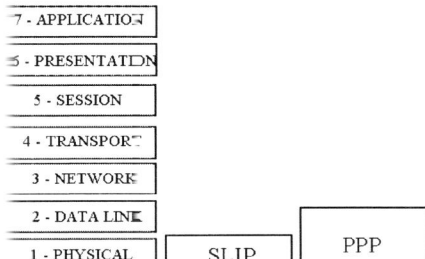

Extended networks

## D. PPP (Point-to-Point Protocol)

PPP was developed as an improvement to SLIP. With reference to the OSI model, it provides a physical layer and a data link layer.

PPP offers extra features such as error checking (supplied by the Logical Link Control sub-layer), security, dynamic IP address allocation and support for various LAN protocols such as IP, IPX, AppleTalk and NetBEUI.

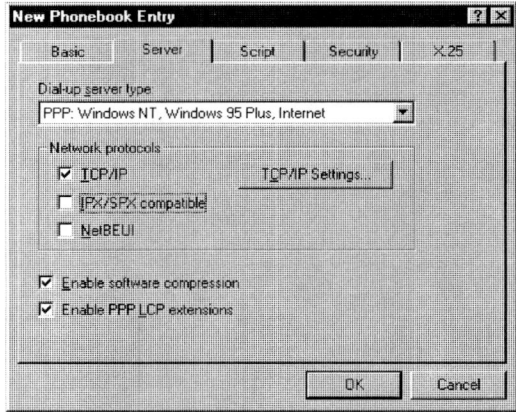

Thus, PPP is able to negotiate all the configuration parameters at the beginning of the connection. It offers two methods of automating connections: Password Authentication Protocol (PAP) and Challenge-Handshake Authentication Protocol (CHAP).

PPP can also negotiate compression of the headers. This is possible because with the headers that are transmitted in a TCP connection, only a few of the fields are modified, and only these fields need be transmitted.

A number of software components are available that allow SLIP or PPP connections to be set up automatically. All you have to do is to configure essential parameters such a your **name and password**, along with the **telephone number** of your access provider.

In summary then, PPP must be chosen, if available. Otherwise, SLIP can be used (in the case of older systems on which no update has been made).

# E. X.25

The ITU specified X.25 in 1974. It was originally designed to connect remote terminals to large systems. At the time, the Telephone Switching Network was used very little as it was not very reliable.

X.25 appeared before the OSI model. It describes a set of protocols that are integrated in a packet switching network using virtual circuits.

| | | | |
|---|---|---|---|
| 7 - APPLICATION | | | |
| 6 - PRESENTATION | | | |
| 5 - SESSION | | | |
| 4 - TRANSPORT | | | |
| 3 - NETWORK | X.25 | | |
| 2 - DATA LINK | LAPB | | |
| 1 - PHYSICAL | X.21 | V.32 | Others |

X.25 covers the first three layers of the OSI model. It is supported by LAPB (Link Accessed Procedures, Balanced), which is a character-oriented protocol. A number of standards are available for the physical layer.

X.25 includes packet identification and acknowledgements. In addition, it manages virtual circuits, provides transmission control and offers an error recovery facility. This is very important as the X.25 physical architecture was originally designed to work with existing, unreliable telephone networks. Unfortunately, the transmission error correction features slow down considerably the X.25 implementations, on lines that do not exceed transmission rates of 64 Kbps.

Such speeds are not very suitable for interconnecting LANs. In spite of this, X.25 is an internationally used standard and is tending to expand into those areas of the world where modern infrastructures have not yet been installed (such as Africa, South America, Asia and some Eastern European countries).

*Extended networks*

## 1. Terminology

An X.25 network includes the terminal hardware (DTE) and the equipment that provides access to the switched network (DCE). In addition there are the PSE (Packet Switching Exhanges), which identify the X.25 switches.

Finally, the PADs (Packet Assembler/Disassemblers) provide network access to non-X.25 terminals. You can also access the X.25 network from the Switched Telephone Network (as defined by the X.32 standard).

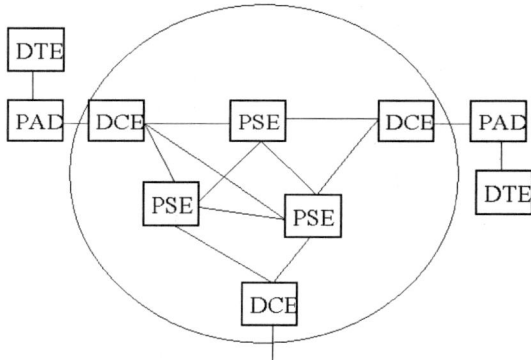

## 2. Example of X.25 access offered in Europe

### a. With a direct connection to X.25

This solution supports transmission speeds from 9.9 Kbps to 1920 Kbps. It allows universal connectivity with all subscribers of Transpac and Global One, along with all users of the X.25 public network, via the international transit node.

☞ *Global One is an international consortium including France Telecom, Deutsche Telekom and Sprint.*

### b. With an indirect connection to X.25

This is an economical, simple and universal solution. It is suitable for applications that require short communication times.

In this case, you can access the X.25 network, either from the Telephone Switching Network or via an ISDN connection. Transmission speeds vary from 0.3 Kbps to 28.8 Kbps in asynchronous mode, and from 2.4 Kbps to 19.2 Kbps (or 64 Kbps) in synchronous mode.

## F. Frame relay

Frame relays were designed to function as a means of transporting other protocols in a packet switched network on a digital medium. Today, the frame relay is very standardized: by ANSI, ITU-T, IETF (Internet Engineering Task Force) and Frame Relay Forum.

It is often referred to as Fast Packet Switching. This underlines the fact that all frame relay does is to switch the frames (in contrast, X.25 uses a store and forward technique).

The idea was to use a more reliable physical medium (such as fiber optics) so as to avoid the need for time-consuming error correction. In addition, and unlike X.25, frame relay describes only two protocols, on two levels (1 and 2). Consequently, a layer-3 network protocol is integrated directly into level 2. This technique has allowed the implementation of a more efficient algorithm, so that frame relay supports higher transmission speeds (up to 8 Mbps).

☞ *In fact, the level 3 protocol of X.25 encapsulates other level 3 packets, which incurs considerable overheads.*

| 7 - APPLICATION |
| 6 - PRESENTATION |
| 5 - SESSION |
| 4 - TRANSPORT |
| 3 - NETWORK |
| 2 - DATA LINK |
| 1 - PHYSICAL |

Frame relay

The data is forwarded from a network, via a digital leased line to a frame relay switch (this requires the presence of a router or a bridge in order to handle the frames and access the private frame relay network).

## G.ATM (Asynchronous Transfer Mode)

ATM is derived from packet switching. It carries out uniform data transmission, in the form of low level switching of very small packets (53-byte cells). ATM supports high transmission speeds: from 155 Mbps to 622 Mbps. ATM offers a high speed, real time, switched solution, in broadband or baseband, for both LAN and WAN connections.

The following diagram illustrates the relationship between ATM and the OSI model:

| 7 - APPLICATION    |       |      |        |
|--------------------|-------|------|--------|
| 6 - PRESENTATION   |       |      |        |
| 5 - SESSION        |       |      |        |
| 4 - TRANSPORT      |       |      |        |
| 3 - NETWORK        | ATM   |      |        |
| 2 - DATA LINK      |       |      |        |
| 1 - PHYSICAL       | SONET | FDDI | Others |

## Exercises

To be absolutely sure that you have assimilated this chapter, work through the corresponding exercises. These are set out from page 400.

☒ Topologies and interconnections.

## Assessing your skills

Try the following questions if you think you know this chapter well enough

*General points on WAN connections*

1 What are the four characteristics of a WAN connection? ☐

2 What is the most common method of transmitting information at relatively low transmission speeds? ☐

3 Which solution provides you with a standing-charge connection between two subscribers? ☐

4 What is the least expensive way of publishing information on a server on the Internet, so that your data is available 24 hours a day? ☐

5 What transmission speed is provided by a type T1 connection in the USA? ☐

6 Which type of line provides transmission speeds of around 45 Mbps?

7 In Europe, which names are used for multiple transmission speeds?

## ISDN

8 What does ISDN signify?

9 What is the name of the ISDN version that offers higher transmission speeds?

10 What are the two main advantages of an all-digital solution?

11 Which protocol is used with ISDN to manage the D channel?

12 Which basic transmission speed is offered by ISDN?

13 Which channels are used with basic rate access?

14 What is the name of the RJ-45 interface used for local ISDN connections?

15 What is the name of automatic switching ISDN?

16 On which basis is an ISDN user invoiced?

## SLIP and PPP

17 Which WAN protocol that supports IP, is old and non-secure?

18 Which WAN protocol supports different LAN protocols?

19 Which authentication methods are supported by PPP?

20 Does SLIP support header compression?

21 Which WAN protocol that is based on IP, can be a DHCP client?

22 Does SLIP incorporate error checking?

23 On which layer(s) of the OSI model does SLIP operate?

24 On which layer(s) of the OSI model does PPP operate?

25 Which Data Link sub-layer does PPP use? ☐

26 Which WAN protocol would you probably use to implement an automatic, secure WAN connection for a client with recent equipment? ☐

### X.25, Frame Relay and ATM

27 What is the main drawback of X.25? ☐

28 On which layer(s) of the OSI model does X.25 operate? ☐

29 Which type of network does X.25 implement? ☐

30 Which protocol underlies layer 3 of X.25? ☐

31 Is X.25 still used today? ☐

32 What does DTE and DCE signify? ☐

33 Which are the two ways of accessing an X.25 network? ❏

34 Which type of X.25 connection supports the highest transmission speeds? ❏

35 What is the purpose of Frame Relay, with respect to X.25? ❏

36 Which nickname is often given to Frame Relay? ❏

37 On which layers of the OSI model is Frame Relay defined? ❏

38 Which interconnection solution incurs considerable operational overheads? ❏

39 Which type of switching does ATM implement? ❏

40 For which data types is ATM suitable? ❏

41 Which transmission speeds are theoretically available with ATM? ❏

42 What is the length of an ATM packet?  ☐

## Results

Check your answers on pages 313 to 317. Count one point for each correct answer.

Number of points ☐ /42

For this chapter you need to have scored at least 32 out of 42.

Look at the list of key points that follows. Pick out the ones with which you have had difficulty and work through them again in this chapter before moving on to the next.

## Key points of the chapter

☐ General points on WAN connections.
☐ ISDN.
☐ SLIP and PPP.
☐ X.25, Frame Relay and ATM.

# Solutions

### General points on WAN connections

1 What are the four characteristics of a WAN connection?

*A WAN connection can be point-to-point or multipoint, analog or digital, switched or leased and public or private.*

2 What is the most common method of transmitting information at relatively low transmission speeds?

*Using the Switched Telephone Network, with a modem.*

3 Which solution provides you with a standing-charge connection between two subscribers?

*Leased line.*

4 What is the least expensive way of publishing information on a server on the Internet, so that your data is available 24 hours a day?

*Leased line.*

5 What transmission speed is provided by a type T1 connection in the USA?

*1.544 Mbps*

6 Which type of line provides transmission speeds of around 45 Mbps?

*A T3 line.*

7 In Europe, which names are used for multiple transmission speeds?

*Transmission speeds E1, E2 E3...*

## ISDN

8 What does ISDN signify?

*Integrated Services Digital Network.*

9 What is the name of the ISDN version that offers higher transmission speeds?

*Broadband ISDN.*

10 What are the two main advantages of an all-digital solution?

*All-digital solutions offer better transmission quality and allow you to transmit all types of information.*

11 Which protocol is used with ISDN to manage the D channel?

*LAP-D (Link Access Procedure, D channel).*

12 Which basic transmission speed is offered by ISDN?

*64 Kbps and 128 Kbps using line aggregation techniques.*

13 Which channels are used with basic rate access?

*Two B channels and a D channel.*

14 What is the name of the RJ45 interface used for local ISDN connections?

*The S0 interface.*

15 What is the name of automatic switching ISDN?

*PABX (Private Automatic Branch Exchange).*

16 On which basis is an ISDN user invoiced?

*ISDN is a switched service that is invoiced according to usage time.*

## SLIP and PPP

17 Which WAN protocol that supports IP, is old and non-secure?

*SLIP.*

18 Which WAN protocol supports different LAN protocols?

*PPP.*

19 Which authentication methods are supported by PPP?

*CHAP and PAP.*

20 Does SLIP support header compression?

*No, SLIP does not support header compression in its standard version. However the C-SLIP version does support header compression.*

21 Which WAN protocol that is based on IP, can be a DHCP client?

*PPP (and not SLIP).*

22 Does SLIP incorporate error checking?

*No. However, modems implement this feature nowadays.*

23 On which layer(s) of the OSI model does SLIP operate?

*Physical layer.*

24 On which layer(s) of the OSI model does PPP operate?

*Physical and Data Link layers.*

25 Which Data Link sub-layer does PPP use?

*LLC.*

26 Which WAN protocol would you probably use to implement an automatic secure WAN connection for a client with recent equipment?

*PPP with IP.*

### X.25, Frame Relay and ATM

27 What is the main drawback of X.25?

*It is slow. This is because it incorporates an error correction feature.*

28 On which layer(s) of the OSI model does X.25 operate?

*The three first layers (Physical, Data link and Network).*

29 Which type of network does X.25 implement?

*A private, multipoint, packet switched network.*

30 Which protocol underlies layer 3 of X.25?

*LAPB (Link Accessed Procedures Balanced).*

31 Is X.25 still used today?

*Yes, it is implemented in unreliable telephone infrastructures. It is very suitable for such applications. In addition, X.25 is a proven international standard.*

32 What does DTE and DCE signify?

*DTE is terminal equipment, whilst DCE provides access to the switched network.*

33 Which are the two ways of accessing an X.25 network?

*You can connect to a private network via a modem, or via an ISDN connection. Alternatively you can connect directly using an X.25 card or an X.25 switch (PAD).*

34 Which type of X.25 connection supports the highest transmission speeds?

*Direct connection.*

35 What is the purpose of Frame Relay, with respect to X.25?

*Frame Relay was designed as an alternative to the X.25 network. Frame Relay is a fast protocol for use with a reliable physical medium.*

36 Which nickname is often given to Frame Relay?

*Fast Packet Switching.*

37 On which layers of the OSI model is Frame Relay defined?

*The first two layers.*

38 Which interconnection solution incurs considerable operational overheads?

*X.25.*

39 Which type of switching does ATM implement?

*Cell switching.*

40 For which data types is ATM suitable?

*For all types of voluminous data, such as multimedia.*

41 Which transmission speeds are theoretically available with ATM?

*Transmission speeds of 155 Mbps, 622 Mbps and even 1 Gbps.*

42 What is the length of an ATM packet?

*An ATM packet is known as a cell and has a constant length of 53 bytes.*

Essentials

# Prerequisites for this chapter

- ☒ Knowledge of point-to-point and centralized models.
- ☒ Knowledge of backup strategies and techniques for implementing levels of fault tolerance.

# Objectives

When you have completed this chapter you will be able to:
- ☒ Distinguish between network administration in a point-to-point environment and in a centralized environment.
- ☒ Define the characteristics of a Windows NT user.
- ☒ Explain the approach of implementing Windows NT groups organization of users and resource access. Describe predefined groups in a Windows NT Server domain.
- ☒ Implement password life policy and intrusion management.
- ☒ Define a resources audit policy.
- ☒ Explain the functioning of the Windows NT tools that are provided to monitor network traffic.
- ☒ Define the means that are required to implement a recovery plan.

**Network administration**

# Summary

- A. Accessing resources . . . . . . . . . . 321
    1. Connecting to a workgroup or to a domain . . 321
    2. Types of security . . . . . . . . . . . . . 322
    3. Sharing folders and printers . . . . . . . . . . 322

- B. Accounts management . . . . . . . . 323
    1. User accounts . . . . . . . . . . . . . . . . . 323
    2. Organizing the users . . . . . . . . . . . . 325
    3. Predefined local group accounts . . . . . . . 325
    4. Creating new groups . . . . . . . . . . . . 327
    5. Global group accounts . . . . . . . . . . . . . 327

- C. Security management . . . . . . . . . 328
    1. Accounts policy . . . . . . . . . . . . . . . 328
    2. Audit policy . . . . . . . . . . . . . . . . . 329

- D. Monitoring the network . . . . . . . . 333
    1. Network monitoring tools . . . . . . . . . . . 333
    2. Identifying and resolving network performance problems . . . . . . . . . . . . . . . . . . 335
    3. Resolving broadcast storm problems . . . . . 336

- E. Choosing a recovery plan for different catastrophic scenarios . . . . . . . . . 337
    1. Preventing breakdown of server power supplies . . . . . . . . . . . . . 337
    2. Backup strategies . . . . . . . . . . . . . . 337
    3. Data redundancy and fault tolerance . . . . . 338

Once you have installed the network operating system, you must define the rules that are required to administer life on the network. This involves the following activities:
- definition of an administration plan,
- definition of user accounts,
- definition of backups that must be made,
- monitoring of user activities,
- monitoring of work loading on each workstation,
- incident management (avoidance and handling).

All these items contribute to the implementation of a global security policy. They allow you to create a flexible organizational tool, and to prevent all destructive actions, whether they are intentional or not. In addition, a recovery plan must be devised that is capable of restoring data or damaged system elements, in the event of an incident.

This chapter will illustrate these techniques using Microsoft Windows NT Server. This system provides a number of tools that are essential for the implementation of an administration plan.

## A. Accessing resources

Resource access must be pertinent, flexible and secure.

### 1. Connecting to a workgroup or to a domain

Resource access security is ensured with respect to the network architecture implemented and the operating systems used.

In the first chapter of this book we saw that there were two basic types of network architecture: **networks that are organized around a server** and networks that are based on **peer-to-peer architectures**.

In most environments that include more than a few dozen users, a centralized architecture must be implemented. This architecture must allow the opening of sessions, resource access and the monitoring of backups.

On Windows NT Server operating systems, you can work in a domain environment. A **domain** is a group of computers that share the same security system and the same authentication basis for opening sessions.

You can also work in a machine-to-machine environment using **workgroups**. The purpose of the workgroup is to implement resource access, in a hierarchical organization.

In a domain, each user has a **name** and a **password**. This information must be supplied when opening a session on the network, so that it can be authenticated. The database of network users is centralized. In this way, access to resources can be controlled at the user level: this means that permissions are customized for each user, for each available resource.

This technique makes it much easier to know who is doing what and when. One specific user is called the **administrator** and has the task of managing all the resources on the network. The administrator is the most powerful user on the whole network.

## 2. Types of security

### a. Security at resource level

Security at resource level means that the resource is at the center of the security system. Passwords are attributed to resources, independently of the users.

### b. Security at user level

Security at user level allows more specific permissions to be attributed to each user for a given resource. First, a user must identify himself/herself for the reference entity (for example, the NT domain). Then, customized permissions allow specific access to the shared resources.

## 3. Sharing folders and printers

Identified resources include directories, which contain files, and spool queues for printers.

## B. Accounts management

In the accounts database of the domain, different accounts are managed these include user accounts, local and global group accounts and computer accounts.

### 1. User accounts

In order to identify resource access precisely, individual accounts are created: these are called **user accounts**. The following example illustrates the information that must be supplied when you create a user.

You can also specify numerous parameters that allow you to customize the environment of the created user. These include the User Profile **Path**, which specifies the location in which the user environment is stored; the Logon **Script**, which allows the execution of specific user commands and the **Home Directory**, which defines a path for the storage of user documents.

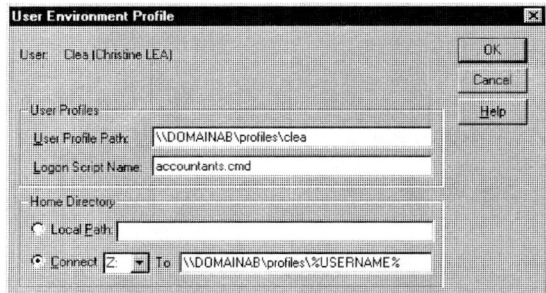

Each user has a name and a password. This information is identified internally by a SID (Security IDentity). This number can be viewed in the Windows NT Registry Editor, when the user accesses his/her configuration:

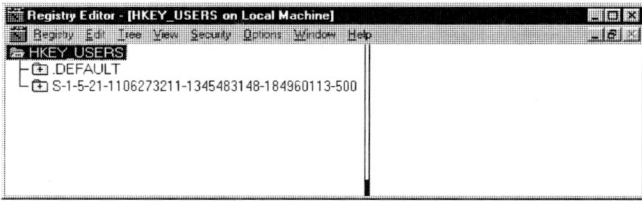

A SID is associated with each process that is generated. This means that it is possible to know who does what on the network. It also determines what the processes that are generated by the users are allowed to do.

Users can be managed using a specific tool that is available on most Microsoft clients. The following example shows the **User Manager** window, which allows you to administer the users in a domain environment.

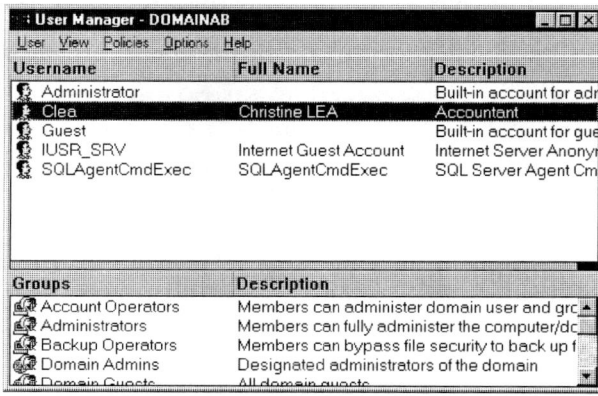

## 2. Organizing the users

The management of a large number of users in a network requires planning of the resources that must be used and the types of access that must be associated with them. It also requires that the Users receive their access authorization It is useful to gather users into groups that reflect the organization of the enterprise. Then, types of access to resources must be chosen not only so that they are coherent with each other, but also so that they will be easy to manage in the future.

In this way, when a new employee joins the company with a well-defined role, you will not need to implement a complex sequence of actions. You will need to create, only a new user, with respect to a specific model.

More specifically, we will examine the group model implemented in Windows NT networks and organized with respect to a domain.

## 3. Predefined local group accounts

For everyday tasks, a certain number of groups have been predefined, with specific predefined rights. This technique allows you to organize your administration policy, by decomposing your administration activities into elementary tasks.

These tasks include the management of shared resources (such as folders and printer spool queues and software applications), user management, computer management (shutdown and time changes), backups and restores

Different permissions are granted to predefined local groups. The members of these groups benefit from these associated permissions.

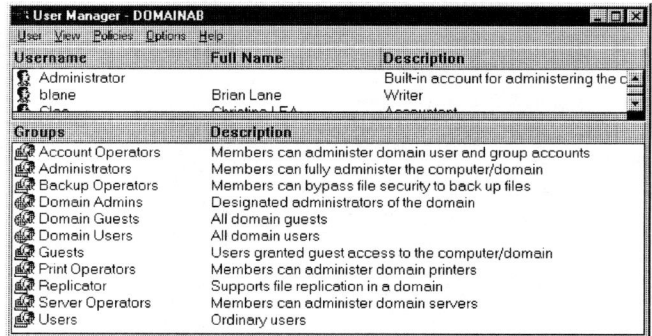

The above example describes the rights associated with certain predefined Windows NT Server groups.

### Account operators

These users can create users and groups. They can also manage (modify and delete) the users and groups that they create. They have the right to work interactively on NT servers that manage the users of the domain (domain controllers). They can also shutdown a server and add a new computer into a domain.

### Print Operators

Members of this group manage and administer printer sharing on all the servers. In addition, they can shutdown servers.

### Server Operators

These users manage servers. They can create, delete and administer shared printers and shared folders. They can backup and restore files, lock and unlock servers, format hard disks and change the system time. They can also open a session locally and shutdown servers.

### Backup Operators

Members of this group can backup and restore files on all the servers. They can also open a session locally and shutdown servers.

## 4. Creating new groups

The administrator can also define other groups. Rights of group members can be attributed implicitly. Alternatively, a group can be associated with a resource and permissions can be specified for this resource (user level security).

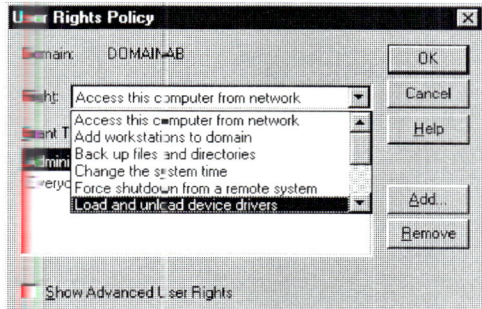

## 5. Global group accounts

On Windows NT Server, users in a domain environment are organized into global groups. This technique allows you precisely to define the logical organization of the company.

Some global groups are predefined, such as **Domain Admins**, **Domain Users** and **Domain Guests**. These global groups belong to predefined local groups with similar names: for example, **Domain Guests** is a member of the Guests group, and has restricted rights.

☞ *It is important to remember that a global group must not have direct rights. These rights must be indirectly granted by membership of local groups, which do have specific rights. This technique allows you to manage separately the organization of users and the rights that the users have as members of local groups (these rights are associated with access to a particular resource).*

## C. Security management

Predefined groups allow you to reuse certain permissions, by decomposing tasks into functional subsets. The creation of new groups allows you to define and associate rights according to your needs.

### 1. Accounts policy

When you have defined your groups and users, you must then manage the user accounts. This involves controlling the life cycle and renewing the passwords, in order to prevent unauthorized intrusion. Also, in the worst-case scenario, this can involve locking the accounts.

For example, it is important to oblige the users to change their passwords regularly and to prevent them from reusing old passwords. However, making your users change their passwords four times a month is not very useful if the users are able to change their passwords four times in one day, so that they need not touch them again for the rest of the month! In addition then, you must define a minimum time for which a password must remain valid without being modified.

Windows NT account policy allows you to implement this management, globally.

## 2. Audit Policy

Users must be monitored on a continuing basis. Precise rules must be defined in order to limit their actions, in particular concerning intrusions. To this end, the account policy is defined.

Another essential issue is the confidentiality associated with resources and with access to resources. Resource usage must be monitored. Any users who misuse a resource must be identified, and if necessary their access permission to the resource must be withdrawn.

This aspect is defined by using the **Audit Policy** and by monitoring system resources.

The **User Manager** of the Windows NT domain allows you to define the types of resources you wish to audit. When you have done this, you must monitor the resources themselves.

The first step consists of activating a type of event with respect to a class of user account, and with respect to a type of audit: **Success** (in the case of successful actions) and **Failure** (in the case of unsuccessful actions). Windows NT allows you to monitor several types of event:

| Audit Policy | Success | Failure |
|---|---|---|
| Logon and Logoff | ☐ | ☐ |
| File and Object Access | ☑ | ☑ |
| Use of User Rights | ☐ | ☑ |
| User and Group Management | ☑ | ☐ |
| Security Policy Changes | ☑ | ☐ |
| Restart, Shutdown, and System | ☐ | ☐ |
| Process Tracking | ☐ | ☐ |

Domain: DOMAIN_B — Do Not Audit / Audit These Events

These different types of event include logging-on and logging-off, connection to shared resources and the monitoring of Windows NT files and printers (**File and Object Access**).

When you have defined the overall audit policy, you can define precisely the monitoring that must be carried out for a Windows NT object. This is defined at the **Properties** level for the object.

For example for a file situated in a Windows NT, NTFS file system, here are the different actions that can be audited.

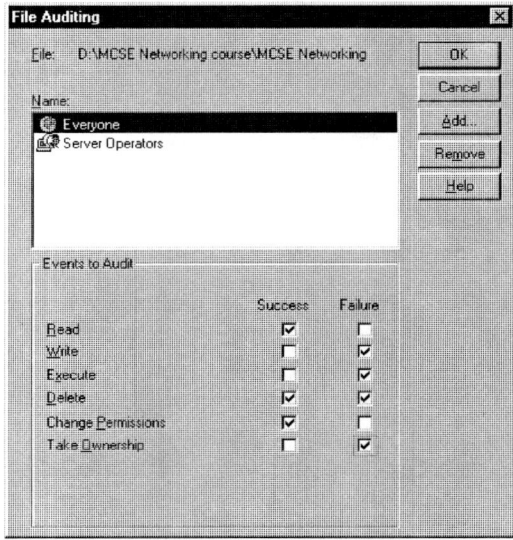

Similarly, you can define the auditing actions for a Windows NT, NTFS folder.

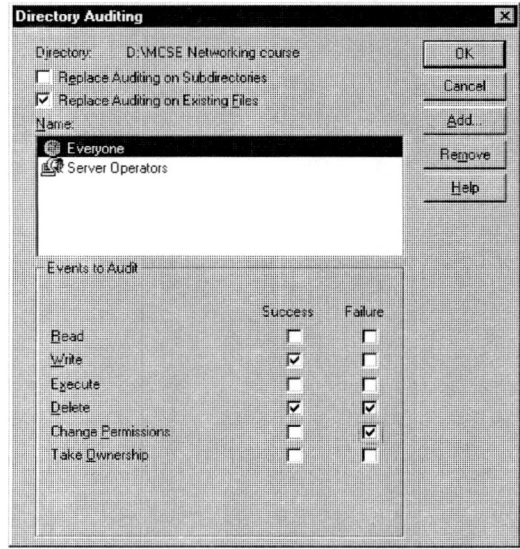

In addition, you can monitor a printer spool queue.

**Essentials**

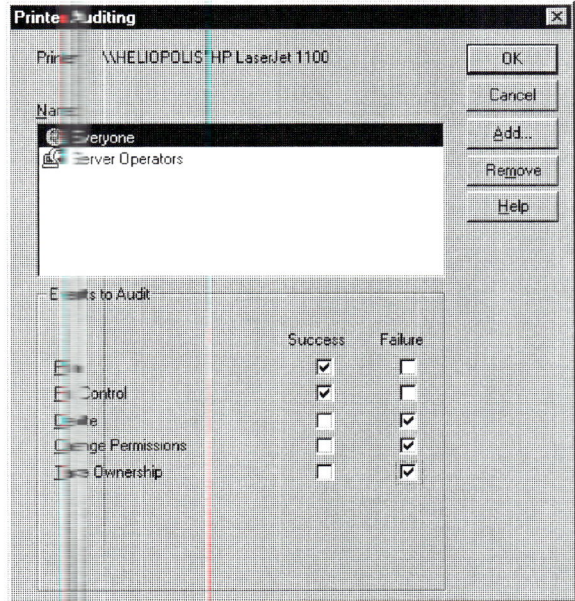

When you have configured your audit policy, you can monitor events by consulting the **Event Viewer**.

For each line in the security (audit) log a certain amount of information is recorded.

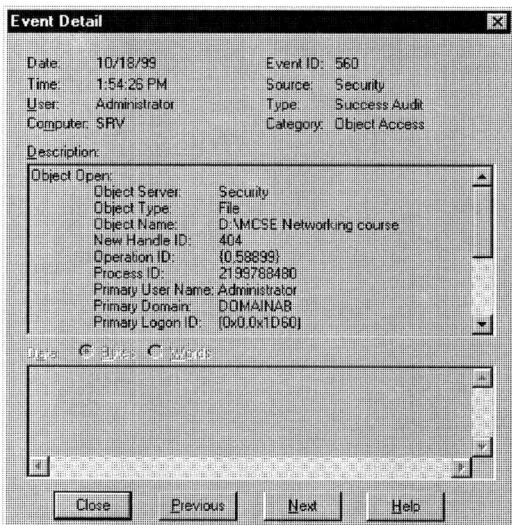

## D. Monitoring the network

It is important to monitor the workload of a network. It is essential to check that your network is able to support the load for which it has been defined. Following the installation of a network, demands on resources often increase and the services that were defined no longer meet the new requirements. This situation produces **bottlenecks** that slow down the system.

In order to avoid such problems, the administrator can implement the necessary tools and then detect problems by monitoring performance. These techniques even allow you to identify the component that must be updated in order to improve the global performance.

### 1. Network monitoring tools

The network bandwidth is one of the key elements that must be monitored. If data cannot be exchanged properly between network peripherals then the overall performance will suffer.

Each network operating system has its own tools that allow you to monitor network traffic. Windows NT Server has two very powerful, standard tools: the **Performance Monitor** and the **Network Monitor**.

#### a. Performance Monitor

The Performance Monitor allows you to monitor all resources. Resources can be divided into four categories: **network**, **memory**, **processor** and **disk**. The Performance Monitor allows you to monitor such diverse resources as a process, a partition, a processor, a protocol or a service.

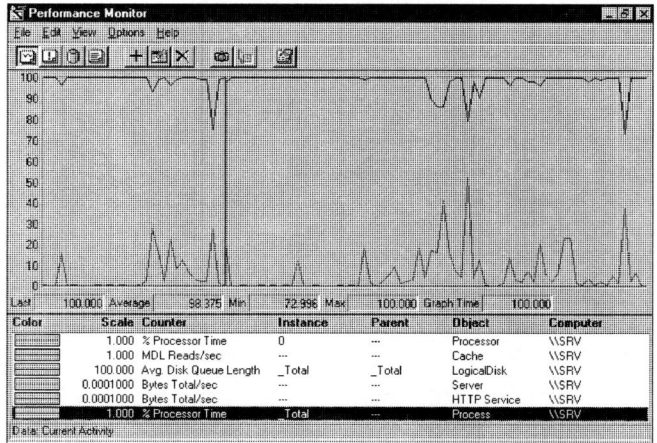

By using the various options offered by this tool, you can monitor performance and record the results for future analysis. Alternatively, you can consult a performance chart of resource usage in real time. In addition, alert thresholds can be defined in order to warn the administrator that a specific resource is heavily loaded. For example, you can send a message to the administrator if a partition is almost full or if a processor has reached its maximum processing capacity.

#### b. Network Monitor Agent

The Network Monitor Agent allows you to capture and analyze frames that are circulating on the network. For example, you can identify messages exchanged between a client and a server.

Here is an example of a frame capture.

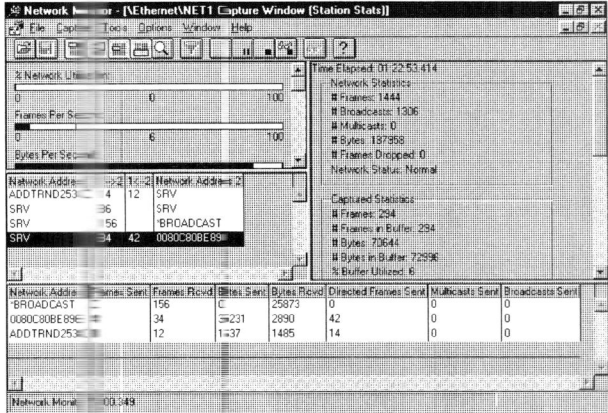

Once the frame capture has been made, you can analyze each of the captured packets.

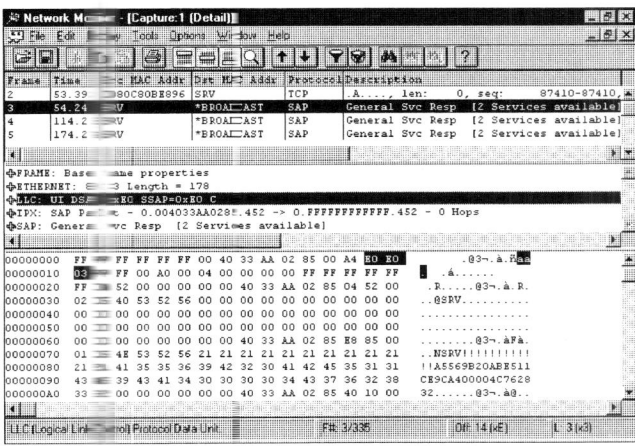

## 2. Identifying and resolving network performance problems

Network performance is monitored by using tools such as the Windows NT **Performance Monitor**, and by studying the use of network components: protocols, services or use of the network itself with objects such as **Network Segment**, **% Network utilization**.

As part of this monitoring, you can configure alerts so that the administrator will be informed as soon as there is too much activity on the network.

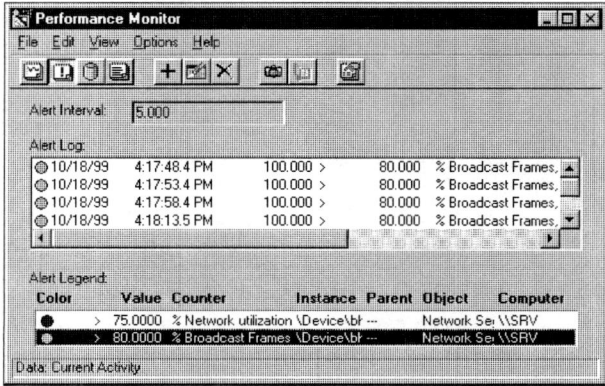

### 3. Resolving broadcast storm problems

A broadcast storm occurs when a broadcast overloads the bandwidth of the network, up to the limits of the physical medium used. This excessive traffic can result in a network meltdown whereby the network comes to a halt.

Defective network interface cards often cause these problems.

Reducing the size of the broadcast domain can solve these problems. You can do this by segmenting the network using routers.

On broadcast oriented networks such as Ethernet, you can segment the network into collision domains using bridges.

## E. Choosing a recovery plan for different catastrophic scenarios

First, you must monitor your network in order to detect the deletion of information (voluntary or otherwise). You must also be prepared to react rapidly should such a problem occur. To this end, a number of techniques allow you to safeguard your network environment (these techniques were presented in chapter 2).

A number of solutions allow you to protect your system against loss of data: these include data redundancy, UPS (Uninterruptible Power Supply) and the implementation of backup strategies.

### 1. Preventing breakdown of server power supplies

Your servers should be protected against power breakdown. They should also be protected from low quality power supply (by voltage filtering). UPS devices provide a suitable solution to both of these problems. These devices provide warning of an imminent power cut. In addition, they maintain the power supply for enough time to allow the shutdown of your servers.

### 2. Backup strategies

The regular backing-up of data is an essential activity in a company. The backup strategy must be chosen carefully to suit the needs of the enterprise, particularly with respect to the recovery time required after an incident. A number of factors must be taken into account. These include storage media rotation strategy, storage media life, good physical storage conditions and storage in a geographically remote location.

## 3. Data redundancy and fault tolerance

Whether you simply duplicate your data elsewhere on the network, or whether you implement a hardware RAID solution, you must be sure that you will be able to react quickly should an incident occur.

Disk mirroring is a useful technique to ensure that a partition that contains operating system data is permanently available. Similarly, data that must be accessed simultaneously should be protected using a technique such as disk striping with parity. In addition, to these techniques, regular backups must be implemented.

# Exercises

To be absolutely sure that you have assimilated this chapter, work through the corresponding exercises. These are set out from page 406.

☒ Network troubleshooting.

# Assessing your skills

Try the following questions if you think you know this chapter well enough

### Account policy

1 Which items allow the system to authenticate security at user level? ☐

2 Which items are associated with the profile of a Windows NT user? ☐

3 Which types of group are used to organize users in a Windows NT domain? ☐

4 Which types of group are used to grant access rights to users in a Windows NT domain? ☐

5 How can you define a set of permissions without creating new Windows NT groups? ☐

6 Which important item allows you to define the life of a password and the locking of user accounts? ☐

7 Is it possible to make a user change his/her password every Friday? ☐

## Resource monitoring

8 Which items must be associated with each other in order to monitor resources using the Windows NT Audit Policy? ☐

9 In order to monitor the connection to the resources of an NT server, which audit class must be activated, and which tool must be used? ☐

10 Which Windows NT tool tells you clearly which password was transmitted on the network via ftp? ☐

11 Which Windows NT tool allows you to record the usage of an NT server processor? ☐

12 What are the four fundamental components that must be monitored on a system? ☐

## Recovery plans

13 Which data protection technique must be used in all cases? ☐

14 Which technique allows you to improve input/output performance whilst providing fault tolerance? ☐

15 How can you protect a server against power failure? ☐

___

## Results

Check your answers on pages 342 to 343. Count one point for each correct answer.

Number of points ☐ /15

For this chapter you need to have scored at least 11 out of 15.

Look at the list of key points that follows. Pick out the ones with which you have had difficulty and work through them again in this chapter before moving on to the next.

## Key points of the chapter

☐ Account policy.
☐ Resource monitoring.
☐ Recovery plans.

# Solutions

## Account policy

1 Which items allow the system to authenticate security at user level?

*Name and password.*

2 Which items are associated with the profile of a Windows NT user?

*The user profile path, the logon script and the home directory.*

3 Which types of group are used to organize users in a Windows NT domain?

*Global groups.*

4 Which types of group are used to grant access rights to users in a Windows NT domain?

*Local groups.*

5 How can you define a set of permissions without creating new Windows NT groups?

*By using predefined Windows NT groups.*

6 Which important item allows you to define the life of a password and the locking of user accounts?

*Account Policy.*

7 Is it possible to make a user change his/her password every Friday?

*Yes.*

## Resource monitoring

8 Which items must be associated with each other in order to monitor resources using the Windows NT Audit Policy?

*An association must be defined between the users and the resource that must be audited.*

9 In order to monitor the connection to the resources of an NT server, which audit class must be activated, and which tool must be used?

*You must activate the Audit Policy class, File and Object Access using the User Manager for Domains.*

10 Which Windows NT tool tells you clearly which password was transmitted on the network via ftp?

*The Network Monitor, by capturing data frames.*

11 Which Windows NT tool allows you to record the usage of an NT server processor?

*The Performance Monitor, in log mode.*

12 What are the four fundamental components that must be monitored on a system?

*The disk, the memory, the processor and the network.*

### Recovery plans

13 Which data protection technique must be used in all cases?

*Data backup.*

14 Which technique allows you to improve input/output performance whilst providing fault tolerance?

*Disk striping with parity.*

15 How can you protect a server against power failure?

*By connecting it to a UPS (Uninterruptible Power Supply)*

Essentials  Chapter 10 - Page 345

## Prerequisites for this chapter

☒ Knowledge of network topologies and physical media.
☒ Knowledge of standards for lower-level layers.

## Objectives

When you have completed this chapter you will be able to:
☒ Describe the different connectivity problems that are commonly met.
☒ Describe the tools that allow you to resolve connectivity problems: cable testers, voltmeters, reflectometers and protocol analyzers.
☒ Identify common problems in Ethernet, Token Ring, FDDI and ArcNet networks.

# Network troubleshooting

# Summary

**A. Diagnosing common connectivity problems involving network interface cards, cables and associated hardware . . . 347**
   1. Cable testers . . . . . . . . . . . . . . . . . . . . 347
   2. Reflectometers . . . . . . . . . . . . . . . . . . . 348
   3. Using a terminator plug on an Ethernet coaxial cable . . . . . . . . . . . 348
   4. Voltmeters . . . . . . . . . . . . . . . . . . . . . 349
   5. Protocol analyzers . . . . . . . . . . . . . . . . . 349

**B. Solving connection problems . . . . . 350**
   1. Ethernet . . . . . . . . . . . . . . . . . . . . . . 350
   2. IPX and Ethernet . . . . . . . . . . . . . . . . . 351
   3. Cable problems and testing tools . . . . . . . 352
   4. Problems with Token Ring . . . . . . . . . . . 352
   5. Problems with FDDI . . . . . . . . . . . . . . . 354
   6. Problems with ArcNet . . . . . . . . . . . . . . 355

There are a number of tools that allow you to detect network problems. Functional problems can be caused by a number of different components: cables, connectors (for example a thin coaxial Tee-connector) or network interface cards.

This chapter will describe the different hardware techniques that you can use in order to identify the component that is causing the problem.

## A. Diagnosing common connectivity problems involving network interface cards, cables and associated hardware

### 1. Cable testers

Cable testers allow you to check that a cable is working correctly. They can be used to check that the cable is not broken. They can also measure attenuation, resistance and other characteristics. Thus, they provide detailed information on the mechanical and electrical properties of a cable. It must be remembered that, the longer the physical medium, the higher the risk of it malfunctioning.

☞ *Nowadays, sophisticated cable testers are available that provide information on collisions and on other important items that can lead to degradation of performance*

These cable testers (Ohmeters) allow you to check the correct impedance of the different components. For example, a thin coaxial cable, together with its terminations, must have a resistance of 50 Ohms. On the other hand, if a short-circuit has occurred, and you measure the resistance between the central core and the external braiding, you will obtain a reading of 0 Ohms. Similarly, if you measure the resistance between two extremities of a segment, and you obtain an infinite value, you can conclude that the segment is broken.

## 2. Reflectometers

Reflectometers allow you to measure the distance to a break in the network. Models exist that can be used with coaxial or with fiber optics cables. If the cable is broken, the signal is reflected back. By measuring the return time of the signal for a given physical medium, the distance from the break can be deduced.

To ensure that the relectometer gives a correct reading, you must use it at the extremity of a segment. Before you use these devices, you must ensure that any repeater or bridges in the LAN have been switched off, as they may disrupt your test results. It is even advisable to stop the network completely, unless you are sure that the reflectometer can function correctly in an operational network.

A simpler and cheaper solution is to use the test software that is supplied with the network interface cards. These programs allow you to isolate the defective component (cable or tee-connector) by changing the position of a terminator plug.

## 3. Using a terminator plug on an Ethernet coaxial cable

If you suspect that you have a problem on a coaxial cable, you can move the position of the terminator plug progressively, in order to test each portion of the cable (situated between the two plugs). You can then test the transmission of packets onto the network using the tools supplied with the network interface card. If there is a break in the cable between the two plugs on the segment connected to the card, then the signal will be reflected back and collisions will take place.

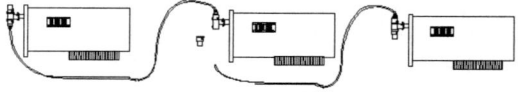

Placing a terminator plug on a thin coaxial cable

### 4. Voltmeters

You can also use a voltmeter to detect a broken cable or a short-circuit. This instrument detects problems by applying a voltage across a cable.

### 5. Protocol analyzers

This tool allows you to monitor network activity and to optimize network performance. Protocol analyzers are able to identify, the most verbose network protocol, the computer that exchanges the most information or the protocol that makes the most broadcasts. Protocol analyzers can even detect if a protocol exceeds its limits.

However, this tool is not designed to detect a broken cable or a short-circuit.

☞ *The best known protocol analyzers include Novell's LAN Analyzer for Windows, HP's Network Advisor and Network General's Sniffer.*

In general, these tools include a graphic interface with a control panel showing the different elements that you can monitor.

## B. Solving connection problems

A number of problems can be identified from the viewpoint of the client who wishes to access network servers. In fact, even after a network has been installed and configured, various problems often remain. A few typical situations are described below:

### 1. Ethernet

Ethernet problems include difficulties with cards (parameter verifications, IRQ, input/output addresses, connector types) and with connectors (cables, plugs, and Tee-connectors; particularly with thin Ethernet).

#### a. MAC addresses

Each network interface card on the same logical network should have a unique MAC address. In principle, this should not cause any problems in Ethernet networks in which predefined IEEE addresses are used.

 *However, problems can occur in some rare cases. To solve such problems, some Ethernet network interface cards allow you to modify their MAC addresses.*

#### b. Types of connector

Some cards are equipped with multiple connectors. These are known as COMBO cards and can have AUI, BNC, TP or fiber optic connectors. For this type of card, the configuration must be carefully checked on each machine. In fact, even with some PCI cards, the **connector type autodetection** feature does not work correctly (particularly when used with a thin coaxial cable).

### c. Network interface cards

Some network interface cards produce packets with lengths that are longer than the maximum authorized (this is 1518 bytes for Ethernet). These packets can be detected on a hub when the **jabber** indicator is switched on. You can then identify the machine causing the problem by progressively switching the machines off, until only one machine remains and the indicator is still lit.

### d. Conflicting parameters

When you are unable to make a card function correctly, the first thing to do is to check that the configuration recorded in the EEPROM is the same as that specified in the operating system environment.

☞ *It must be remembered that, although most operating systems are able to detect the network interface card, they cannot generally detect its exact configuration.*

The second step involves checking that there is no conflict between the different peripherals that are connected to the machine. For this purpose, you can refer to the table shown in chapter 3, concerning available IRQ and input/output addresses. In all cases, the manufacturer supplies tools that allow you to choose a non-conflicting configuration for the working environment concerned.

## 2. IPX and Ethernet

The most common IPX problems concern incompatibility between frame types. Here are the different types of frame that are used:

Ethernet 802.2,
Ethernet 802.3,
Ethernet II,
Ethernet SNAP.

Although these types of frame have only minor differences, they are incompatible with each other. Consequently, two machines that communicate with each other using IPX on an Ethernet network must use the same types of frame. At present, Microsoft and Novell recommend the use of the 802.2 frame.

☞ *802.2 type frames are installed automatically on Novell Netware servers as from version 3.12.*

In most cases, the frame type is detected automatically and no action is required: the RIP IPX protocol determines information such as the type of frame that is needed for communication with the rest of the network. The problem occurs when several frame types circulate simultaneously on the network and the client is configured to use only one by default.

☞ *For example, with Windows NT, where frame types 802.2 and 802.3 are detected automatically, the client uses only frame type 802.2.*

### 3. Cable problems and testing tools

You must ensure that cables are not exposed to disruptive electrical or electromagnetic sources. For example, functional problems can be caused when a network cable uses the same conduit as electrical cables. Similarly, electromagnetic disturbances can be caused if a cable runs too close to a fluorescent tube. In addition, cabling that runs too close to a motor can also cause problems. These problems can often be solved by using a shielded cable (STP), or even by protecting the cable passage with a metallic sheath.

### 4. Problems with Token Ring

Problems in a Token Ring environment can have a variety of causes: for example a card that is in conflict with other resources, badly specified addresses, unsuitable speeds and inappropriate types of cable.

### a. Conflicting configurations

The first thing to check is that the configuration of the network interface card does not conflict with the other peripheral devices installed on the machine.

The statistics produced by the interface cards must be monitored to check for any internal errors. Internal errors indicate that the peripheral is malfunctioning and that it must be replaced.

### b. Configuration of the Token Ring card

The driver that is supplied with the Token Ring card must allow you to adjust four essential parameters of the card: the ring speed, the card address, the shared memory used and the release of the token just after the data frame (at 16 Mbps only).

## Ring speed

You must check that all the cards used in the network run at the same speed (4 or 16 Mbps). If you work with an IBM PS/2 machine, you will probably use a configuration floppy disk to reinitialize your system and implement a card speed of 4 Mbps.

It must be noted that if a Token Ring card runs at a different speed from that of the ring, it will generate a complete reconfiguration of the ring.

## Address of the Token Ring card

Although Token Ring addresses are generally coded into ROM, some Token Ring cards allow you to modify their addresses. As with Ethernet, you must ensure that no two cards in a network have the same physical address. You can modify the address of a Token Ring card by configuring the driver.

## Shared memory

You will certainly need to specify the address of the shared memory used for a Token Ring card.

### Release of the token just after the data frame

With a Token Ring network running at 16 Mbps, the token can be released just after the data frame that is emitted. This feature, which is similar to that provided by FDDI, allows you to increase the effective transmission speed of the ring.

### c. MAU connectors and cabling

You must ensure that you have all the necessary documentation for the cabling and the hardware that you are using. This can help you to solve any problems you might meet. It is not advisable to mix equipment of different manufacturers who use different internal electrical characteristics.

## 5. Problems with FDDI

FDDI problems generally concern connectors, cabling or communication delays.

### a. FDDI connectors

Dirty connectors, and even grains of dust, can cause transmission errors with fiber optics. FDDI connectors can be cleaned using a clean cloth and alcohol.

A defective connector or a broken cable can also cause problems.

### b. Cabling

Problems may occur if you do not use the correct type of cabling between two nodes. Multimode fibers can be used for segments of up to two kilometers long. For greater distances it is advisable to use monomode fibers. Transmission speeds vary according to the type of fiber used. Fibers with plastic cores can be used to transmit over 50 meters only. Fibers with glass cores can transmit much further.

A break in the cable can be detected using an optical reflectometer (although these devices are very expensive).

## 6. Problems with ArcNet

As with Ethernet and Token Ring, ArcNet problems are often caused by incorrect or conflicting configuration, or by the connector hardware used.

### a. Network interface card

ArcNet cards are configured in the factory with an address of 0. You must therefore configure the card manually so that it has a unique address on the network. On an ArcNet bus, you must also ensure that all the cards have the same impedance level. If this is not the case, the signal may attenuate too much and may rebound.

### b. Connector hardware

With an ArcNet network, you must take particular care to respect the specifications laid down by the manufacturer, concerning the length of cables used and the number of nodes per segment.

## Exercises

To be absolutely sure that you have assimilated this chapter, work through the corresponding exercises. These are set out from page 413.

☒ Choosing network components.

## Assessing your skills

Try the following questions if you think you know this chapter well enough.

### Connectivity problems

1 Which tool allows you to measure the various characteristics of a copper cable? ☐

2 Can a cable tester provide information relating to collisions occurring on an Ethernet network? ☐

3 Which hardware device allows you to measure the impedance of a cable? ☐

4 What impedance must a thin Ethernet coaxial cable have? ☐

5 What impedance must a thick Ethernet coaxial cable have? ☐

6 What impedance should a multimeter measure between the core and the external braiding of a correctly functioning coaxial cable? ☐

7 What conclusion can be drawn if there is infinite impedance between the two ends of a thin coaxial cable?

### Test tools

8 What information does a reflectometer provide?

9 What is the least expensive way of repairing a 10Base2 network, which has a broken cable?

10 Which tool can warn the administrator that the network is starting to become overloaded?

11 Which device can be used to detect a break in a fiber?

12 What are the main elements of a network interface card for which you must ensure the correct configuration?

13 What is a Combo card?

14 What is a Jabber?

15 Which item must be monitored when an IPX connectivity problem occurs? ❏

16 Which items can cause problems by their proximity to copper cables? ❏

**Common problems with Ethernet, Token Ring and ArcNet Networks**

17 How can you improve the performance of a Token Ring 16 network? ❏

18 What must be checked when a problem occurs with FDDI connector hardware? ❏

19 Which type of fiber can be used for long segments? ❏

20 What is the address of an ArcNet card when it leaves the factory? ❏

## Results

Check your answers on pages 360 to 362. Count one point for each correct answer.

Number of points [ /20 ]

For this chapter you need to have scored at least 15 out of 20.

Look at the list of key points that follows. Pick out the ones with which you have had difficulty and work through them again in this chapter before moving on to the next.

## Key points of the chapter

- ☐ Connectivity problems.
- ☐ Test tools.
- ☐ Common problems with Ethernet, Token Ring and Archnet networks.

# Solutions

### Connectivity problems

1 Which tool allows you to measure the various characteristics of a copper cable?

*A cable tester.*

2 Can a cable tester provide information relating to collisions occurring on an Ethernet network?

*Yes, if it is a modern cable tester.*

3 Which hardware device allows you to measure the impedance of a cable?

*An ohmmeter. This functionality can be included in a tool that offers other features as well, such as a digital multimeter.*

4 What impedance must a thin Ethernet coaxial cable have?

*50 Ohms.*

5 What impedance must a thick Ethernet coaxial cable have?

*50 Ohms.*

6 What impedance should a multimeter measure between the core and the external braiding of a correctly functioning coaxial cable?

*Infinite.*

7 What conclusion can be drawn if there is infinite impedance between the two ends of a thin coaxial cable?

*This means that the cable will not be transmit a signal. It indicates that the cable has either been crushed or broken.*

## Test tools

8 What information does a reflectometer provide?

*The distance between the extremity of the segment and a break in the cable.*

9 What is the least expensive way of repairing a 10Base2 network, which has a broken cable?

*You can progressively change the position of a terminator plug and send a data frame to determine if the segment concerned has a break in it.*

10 Which tool can warn the administrator that the network is starting to become overloaded?

*A protocol analyzer.*

11 Which device can be used to detect a break in a fiber?

*An optical reflectometer.*

12 What are the main elements of a network interface card for which you must ensure the correct configuration?

*IRQ, input/output address and the type of connector used.*

13 What is a Combo card?

*A combo card is a card that is equipped with several types of network connector.*

14 What is a Jabber?

*A jabber is a packet that has a length greater than that authorized. Jabbers are generated by defective Network Interface Cards.*

15 Which item must be monitored when an IPX connectivity problem occurs?

*The type of frame used.*

16 Which items can cause problems by their proximity to copper cables?

*Electric or electromagnetic sources.*

## Common problems with Ethernet, Token Ring and ArcNet Networks

17 How can you improve the performance of a Token Ring 16 network?

*By freeing the token immediately after the emitted data frame.*

18 What must be checked when a problem occurs with FDDI connector hardware?

*It must be ensured that the passage of the light is not obstructed by fine particles of dust.*

19 Which type of fiber can be used for long segments?

*Fibers with a glass core.*

20 What is the address of an ArcNet card when it leaves the factory?

*0.*

## Prerequisites for this chapter

☒ To have read the previous chapters.

## Objectives

When you have completed this chapter you will be:
☒ Aware of information access development problems, and the issues involved.
☒ In a position to observe the various networking elements currently being developed.

# Future prospects

## Summary

A. Introduction . . . . . . . . . . . . . . 365

B. The global internetwork . . . . . . . . 366

C. Mobile networks . . . . . . . . . . . . 367

D. Network management . . . . . . . . . 369

## A. Introduction

Today, interconnection has become a major issue in the field of communications between industrialized countries.

The modern tendency is to control everything via networks: for example, telephone calls, reserving a seat in a train or on a plane, reserving a hotel, and paying for it all with a credit card

The development of mobile phones and pagers are developments that have enabled modern man and woman to become *homo sapiens communicans*, with just one objective to get information as quickly as possible so as to be able to use it in real time. This vicious circle is suffocating people, who believe that they are the only ones able to use their communication tools. Ironically, this situation may lead to a gradual acceleration in life styles. Furthermore, users may become so dependent of their communication modes and faculties that they will no longer be able to manage without them.

## B. The global internetwork

The Internet's influence increases every day. Already, it has **abolished all frontiers**. Developing countries have access to the same information as the rich countries. A gigantic distributed database is made available to everyone irrespective of age, sex or color of skin. For all these reasons, the Internet bothers people. It can be involved in politics as well as expressing the most repugnant vices that are buried deep in each of us. In fact, the Internet is a reflection of what we are, nothing more, nothing less. It allows people to listen and to communicate, but it also allows people to manipulate...

One of the Internet's principal characteristics is that it is **uncontrollable**. For example, if a book is banned, its author can still diffuse it on the Internet. In some countries, opinion polls must not be published for a week or so before an election. However, nothing stops them being published in a neighboring country. A message encrypting algorithm called PGP (Pretty Good Privacy) was forbidden on the Internet. In spite of this its author photocopied it, scanned it and disseminated it freely. The lawsuits against the author were dropped as being in vain.

API's using the SSL (Secure Sockets Layer) protocol for transmitting private documents is authorized in many countries. This protocol is controlled by an irreproachable, independent organization. This organization manages the public key that authorizes the encrypting. Corresponding Web pages are identified with a HTTPS:// prefix. This technique has resulted in the appearance of an increasing number of commercial Websites. An example of a European commercial site is *https://www.monaco-shopping.com*. Monaco shopping offers a range of electronic luxury products with secure payment by SSL.

Apparently, the saying '*you cannot see the wood for the trees*' highlights an inherent problem with the Web. We believe, however, that people will be able to rationalize and adapt themselves to sets of references in order to classify data and validate its use accordingly.

## C. Mobile networks

An increasingly popular concept is the NC (**Network Computer**). The NC is a client with limited resources that is able to access the Internet thanks to a built-in modem. A number of NC versions are available: for example the Internet decoder, the NetBox (which you can connect to your TV to obtain all the multimedia features) or the NCs that are commercialized by a number of manufacturers such as Wyse who offer a model with an infrared keyboard. All these versions offer the same basic service: easy connection to the Internet.

Some European countries are behind the times in this field. Many of them are leading a variety of operations to encourage educational establishments to connect to the Internet

Internet tools are developing naturally towards **client/server** functioning modes. An important factor in this respect is the use of ActiveX controls. These are downloaded automatically onto a client machine in order to provide it with specific features, such as the means of consulting a database and the teledistribution of multimedia data.

The virus problem remains a major threat. Inevitably interconnection involves a certain risk of infection. Increasingly prevalent, is the macro type of virus, which attacks model file documents. These viruses are often transmitted in the form of attached files.

The development of transmission technologies has resulted in the possibility of transmitting voice, data and multimedia along the same physical medium. This means that telephone, television and computer networks are converging towards the use of the same transmission medium.

In Europe, an important event in this respect was the opening up of free competition for all telecommunications services, including public telephone services, which represent around 70% of the market.

This has led to alliances being set up between European operators such as Cegetel and **British Telecom**, and the private operation of large networks; for example the French railways fiber optics network with its 6000 miles (9000 kilometers) of cables.

Other telephone operators specialize in services to small companies and individual users.

These developments mean that the big national telephone operators may well have big efforts to make.

Another important aspect is the **IP telephone gateways**. One possible development of these techniques is the prospect of using the Internet to telephone to the other side of the world for the price of a local call. Solutions already exist for such projects, with all the unfair competition that they entail for the classical telephone operators.

## D. Network management

Network management has also been undergoing important developments. Microsoft now offers its Zero Administration Kit for NT4 on the Internet. Moreover, Microsoft has announced this feature as standard supply with Windows 2000. Intelli-mirror agents, which are to be supplied with the new NT version, will allow you to download automatically any components (files) that you do not have locally. For example, you could obtain a wordprocessor application that has not yet been installed.

Tools in the **distributed administration** field are becoming more and more numerous. These tools cover such applications as the administration of physical cabling, inventory control, performance management and even tele-distribution (management and distribution of applications).

Remote administration tools such as SNMP agents and RMON (Remote MONitoring) probes are becoming increasingly common. Intelligent agents spread across all hardware and systems allow you to supervise an entire network from an administration console (for example, HPOV: HPOpen View on HPUX). These agents manage local databases and can be commanded from an administration console, to access the local configuration, and even to modify it.

Another important development field is that of simulation. **Network loading simulators** are available to deal with a broken-down router and physical topology simulators help you design the architecture of your future network. For example, *Delta Partners*' NetQUAD application allows you to design an optimized network according to several criteria (such as budget, performance and existing hardware to be reused). It works with a database that incorporates two types of information: on the one hand technical characteristics (performance) and financial characteristics (acquisition and maintenance costs), and on the other hand the tariffs of telecommunications operators.

# Networking overview . . . . . . . . . . . . . 373

1.1 History of networking . . . . . . . . . . . . 373
1.2 Definitions relating to LANs and extended LANs . . . . . . . . . . . . . . . . 373
1.3 Comparison of the different network services . . . . . . . . . . . . . . . . . . . . 374
1.4 Comparison of a centralized network and a machine-to-machine network . . . . . 375
1.5 Comparison of user level security and resource level security . . . . . . . . . . 376
   Solutions . . . . . . . . . . . . . . . . . . . 377

# Types of communication . . . . . . . . . . . 381

2.1 Types of communication with and without connection . . . . . . . . . . . . . 381
   Solutions . . . . . . . . . . . . . . . . . . . 382

# Troubleshooting connectivity problems . . 383

3.1 Choice of the appropriate tools to monitor a network . . . . . . . . . . . . 383
3.2 Common communications problems . . 383
   Solutions . . . . . . . . . . . . . . . . . . . 384

# Network planning . . . . . . . . . . . . . . . 385

4.1 Choice of an administration plan . . . . 385
4.2 Choice of a recovery plan . . . . . . . . 386
   Solutions . . . . . . . . . . . . . . . . . . . 387

# Extended networks . . . . . . . . . . . . . . 388

5.1 SLIP and PPP . . . . . . . . . . . . . . . . 388
5.2 Characteristics of extended networks . . 389
   Solutions . . . . . . . . . . . . . . . . . . . 390

# LANs . . . . . . . . . . . . . . . . . . . . . . . 391

6.1 Selection of protocols . . . . . . . . . . . 391
6.2 Implementation of a NetBIOS naming scheme . . . . . . . . . . . . . . 392
   Solutions . . . . . . . . . . . . . . . . . . . 393

## Standards and terminology . . . . . . . . . 395

7.1 Characteristics of 802.3 standards . . . . . 395
7.2 Terms used with thick Ethernet . . . . . . . 395
7.3 Terms used with thin Ethernet . . . . . . . 396
7.4 Terms used with twisted pair Ethernet . . . 396
7.5 Characteristics of the 802.5 standard . . . 397
     Solutions . . . . . . . . . . . . . . . . . . 398

## Topologies and interconnections . . . . . . 400

8.1 Choice of a suitable topology . . . . . . . 400
8.2 Choice of suitable interconnection components . . . . . . . . . . . . . . . . . 401
8.3 Interconnection components and the OSI model . . . . . . . . . . . . . . . 402
     Solutions . . . . . . . . . . . . . . . . . . 403

## Network troubleshooting . . . . . . . . . . . 406

9.1 NDIS and ODI specifications . . . . . . . . 406
9.2 Identification of broadcast storm problems . . . . . . . . . . . . . . . . . . 407
9.3 Identification of performance problems . 407
     Solutions . . . . . . . . . . . . . . . . . . 410

## Choosing network components . . . . . . . 413

10.1 Choosing a transmission medium according to cost . . . . . . . . . . . . . 413
10.2 Choosing a physical medium according to maximum segment length . . . . . . 413
10.3 Choosing a wireless network system . . . 414
10.4 Identification of available IRQs . . . . . . 416
     Solutions . . . . . . . . . . . . . . . . . . 417

# Networking overview

## 1.1 History of networks

Match up the elements in the left hand column below, with their correct definitions.

| | |
|---|---|
| ARPANET | · IBM centralized network. |
| System Network Architecture | · is responsible for the lower layer standards. |
| DECNet | · proposes a network model composed of 7 layers. |
| TCP IP | · the PC XT in 1981. |
| Unix BSD | · helped to distribute the sources of TCP/IP. |
| Personal computer | · DIGITAL centralized network. |
| IEEE | · de facto standard. |
| ISO | · first packet switched network. |

## 1.2 Definitions relating to LANs and extended LANs

Match up the elements in the left hand column below, with their correct definitions.

| | |
|---|---|
| A LAN | · is a News forum. |
| A MAN | · is made up by interconnecting several LANs of a company. |
| A WAN | · is defined on the scale of a geographical district. |
| The Company Network | · is to share common resources. |
| USENET | · is defined on the scale of a building or a company. |
| The purpose of a network | · is often made up of several interconnected LANs. |

## 1.3 Comparison of the different network services

For each element in the left hand column, indicate all the descriptions that apply.

| | |
|---|---|
| File Service | • implements file transfer. |
| | • implements a queue in order to ensure concurrent access to the peripheral device. |
| Print Service | • implements peer-to-peer communication. |
| | • implements the storage and the migration of data. |
| Electronic mail service | • generally assigns to clients, job formulation tasks and the processing of the response, whereas servers analyze the requests and provide the required data. |
| | • implements backups. |
| | • allows you to work with groupware. |
| | • implements the ftp service. |
| Applications service | • allows you to control and to manage peripheral devices such as printers and faxes. |
| | • requires considerable processing power. |
| Data service | • implements synchronization of file updates. |
| | • allows you to share processing power. |
| | • requires a lot of memory for caching. |
| | • implements the SMB service. |

## 1.4 Comparison of a centralized network and a machine-to-machine network

For each element in the right hand column, indicate if it applies to a centralized network or to a machine-to-machine network.

| | |
|---|---|
| | • In order to be able to work, a user must first be authenticated. |
| | • the machines are both clients for some resources and servers for others. |
| | • is referred to as a peer-to-peer network. |
| | • each user has a name and a password. |
| Centralized network | • users are often administrators of their own machines. |
| | • users are not complete novices. |
| | • is based on user level security. |
| Machine-to-machine network | • for each user, permissions can be customized for each resource. |
| | • a user is designated to manage the whole network. |
| | • all the machines play an identical role. |
| | • generally include few machines. |
| | • the user database is centralized. |
| | • administration is distributed. |
| | • are used by workgroups. |

## 1.5 Comparison of user level security and resource level security

For each element in the right hand column, indicate if it applies to user level security or to resource level security.

| | |
|---|---|
| | • allows you to attribute permissions for a given resource that are more specific to each user. |
| | • there is no initial authentication |
| User level security | • passwords are attributed for a given resource. |
| | • each user must provide identification with respect to a reference entity. |
| | • allows you to define distinct customized access whilst sharing the resource. |
| Resource level security | • the resource is at the heart of the security system. |
| | • access to resources is independent of the user concerned. |
| | • to prevent a user from working with a resource you must change the resource password. |

# Solutions

## 1.1 History of networks

| ARPANET | first packet switched network. |
|---|---|
| TCP IP | de facto standard. |
| DECNet | DIGITAL centralized network. |
| System Network Architecture | IBM centralized network. |
| Unix BSD | helped to distribute the sources of TCP/IP. |
| Personal computer | the PC XT in 1981. |
| IEEE | is responsible for the lower layer standards. |
| ISO | proposes a network model composed of 7 layers. |

## 1.2 Definitions relating to LANs and extended LANs

| A LAN | is defined on the scale of a building or a company. |
|---|---|
| A MAN | is defined on the scale of a geographical district. |
| WAN | is often made up of several interconnected LANs. |
| The Company Network | is made up by interconnecting several LANs of a company. |
| USENET | is a News forum. |
| The purpose of a network | is to share common resources. |

## 1.3 Comparison of the different network services

| | |
|---|---|
| File service | · implements file transfer.<br>· implements the storage and the migration of data.<br>· implements synchronization of file updates.<br>· implements backups.<br>· implements the ftp service.<br>· implements the SMB service.<br>· requires a lot of memory for caching. |
| Print service | · allows you to control and to manage peripheral devices such as printers and faxes.<br>· implements a queue in order to ensure concurrent access to the peripheral device.<br>· requires a lot of memory for caching. |
| Electronic mail service | · allows you to work with groupware. |
| Applications service | · allows you to share processing power.<br>· implements peer-to-peer communication.<br>· requires considerable processing power. |
| Data service | · generally assigns to clients, job formulation tasks and the processing of the response, whereas servers analyze the requests and provide the required data. |

## 1.4 Comparison of a centralized network and a machine-to-machine network

| Centralized network | · each user has a name and a password.<br>· In order to be able to work, a user must first be authenticated.<br>· the user database is centralized.<br>· is based on user level security.<br>· for each user, permissions can be customized for each resource.<br>· a user is designated to manage the whole network. |
|---|---|
| Machine-to-machine network | · the machines are both clients for some resources and servers for others.<br>· all the machines play an identical role.<br>· is referred to as a peer-to-peer network.<br>· generally include few machines.<br>· administration is distributed.<br>· users are often administrators of their own machines.<br>· users are not complete novices.<br>· are used by workgroups. |

## 1.5 Comparison of user level security and resource level security

| User level security | • allows you to attribute permissions for a given resource that are more specific to each user.<br>• each user must provide identification with respect to a reference entity.<br>• allows you to define distinct customized access whilst sharing the resource. |
|---|---|
| Resource level security | • passwords are attributed for a given resource.<br>• the resource is at the heart of the security system.<br>• access to resources is independent of the user concerned.<br>• there is no initial authentication.<br>• to prevent a user from working with a resource you must change the resource password. |

# Types of communication

## 2.1 Types of communication with and without connection

For each item in the right-hand column, indicate if it applies to connection oriented mode or connectionless mode.

|  |  |
|---|---|
|  | · HDLC |
|  | · The network layer |
|  | · IP |
| Connection | · UDP |
| oriented mode | · SDLC |
|  | · LLC |
|  | · IPX |
|  | · The transport layer |
| Connectionless | · CNLP |
| mode | · TCP |
|  | · SPX |
|  | · The session layer |
|  | · CONS |

# Solutions

## 2.1 Types of communication with and without connection

| Connection oriented mode | HDLC |
| --- | --- |
| | SDLC |
| | LLC |
| | TCP |
| | SPX |
| | The transport layer |
| | The session layer |
| | CONS |
| Connectionless mode | IP |
| | UDP |
| | IPX |
| | The network layer |
| | CNLP |

# Troubleshooting connectivity problems

## 3.1 Choice of the appropriate tools to monitor a network

Match up the different items from the right-hand column, that allow you to follow the network aspects in the left-hand column.

| Tools | Choice |
|---|---|
| Audit policy | · Allows you to detect a break in a cable. |
| Reflectometer | · Allows you to capture frames on the network. |
| Frame analyzer | · Warns the administrator when a protocol is too verbose. |
| Protocol analyzer | · Allows you to monitor access to network resources. |

## 3.2 Common communications problems

Reconstruct the sentences below by rematching the elements of the first column with those of the second column.

| | |
|---|---|
| A cable tester | Allows you to measure the impedance of a cable. |
| An ohmmeter | · Must have an impedance of 50 Ohms. |
| A thin coaxial cable | · To enable two machines to communicate. |
| A thick coaxial cable | · Must have an impedance of 50 Ohms. |
| A Jabber | · Must not pass too close to an electric or to an electromagnetic source. |
| With IPX | · Allows you to measure various characteristics of a copper cable. |
| Copper cables | · Is an abnormally long packet that is generated by a defective network interface card. |

# Solutions

## 3.1 Choice of the appropriate tools to monitor a network

| Audit policy | Allows you to monitor access to network resources. |
|---|---|
| Reflectometer | Allows you to detect a break in a cable. |
| Frame analyzer | Allows you to capture frames on the network. |
| Protocol analyzer | Warns the administrator when a protocol is too verbose. |

## 3.2 Common communications problems

**A cable tester**
> allows you to measure various characteristics of a copper cable.

**An ohmmeter**
> allows you to measure the impedance of a cable.

**A thin coaxial cable**
> must have an impedance of 50 Ohms.

**A thick coaxial cable**
> must have an impedance of 50 Ohms.

**A Jabber**
> is an abnormally long packet that is generated by a defective network interface card

**With IPX**
> for two machines to be able to communicate, the type of frame used must be the same on both machines.

**Copper cables**
> must not pass too close to an electric or to an electro-magnetic source.

# Network planning

## 4.1 Choice of an administration plan

A company wishes to reorganize its network. It would like to convert its network from a peer-to-peer architecture, to a centralized architecture, which is organized around a Windows NT server and a domain. The machines currently run Windows 95 and are autonomous. In addition, all the users have a high degree of autonomy. This organization leads to frequent problems, such as loss of data, crashed machines, software piracy and intrusion.
Which networking elements would you implement so that the users can work in an environment that is both secure and familiar, without being able to pirate data? How would you implement regular backups whilst sensitizing the users to a centralized network?

### Developing your ideas

**Working in small groups of three or four people, develop your ideas on the case study outlined above. Refer to the information contained in chapter 4 for this purpose.**

- 
- 
- 
- 
- 
- 
- 
- 
- 
- 
- 
- 
- 
- 

### Open discussion

With the participation of your discussion leader, present to the rest of the group the ideas that you have prepared in order to start an open discussion on this subject.

## 4.2 Choice of a recovery plan

You wish to implement a strategy to protect your server and its data, whilst ensuring that you recover your data and your system in the event of an incident occurring.
Which hardware means can you use to protect your server? How can you protect your operating system and its data: in terms of reliability, and in terms of confidentiality?

*Developing your ideas*

**Protecting your server**
 - 
 - 
 - 
 - 

**Protecting your operating system**
 - 
 - 

**Protecting the data on your server**
 - 
 - 
 - 
 - 
 - 

*Open discussion*

With the participation of your discussion leader, present your ideas to the rest of the group in order to start an open discussion on this subject.

## Solutions

### 4.1 Choice of an administration plan

There are a number of valid solutions to this exercise.

### 4.2 Choice of a recovery plan

Solution items:

**Protecting your server**
- UPS (Uninterruptible Power Supply)
- Transactional file system.

**Protecting your operating system**
- RAID 1.

**Protecting the data on your server**
- RAID 3
- RAID 5
- Full backups on Fridays and differential backups on the other days
- Secure file systems
- Isolating the server in a separate room.

# Extended networks

## 5.1 SLIP and PPP

Indicate which features are associated with each of these protocols.

### Protocols

SLIP

PPP

### Features

a - takes charge of NetBEUI, IPX and IP
b - requires that you know your own IP address
c - requires TCP/IP
d - allows numbering
e - uses CHAP and PAP
f - does not provide error checking
g - allows compression.

## 5.2 Characteristics of extended networks

Indicate which characteristics are associated with each of the following types of WAN connection.

*Protocols*

X.25

ISDN

Frame Relay

ATM

*Characteristics*

a - It is slow because it has built-in error correction.
b - It provides superior transmission quality and can be used to transmit all types of information.
c - The LAP-D protocol is implemented to manage the D channel.
d - The basic rate access corresponds to two B channels and one D channel.
e - It was designed as a light alternative to the X.25 network, using a reliable physical medium.
f - It is called Fast Packet Switching.
g - LAP-B underlies this protocol.
h - You can access it via a modem or via a PAD.
i - Implements cell switching.
j - Works with frames of 53 bytes in length.

# Solutions

## 5.1 SLIP and PPP

### SLIP
**b** - requires that you know your own IP address
**c** - requires TCP/IP
**f** - does not provide error checking.

### PPP
**a** - takes charge of NetBEUI, IPX and IP
**d** - allows numbering
**e** - uses CHAP and PAP
**g** - allows compression.

## 5.2 Characteristics of extended networks

### X.25
**a** - It is slow because it has built-in error correction.
**g** - LAP-B underlies this protocol.
**h** - You can access it via a modem or via a PAD.

### ISDN
**b** - It provides superior transmission quality and can be used to transmit all types of information.
**c** - The LAP-D protocol is implemented to manage the D channel.
**d** - The basic rate access corresponds to two B channels and one D channel.

### Frame Relay
**e** - It was designed as a light alternative to the X.25 network, using a reliable physical medium.
**f** - It is called Fast Packet Switching.

### ATM
**i** - Implements cell switching.
**j** - Works with frames of 53 bytes in length.

# LANs

## 6.1 Selection of protocols

Indicate which protocol must be installed for each of the following services:

### Service or type of access required

ftp

Access to a Netware 3.12 server

Access to a shared directory on Macintosh

Telnet

SMB

HTTP

NFS

Connection to SNA gateways

Direct connection to network print peripherals.

### Protocols

TCP/IP

NetBIOS

DLC

IPX/SPX

AppleTalk

## 6.2 Implementation of a NetBIOS naming scheme

In a company that is equipped with 5 interconnected sites and 300 machines, an administrator wishes to implement a NetBIOS naming scheme for the computers that he/she uses.

Define a naming scheme, given the following information:
- There are 5 sites.
- The following types of machine are present: NT 4 and NT3.51 servers, NT 4 workstations, Windows 95 machines, and Novell 3.12 and 4.11 servers.
- Each site includes a maximum of 10 rooms, spread out over a maximum of 5 floors.
- Each room contains a maximum of 50 machines.

# Solutions

## 6.1 Selection of protocols

**ftp**
TCP/IP

**SMB**
NetBIOS

**HTTP**
TCP/IP

**Telnet**
TCP/IP

**Connection to SNA gateways**
DLC

**Connection to network print peripherals**
TCP/IP
DLC

**NFS**
TCP/IP

**Access to a Netware 3.12 server**
IPX/SPX

**Access to a shared directory on Macintosh**
AppleTalk

## 6.2 Implementation of a NetBIOS naming scheme

The first two characters identify the site concerned: S1, S2, S3, S4 and S5

The next five characters identify the operating system that is used, for example:

| | |
|---|---|
| NTS40 | NT Server 4.0 |
| NTS35 | NT Server 3.51 |
| NTW40 | NT Workstation 4.0 |
| WIN95 | Windows 95 |
| NW312 | Netware 3.12 |
| NW411 | Netware 4.11. |

One character indicates the floor:
1, 2, 3, 4 or 5

Two characters indicate the room:
01 to 99

Two characters indicate the number of the machine in the room
01 to 99

For example, on site 2, NT 4.0 server, number 4, in room 7 on the 3rd floor will be called:
\\S2NTS4030704

# Standards and terminology

## 7.1 Characteristics of 802.3 standards

Indicate the characteristic that is associated with each of the following standards:

| 802.3 Standard | Characteristics |
|---|---|
| 10 base 2 | corresponds to a bus topology with maximum segment lengths of 500 meters. |
| 10 base 5 | corresponds to thin Ethernet. |
| 10 base T | runs at 100 Mbps on category 5. |
| 100 base T | is based on fiber optics. |
| 10 base FL | corresponds to Ethernet on twisted pair cables. |

## 7.2 Terms used with thick Ethernet

What are the names of the different elements in the following diagram?

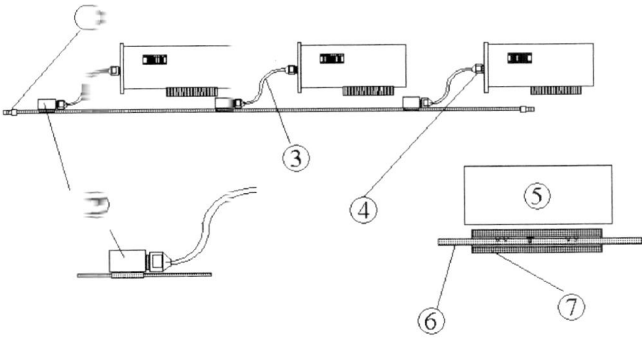

Connector hardware used with thick Ethernet

1 -            5 -
2 -            6 -
3 -            7 -
4 -

## 7.3 Terms used with thin Ethernet

What are the names of the different elements in the following diagram?

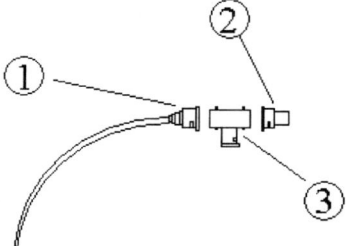

Connector hardware used with thin Ethernet

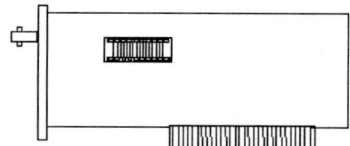

Thin Ethernet card

1 -
2 -
3 -

## 7.4 Terms used with twisted pair Ethernet

What are the names of the different elements in the following diagram?

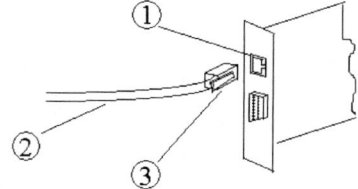

Connector hardware used with twisted pair Ethernet

1 -
2 -
3 -

## 7.5 Characteristics of the 802.5 standard

Which of the following statements apply to the 802.5 standard?

The 802.5 standard is based on the token passing method and a bus topology.

The machines are connected to the MAU in a star configuration.

The logical topology is a point-to-point ring in which each machine acts as a repeater.

The MAUs have a built-in fault tolerance and can be configured to detect the failure of a machine.

The medium used is either a pair of shielded twisted pairs (for example, type 1), or fiber optics.

The connector types are DB9 for network interface cards and male/female connectors for MAU connections.

The *Manchester* encoding type is used.

# Solutions

## 7.1 Characteristics of 802.3 standards

| 10 base 2 | corresponds to thin Ethernet. |
|---|---|
| 10 base 5 | corresponds to Ethernet on twisted pair cables. |
| 100 base T | corresponds to a bus topology with maximum segment lengths of 500 meters. |
| 100 base T | runs at 100 Mbps on category 5 |
| 10 base FL | is based on fiber optics. |

## 7.2 Terms used with thick Ethernet

**1** - Terminator plug
**2** - External transceiver
**3** - AUI cable
**4** - AUI connector
**5** - External transceiver
**6** - Thick coaxial cable
**7** - Vampire tap

## 7.3 Terms used with thin Ethernet

**1** - Thin coaxial cable
**2** - Terminator plug
**3** - Tee-connector

## 7.4 Terms used with twisted pair Ethernet

**1** - RJ-45 socket
**2** - Twisted pair cable
**3** - RJ-45 connector

## 7.5 Characteristics of the 802.5 standard

*The correct solutions are shown in bold type.*

The 802.5 standard is based on the token passing method and a bus topology.

**The machines are connected to the MAU in a star configuration.**

**The logical topology is a point-to-point ring in which each machine acts as a repeater.**

**The MAUs have a built-in fault tolerance and can be configured to detect the failure of a machine.**

**The medium used is either a pair of shielded twisted pairs (for example, type 1), or fiber optics.**

**The connector types are DB9 for network interface cards and male/female connectors for MAU connections.**

The *Manchester* encoding type is used.

# Topologies and interconnections

## 8.1 Choice of a suitable topology

Indicate the characteristics that are satisfied by each of the following topologies:

| Topology | Characteristics |
|---|---|
| Bus | • The least expensive solution is sought. |
| | • The network has a large number of nodes. |
| | • The network configuration is likely to evolve radically in the future. |
| Star | • Ease of reconfiguration is very important (adding and removing machines in the topology). |
| | • It is important to be able quickly to identify network malfunctioning problems. |
| | • Response times must not deteriorate even if the network in heavily loaded. |
| Ring | • The network configuration is fixed (cabling). |
| | • The network will not expand to any great extent. |
| | • The network is small. |
| | • The network configuration is reasonably fixed and will not evolve to any great extent. |

## 8.2 Choice of suitable interconnection components

Indicate the features in the right-hand column that correspond to the components in the left-hand column.

| Component | Features |
|---|---|
| Repeater | • It allows simpler and less costly management than a mixed topology that integrates bridges and routers. |
| | • It is a translator of high and medium level layers. |
| | • It acts like a multiport bridge. |
| | • It acts like a filter. |
| | • It allows you to decongest an overloaded network. |
| Bridge | • It lets through multicasts and broadcasts. |
| | • It lets through frames for which the destinations are unknown. |
| | • It does not allow broadcasts through. |
| Router | • It chooses the best possible path based on logical addresses. |
| | • It cannot work on the semantic level of the frame contents. |
| | • It cannot interconnect networks that run at different speeds. |
| Bridge router | • It is not advisable for use these devices with networks that are already heavily loaded. |
| | • It does not let a packet through if the destination is unknown. |
| | • It requires a routable protocol. |
| Gateway | • It combines the principal characteristics of a bridge and a router. |
| | • It can be used in a centralized architecture by interconnecting other LANs. |
| Switch | • It allows you to extend the maximum length of a segment. |
| | • When twisted pair cabling is used to connect it to the machines. |

## 8.3 Interconnection components and the OSI model

Indicate the levels of the OSI model on which each of the following components work:

| Component | OSI model layer |
|---|---|
| | · data link layer |
| Repeater | · transport layer |
| Bridge | · presentation layer |
| Router | · application layer |
| Gateway | · network layer |
| Switch | · physical layer |
| | · session layer |

# Solutions

## 8.1 Choice of a suitable topology

| Bus | · The network is small. |
| --- | --- |
| | · The least expensive solution is sought. |
| | · The network configuration is fixed (cabling). |
| | · The network will not expand to any great extent. |
| Star | · Ease of reconfiguration is very important (adding and removing machines in the topology). |
| | · It is important to be able quickly to identify network malfunctioning problems. |
| | · The network has a large number of nodes. |
| | · The network configuration is likely to evolve radically in the future. |
| Ring | · Response times must not deteriorate even if the network in heavily loaded. |
| | · The network configuration is reasonably fixed and will not evolve to any great extent. |

## 8.2 Choice of suitable interconnection components

Indicate the features in the right-hand column that correspond to the components in the left-hand column.

| Component | Features |
|---|---|
| Repeater | • It allows you to extend the maximum length of a segment.<br>• It cannot work on the semantic level of the frame contents.<br>• It cannot interconnect networks that run at different speeds.<br>• It is not advisable for use these devices with networks that are already heavily loaded. |
| Bridge | • It acts like a filter.<br>• It allows you to decongest an overloaded network.<br>• It lets through multicasts and broadcasts.<br>• It lets through frames for which the destinations are unknown. |
| Router | • It does not allow broadcasts through.<br>• It chooses the best possible path based on logical addresses.<br>• It does not let a packet through if the destination is unknown.<br>• It requires a routable protocol. |
| Bridge-router | • It combines the principal characteristics of a bridge and a router.<br>• It allows simpler and less costly management than a mixed topology that integrates bridges and routers. |
| Gateway | • It is a translator of high and medium level layers. |
| Switch | • It acts like a multiport bridge.<br>• It can be used in a centralized architecture by interconnecting other LANs.<br>• When twisted pair cabling is used to connect it to the machines. |

## 8.3 Interconnection components and the OSI model

| Repeater | physical layer |
|---|---|
| Bridge | data link layer |
| Router | network layer |
| Gateway | network layer, transport layer, session layer, presentation layer, application layer |
| Switch | data link layer (like a bridge) |

# Network troubleshooting

## 9.1 NDIS and ODI specifications

For each of the characteristics listed below, indicate if it applies to NDIS or to ODI (or to both):

| Specifications | Characteristics |
|---|---|
| NDIS | • allows you to associate several network interface cards with one protocol. |
| | • introduces different specification levels. |
| | • level 4 introduces Plug and Play. |
| | • allows you to associate one network interface card with several protocols. |
| | • refers to drivers that must be installed on an SMB client, Windows 95 computer. |
| | • was developed by Microsoft and 3COM. |
| ODI | • allows you to associate several network interface cards with one protocol. |
| | • allows you to associate one network interface card with several protocols. |
| | • refers to drivers that must be installed on an NCP client, Windows 95 computer. |
| | • was developed by Novell and Apple. |

## 9.2 Identification of broadcast storm problems

You have an inter-network composed of three distinct logical networks in 10BaseT, with star configurations. On one of these logical networks, a large number of communication problems are found to occur. This logical network contains Novell, Windows 95 and NT machines. The Netware machines use an IPX/SPX protocol stack, whereas the Windows machines operate with NetBEUI and TCP/IP. You suspect the presence of a broadcast storm problem.

Which means would you use to identify the protocol(s) that are causing the problem? How would you solve the problem?

**Working in small groups, identify the likely causes of the problem:**

_____
_____
_____
_____

With the participation of your discussion leader, present your ideas to the rest of the group in order to start an open discussion on this subject:

_____
_____
_____
_____
_____
_____

## 9.3 Identification of performance problems

*Case 1*

You have a Windows NT server, which is highly loaded, and you would like monitor the usage of your server. Which tool could you use? Which fundamental resources can be monitored by Windows NT? How can you ensure that you will be notified immediately when a resource has been loaded to its maximum capacity?

**Working in small groups, identify all the items that will allow you to answer the above questions:**

_____
_____
_____
_____
_____
_____
_____

**With the participation of your discussion leader, present your ideas to the rest of the group in order to start an open discussion on this subject:**

_____
_____
_____
_____
_____
_____
_____
_____

*Case 2*

Which circumstances could lead to the following modifications being implemented: adding extra memory on the server, updating the processor, upgrading to a multiprocessor platform, adding an extra network interface card, moving a specific service or specific applications?

**Working in small groups, identify all the items that will allow you to answer these questions:**

Adding extra memory on the server

_____
_____
_____
_____

Updating the processor

_____
_____
_____
_____

Upgrading from a monoprocessor to a multiprocessor

Adding an extra network interface card

Moving an application

**With the participation of your discussion leader, present to the rest of the group the ideas that you have prepared in order to start an open discussion on these subjects:**

Adding extra memory on the server

Updating the processor

Upgrading from a monoprocessor to a multiprocessor

Adding an extra network interface card

Moving an application

# Solutions

## 9.1 NDIS and ODI specifications

| NDIS | · was developed by Microsoft and 3COM.<br>· introduces different specification levels.<br>· level 4 introduces Plug and Play.<br>· allows you to associate several network interface cards with one protocol.<br>· allows you to associate one network interface card with several protocols.<br>· refers to drivers that must be installed on an SMB client. |
|---|---|
| ODI | · was developed by Novell and Apple.<br>· allows you to associate several network interface cards with one protocol.<br>· allows you to associate one network interface card with several protocols.<br>· refers to drivers that must be installed on an NCP client. |

## 9.2 Identification of broadcast storm problems

### Means to be used

You must monitor the network traffic in order to identify the protocol that is causing the problem (the most verbose protocol). You can monitor the network in this way using a protocol analyzer.

### Possible solutions

Broadcast problems are closely linked with the use of NetBIOS and Ethernet. The number of broadcasts increases with the number of distinct protocols that are running on the logical network concerned (which coincides with a broadcast domain).

The first remedy consists of removing certain protocols in order to lighten the load on the network. This involves answering questions such as the following: Can all the machines be served using just one protocol, for example IPX/SPX? Are there any applications that really cannot run without TCP/IP? Do all the machines really need this protocol? Would it be possible to configure a gateway so as to reduce the number of protocols that are used?

The second remedy is to increase the segmentation of the network. However, if you do this you must ensure that you provide for non-routable protocols such as Net-BEUI.

## 9.3 Identification of performance problems

### Case 1

On Windows NT you can use the performance monitor in log mode. This technique allows you to record data on a continuing basis so that you can analyze it later. The fundamental counters that you must monitor are the memory, the disk, the processor and the network. These counters will provide you with fuller information on the resource that is at the heart of the problem.

In addition, you can use the performance monitor to define a certain number of alerts. This technique ensures that messages are sent to the administrator when a resource reaches a certain threshold (for example when the processor usage counter is constantly over 80%).

### Case 2

#### Adding extra memory on the server

When there is not enough memory to provide for all the applications that are running, applications are swapped between the memory and the disk. If this is done frequently, response times will be slowed down considerably. If you cannot reduce the number of applications that run simultaneously, then you must either add more memory, or move certain applications onto other servers.

On a file or print server, part of the memory will be used for the cache. Therefore, it is important to provide enough memory to enable data exchanges to take place as quickly as possible.

### Updating the processor

If your server is being used increasingly as an applications server, you may need to increase the processing power of your processor.

### Upgrading from a monoprocessor to a multiprocessor

If there are a lot of applications that run simultaneously, but few of these applications require a lot of processing power individually, it may be preferable to use several processors, rather than increasing the power of a single processor.

### Adding an extra network interface card

Adding an extra network interface card on a server, is a technique that can allow you physically to segment the network. A possible benefit of this technique could be to divide the number of collisions that take place. You can then choose to use your server as a router. Alternatively you may decide to maintain two separate networks that are isolated from each other for security reasons.

### Moving an application

When response times become too long, one way of improving them considerably is simply to add another server.

# Choosing network components

## 10.1 Choosing a transmission medium according to cost

Using a network catalog supplied by your Course Monitor, sort the following list of media by increasing cost. You could also contact your local network dealer so as to provide a complementary source of information for this purpose.

Indicate the order of increasing cost order, by assigning an order number (1, 2, 3) to each medium and writing it in the Cost column.

| Media | Cost |
|---|---|
| Thin coaxial | |
| Thick coaxial | |
| A pair of UTP cat.3 | |
| A pair of UTP cat.5 | |
| A pair of STP | |
| Optical fiber | |

## 10.2 Choosing a physical medium according to maximum segment length

Match up the following physical media with their corresponding maximum segment lengths:

| Physical Media | Segment length |
|---|---|
| Thin coaxial | 100 meters |
| Thick coaxial | 105 meters |
| A pair of UTP cat.3 | 185 meters |
| A pair of UTP cat.5 | 100 meters |
| A pair of STP | 500 meters |
| Optical fiber | 2000 meters |

## 10.3 Choosing a wireless network system

Match up the following wireless network systems with their corresponding characteristics:

| Wireless system | Characteristics |
|---|---|
| Wideband radio waves | A beam of light is used to transmit the data. These signals are very sensitive to bright lighting. However, they can support transmission speeds of 10 Mbps over a maximum distance of 330 meters. |
| Infrared | They allow you to transfer data on existing analog voice networks, between two telephone calls, when the system is not occupied. Data transmission is very quick and waiting times are less than one second. |
| Radio communication by packets | This technique allows you to transmit signals on a range of frequencies. Transmission speeds between 250 Kbps and 2 Mbps can be attained over distances of 130 meters indoors and 3200 meters outdoors. |
| Cellular LANs | All messages are split up into packets and forwarded to a satellite, which then handles the transmission. |
| Laser | This is the most commonly used method in the European Union for transmission over long distances. Excellent results are obtained between two points by direct visibility (a geostationary orbiting satellite and a land link, between two buildings or over vast expanses). |

| | |
|---|---|
| Narrowband radio waves | This system requires a direct visibility field and is sensitive to misalignment problems. The signal is received by a photo-diode, which resists interference and disturbances but is sensitive to atmospheric conditions. |
| Satellite stations | The user tunes the transceiver into a given frequency. The waves are omnidirectional and broadcasts can be made over 1650 $m^2$. However, the high frequency signal cannot pass through load bearing walls or steel walls. |

## 10.4 Identification of available IRQs

You have a PC equipped with a Pentium processor, a floppy disk drive, a hard disk drive and a CDROM drive on the second IDE controller, a mouse (on the second serial port) and a sound card that is configured on the IRQ that is used by the second parallel port. A modem has been successfully configured on the remaining serial port.

Amongst the IRQs 3, 4, 5, 6, 7, 10, 11, 12, 13, 14 and 15, which are those that can be used to configure your network interface card? Which one of these would you choose?

Fill in the following table for the IRQs that you have used.

| IRQ | Usage on this PC |
|---|---|
| 3 | |
| 4 | |
| 5 | |
| 6 | |
| 7 | |
| 10 | |
| 11 | |
| 12 | |
| 13 | |
| 14 | |
| 15 | |

# Solutions

## 10.1 Choosing a transmission medium according to cost

| Media | Cost |
|---|---|
| Thin coaxial | 2 |
| Thick coaxial | 5 |
| A pair of UTP cat.3 | 1 |
| A pair of UTP cat.5 | 3 |
| A pair of STP | 4 |
| Optical fiber | 6 |

## 10.2 Choosing a physical medium according to maximum segment length

| Physical Media | Segment length |
|---|---|
| Thin coaxial | 185 meters |
| Thick coaxial | 500 meters |
| A pair of UTP cat.3 | 100 meters |
| A pair of UTP cat.5 | 100 meters |
| A pair of STP | 105 meters |
| Optical fiber | 2000 meters |

## 10.3 Choosing a wireless network system

**Radio communication by packets**
  All messages are split up into packets and forwarded to a satellite, which then handles the transmission.

**Cellular LANs**
  They allow you to transfer data on existing analog voice networks, between two telephone calls, when the system is not occupied. Data transmission is very quick and waiting times are less than one second.

**Satellite stations**

This is the most commonly used method in the European Union for transmission over long distances. Excellent results are obtained between two points by direct visibility (a geostationary orbiting satellite and a land link, between two buildings or over vast expanses).

**Wideband radio waves**

This technique allows you to transmit signals on a range of frequencies. Transmission speeds between 250 Kbps and 2 Mbps can be attained over distances of 130 meters indoors and 3200 meters outdoors.

**Infrared**

A beam of light is used to transmit the data. These signals are very sensitive to bright lighting. However, they can support transmission speeds of 10 Mbps over a maximum distance of 330 meters.

**Laser**

This system requires a direct visibility field and is sensitive to misalignment problems. The signal is received by a photodiode, which resists interference and disturbances but is sensitive to atmospheric conditions.

**Narrowband radio waves**

The user tunes the transceiver into a given frequency. The waves are omnidirectional and broadcasts can be made over 1650 $m^2$. However, the high frequency signal cannot pass through load bearing walls or steel walls.

## 10.4 Identification of available IRQs

If there is no paralle printer, IRQ 7 must be used. This is the IRQ with the lowest number and therefore the highest priority.

The available IRQs are presented below:

| IRQ | Usage on this PC |
|---|---|
| 3 | not available (mouse) |
| 4 | not available (external modem) |
| 5 | not available (sound card) |
| 6 | reserved for the floppy disk controller |
| 7 | available (not used by a parallel printer) |
| 10 | available |
| 11 | available (not used by a SCSI peripheral) |
| 12 | available (not used by a PS/2 type mouse) |
| 13 | reserved for the mathematical coprocessor |
| 14 | reserved for the first IDE controller (hard disk) |
| 15 | reserved for the second IDE controller (CDROM) |

## Glossary of networking terms

**ANSI**
*American National Standards Institute*
A US organization that has been responsible for many computing and networking standards.

**ARCNET**
*Attached Resource Computer Network*
A network that is based on a flexible topology for relatively small networks. It is commonly used in the European Union.

**ARP**
*Address Resolution Protocol*
A protocol that is used in TCP/IP to resolve an IP address into a physical address.

**ARPANET**
*Advanced Research Project Agency NETwork*
The first packet switching network. It was developed by the US Department of Defense and was also the first TCP/IP implementation.

**ATM**
*Asynchronous Transfer Mode*
A form of cell switching that provides very high transmission speeds.

**AUI**
*Access Unit Interface*
A DB15 connector that is used to connect a 10Base5 card to an external transceiver.

**AWG**
*American Wire Gauge*
A US specification to define the diameters of copper cables.

**BGP**
*Border Gateway Protocol*
A dynamic routing protocol. BGP allows you to work with routers that are situated in the same peripheral zone.

**BNC**
*British Naval Connector*
A type of connector that is used with 10Base2 to connect a thin coaxial cable to an Ethernet network interface card.

## BSD
*Berkeley Software Development*
A software manufacturer. BSD was responsible for the Unix version that supplied TCP/IP sources to Universities, free of charge. This diffusion contributed greatly to the development of TCP/IP.

## CDDI
*Copper Distributed Data Interface*
A standard that is similar to FDDI, and uses twisted pair cables as its transmission medium.

## CDE
*Common Desktop Environment*
A standard that was developed by the COSE to standardize the graphical interface on Unix.

## CHAP
*Challenge Handshake Authentication Protocol*
An authentication protocol that is used by PPP. CHAP authorizes the encrypting of passwords.

## CODEC
*COder DECoder*
A component that allows you to digitize an analog source into a digital signal.

## COSE
*Common Open Software Environment*
The consortium that was responsible for CDE. COSE is composed of such well known companies such as HP, IBM and SunSoft.

## CRC
*Cyclic Redundancy Check*
A technique for calculating error-check codes, and transmitting them with the frame to provide a first level of error detection.

## CSMA/CA
*Carrier Sense Multiple Access/Collision Avoidance*
A method of accessing the transmission medium used in AppleTalk networks. CSMA/CA is based on the avoidance of collisions by reserving the channel before transmitting the data.

**CSMA/CD**
*Carrier Sense Multiple Access/Collision Detection*
A method of accessing the transmission medium used in Ethernet networks. CSMA/CA is based on the detection of collisions without reserving the channel before transmitting the data.

**CE**
*Data Terminal Equipment*
An intermediary component in a data exchange between DTEs (Data Communications Equipment).

**DEC**
*Digital Equipment Corporation*
A manufacturer that uses OSI protocols.

**DES**
*Data Encryption Standard*
A data encryption algorithm.

**DHCP**
*Dynamic Host Configuration Protocol*
A service that allows you dynamically to attribute TCP/IP parameters to clients that request them.

**DIX**
*Digital Intel Xerox*
Another name for an AUI connector.

**DLC**
*Data Link Control*
A network layer protocol. DLC allows you, either directly to access an HP network print peripheral, or to access the SNA environment.

**DMA**
*Direct Memory Access*
A mechanism that allows you to implement information transfer as a background task using the computer bus, without using the CPU.

**DNS**
*Domain Name System*
A service that is available in a TCP/IP environment. It allows you to resolve names such as www.editions-eni.com into IP addresses.

**DPAM**
*Demand Priority Access Method*
A shared medium management technique that is based on a Polling mechanism. With DPAM the peripheral that is at the heart of the topology, interrogates the other peripherals in order to give them the opportunity to transmit data.

**DQDB**
*Dual Queue Dual Bus (IEEE 802.6)*
A MAN type network that is based on a double-bus architecture in fiber optics. DQDB supports the transfer of multimedia data.

**DTE**
*Data Terminal Equipment*
A terminal component in a data exchange via DCEs (Data Communications Equipment).

**EGP**
*Exterior Gateway Protocol*
A dynamic routing protocol. ECP allows you to work with the routers that are situated at the extremities of a zone.

**ES**
*End System*
A series of OSI standards concerning the network layer. ESES, ESIS, ISIS and ISES define the forwarding of a packet in a switched environment.

**FAT**
*File Allocation Table*
A structure that is used in certain cases with OS/2, MSDOS, Windows 95 and Windows NT. FAT is based on internal linking of information. It does not use internal indexing that would allow access optimization.

**FDDI**
*Fiber Distributed Data Interface*
A token passing standard that supports transmission speeds of 100 Mbps. FDDI is based on a double ring logical topology with a fiber optics transmission medium.

**FTP**
*File Transfer Protocol*
A very popular, connection oriented file transfer protocol. FTP is used in a TCP/IP environment.

**GSNW**
*Gateway Services for NetWare*
A software layer on an NT server. It provides access to Microsoft clients who wish to connect to Netware resources. The NT server shares out the Novell resources to which it has access, to the clients who require them.

**HDLC**
*High level Data Link Control*
A sublayer that is implemented in the data link layer. HDLC offers several service levels. HDLC is used in point-to-point WAN connections.

**HTML**
*Hyper Text Markup Language*
A data formatting language that is used to make graphics mode presentations on an Internet browser.

**HTTP**
*Hyper Text Transfer Protocol*
A file transfer protocol that allows you to forward all types of information.

**ICMP**
*Internet Control error Message Protocol*
A rudimentary protocol that allows you to provide services to the TCP/IP protocol family. In particular, it is useful to warn of the loss of a packet.

**ICS**
*IBM Cabling System*
An IBM cabling standard. In particular, it is referenced in Token Ring.

**IEEE**
*Institute of Electrical and Electronic Engineers*
A standards organization that has been responsible for important network standards concerning lower level layers.

**IPX**
*Internet Packet Exchange*
A routable, connectionless protocol concerning the network and transport layers that is used in a Novell environment.

**IS**
*Intermediate System*
A series of OSI standards concerning the network layer. ESES, ESIS, ISIS and ISES define the routing of a packet in a switched environment.

**IRQ**
*Interrupt ReQuest*
A request to interrupt. Each PC peripheral is connected to the CPU by a line, which allows it to communicate with the CPU when it needs a service such as data transfer via the bus of the machine.

**ISO**
*International Standard Organization*
A world famous standards organization that has been responsible for a large number of standards.

**ISP**
*Internet Service Provider*
An organization that provides Internet access. It provides a gateway between clients.

**ITU-T**
The organization that was responsible for the X. and V. standards series, such as X.25, X.500 and V.32.

**LAN**
*Local Area Network*
A network that covers a limited geographical area.

**LLC**
*Logical Link Control*
A sublayer of the OSI model data link layer that was introduced by the IEEE. LLC offers different types of service.

**LPD**
*Line Printer Daemon*
A TCP/IP print service that is available on various platforms.

**MAC**
*Medium Access Control*
A sublayer of the OSI model data link layer that was introduced by the IEEE. MAC manages access to the physical medium. It integrates the medium access method and physical addressing.

**MAN**
*Metropolitan Area Network*
A network that covers a relatively large geographical area such as an American district.

**MAU or MSAU**
*Multi Station Access Unit*
A Token Ring hub.

**MIB**
*Management Information Base*
The data structure that is implemented by an SNMP (Simple Network Management Protocol) agent. An SNMP agent is a specific application that provides specific information from a hardware or software distributed component.

**MODEM**
*MODutator DEModulator*
A piece of intermediate hardware that allows you to transmit digital data in the form of an analog signal. A MODEM is an example of a DCE.

**NCP**
*Netware Core Protocol*
A protocol that has several functions, including that of providing access to files and printers to Novell clients.

**NDIS**
*Network Device Interface Specification*
A Microsoft/3Com specification. NDIS is used in Microsoft network operating systems for network interface card drivers and medium-level layer protocols.

**NDS**
*Netware Directory Service*
A service supplied by Novell networks. NDS allows distributed management of networking objects according to the X.500 standard.

**NETBEUI**
*NetBios Extended User Interface*
A protocol that covers the network and transport layers as defined by the OSI model. NetBEUI provides access to the NETBIOS interchangeable medium-level layers (session layer).

**NETBIOS**
*NETwork Basic Input Output System*
A network application programming interface. NetBIOS is available for client/server applications on any of the medium-level layer protocols.

**NFS**
*Network File System*
A network file server that runs on TCP/IP. NFS allows you to view a remote file hierarchy as if it was a subdirectory of your local hierarchy.

**NOS**
*Network Operating System*

**NTFS**
*New Technology File System*
A 64-bit secure, transactional system that is provided with Windows NT.

**ODI**
*Open Data Interface*
A specification that was written by Novell/Apple for network interface card divers and for network protocols in a Novell Environment.

**OMG**
*Object Management Group*
A consortium of organizations that has been responsible for many specifications.

**OSF**
*Open Software Foundation*
A foundation that allows different suppliers to combine their experience. OSF was responsible for OSF/Motif, which is a graphical user interface.

**OSI**
*Open System Interface*
A seven-layer reference model that was introduced by the ISO.

**OSPF**
*Open Shortest Path First*
A dynamic routing algorithm that is handled by IP.

**PAD**
*Packet Assembler/Disassembler*
A switch that provides direct access to X.25.

**PING**
*Packet Internet Groper*
A tool that allows you to test connectivity. PING is commonly used on TCP/IP to identify IP configuration or addressing problems.

**PPP**
*Point to Point Protocol*
A WAN protocol that works on the first two layers of the OSI model. PPP is commonly used to connect to the Internet.

**PPTP**
*Point to Point Tunneling Protocol*
A protocol that allows you to manage protected private communications via multipoint IP communications.

**RAID**
*Redundant Array of Inexpensive Disks*
A feature that introduces fault tolerance by the redundant storage of information.

**RFC**
*Request For Comment*
A reference document that defines standards for the TCP/IP family of protocols.

**RIP**
*Routing Information protocol*
A dynamic routing protocol for IPX and IP.

**RISC**
*Reduced Instruction Set Component*
An architecture that is based on a reduced instruction set.

**ROM**
*Read Only Memory*
Non-volatile memory.

**RPC**
*Remote Procedure Call*
A protocol that allows communication between client and server components in a network.

**SAG**
*SQL Access Group*
An organization that develops standards concerning SQL.

**SAP**
*Service Advertisement Protocol*
A protocol that notifies you of the services that are available on a Novell server.

**SCNW**
*Service Client NetWare*
The client for Novell networks that is supplied with Windows NT Workstation.

**SNA**
*System Network Architecture*
An architecture in an IBM environment.

**SFT**
*System Fault Tolerance*
The fault tolerance levels that are defined by Novell.

**SLIP**
*Serial Line IP*
A connectionless point-to-point connection protocol with limited features. Development of this protocol resulted in the creation of PPP, which is progressively replacing it.

**SMB**
*Server Message Block*
A file and print services protocol that is used especially in Microsoft networks.

**SMTP**
*Simple Mail Transfer Protocol*
An elementary protocol that is used for transferring outgoing files.

**SNMP**
*Simple Network Management Protocol*
An elementary protocol that allows you to monitor and administer remote hardware and software components using an information database (an MIB).

**SPX**
*Sequenced Packet eXchange*
Transport layer protocol that provides a connection-oriented service in a Novell environment.

**SQL**
*Structured Query Language*
A very commonly used query language that was standardized by the ANSO in 1992.

**SSL**
*Secure Socket Layer*
A software layer that allows you to filter exchanges between Windows socket applications.

**STP**
*Shielded Twisted Pair*

**TCP/IP**
*Transmission Control Protocol/Internet Protocol*
A world famous family of protocols that is independent from the physical medium used.

**TFTP**
*Trivial File Transfer Protocol*
A file transfer protocol that favors speed to reliability. TFTP is used very little.

**TTL**
*Time To Live*

**UDP**
*User Datagram Protocol*
A connectionless transport layer protocol form the TCP/IP stack.

**UNC**
*Universal Naming Convention*
A network path that allows you to identify a resource in a network that is based on NetBIOS.

**UPS**
*Uninterruptible Power Supply*
A device that is equipped with a battery and is able to provide a temporary power supply in the event of mains failure. A UPS can be connected to one or more servers.

**URL**
*Uniform Resource Locator*
A network path that allows you uniquely to identify a TCP/IP resource.

**UTP**
*Unshielded Twisted Pair*

**UUCP**
*Unix to Unix CoPy*
A family of protocols that allows you to set up a point-to-point connection, as an alternative to using the TCP/IP stack. UUCP allows you to share mail services, to authorize file access and even to run remote programs in a Unix environment.

**WAN**
*Wide Area Network*
A network that covers a large geographical area.

**WINS**
*Windows Internet Name Service*
A dynamic service that allows you to resolve NetBIOS names into IP addresses in an internetwork.

**WWW**
*World Wide Web*
The Internet.

## Networking Essentials

| Skills measured by exam 70-058 | Chapters | Pages | Exercises |
|---|---|---|---|
| **Standards and Terminology** | | | |
| Defining common networking terms for LANs and WANs. | I-B-1 | 14-15 | TD 1 - Ex 1.1<br>TD 1 - Ex 1.2 |
| Comparing a file-and-print server with an application server. | I-B-2 | 15-22 | TD 1 - Ex 1.3 |
| Comparing user-level security with access permission assigned to a shared directory on a server. | I-C-1-c-iii | 28-31 | TD 1 - Ex 1.5 |
| Comparing a client/server network with a peer-to-peer network. | I-C-1-c-ii | 27-28 | TD 1 - Ex 1.4 |
| Comparing the implications of using connection-oriented communications with connectionless communications. | II-A-4-d | 63 | TD 2 - Ex 2.1 |
| Distinguishing whether SLIP or PPP is used as the communications protocol for various situations. | VIII-C, D | 300-302 | TD 5 - Ex 5.1 |
| Defining the communication devices that communicate at each level of the OSI model. | V-D | 172-183 | TD 8 - Ex 8.3 |
| Describing the characteristics and purpose of the media used in IEEE 802.3 and IEEE 802.5 standards. | VI-B-3<br>VI-B-5 | 214-220<br>221-224 | TD 7 - Ex 7.1 to 7.5 |
| Explaining the purpose of NDIS and Novell ODI network standards. | IV-C | 134-135 | TD 9 - Ex 9.1 |
| **Planning** | | | |
| Selecting the appropriate media for various situations. Media choices include: twisted-pair cable, coaxial cable, fiber-optic cable, wireless. Situational elements include: cost, distance limitations, number of nodes. | VI-G<br>III-G | 235<br>100-112 | TD 10 - Ex 10.1 to 10.3 |
| Selecting the appropriate topology for various token-ring and Ethernet networks. | V-B | 163 | TD 8 - Ex 8.1 |
| Selecting the appropriate network and transport protocol or protocols for various token-ring and Ethernet networks. Protocol choices include: DLC, AppleTalk, IPX, TCP/IP, NFS, SMB. | VI-C<br>VII-A, B, C,<br>E-2, D, F | 227-228<br>255-272<br>276-280 | TD 6 - Ex 6.1 |
| Selecting the appropriate connectivity devices for various token-ring and Ethernet networks. Connectivity devices include: repeaters, bridges, routers, brouters, gateways. | V-E | 183-185 | TD 8 - Ex 8.2 |
| Listing the characteristics, requirements, and appropriate situations for WAN connection services. WAN connection services include: X.25, ISDN, Frame Relay, ATM. | VIII-A, B,<br>E, F, G | 295-299<br>303-306 | TD 5 - Ex 5.2 |

## Networking Essentials

| Skills measured by exam 70-058 | Chapters | Pages | Exercises |
|---|---|---|---|
| **Implementation** | | | |
| Choosing an administrative plan to meet specified needs, including performance management, account management, and security. | IX-A, B, C | 321-332 | TD 4 - Ex 4.1 |
| Choosing a disaster recovery plan for various situations. | I-D<br>IX-E | 32-45<br>337-338 | TD 4 - Ex 4.2 |
| Given the manufacturer's documentation for the network adapter, installing, configuring, and resolving hardware conflicts for multiple network adapters in a token-ring or Ethernet network. | IV-D | 136-145 | TD 10 - Ex 10.4 |
| Implementing a NetBIOS naming scheme for all computers on a given network. | VII-E-1-c | 274-275 | TD 6 - Ex 6.2 |
| Selecting the appropriate hardware and software tools to monitor trends in the network. | IX-D-1 | 333-335 | TD 3 - Ex 3.1 |
| **Troubleshooting** | | | |
| Identifying common errors associated with components required for communications. | X-B | 350-355 | TD 3 - Ex 3.2 |
| Diagnosing and resolving common connectivity problems with cards, cables, and related hardware. | X-A | 347-349 | TD 3 - Ex 3.2 |
| Resolving broadcast storms. | IX-D-3 | 336 | TD 9 - Ex 9.2 |
| Identifying and resolve network performance problems. | IX-D-2 | 335 | TD 9 - Ex 9.3 |

100BaseT, 12
100VG AnyLan specification, 168
100VG AnyLan standard, 219
10Base2, 12, 104, 235
10base5, 235
  transceiver, 217
  vampire tap, 216
10BaseFL, 106
10baseT, 235
802.5, 150

Access methods
  collision, 167
  contention, 166 - 167
  polling, 166, 168
  token passing, 166, 169
Account operators, 326
Accounts management, 323
Accounts policy, 328
ACL (Access Control List), 266
Adaptors
  AUI/RJ45 adaptors, 217
AFS (Andrew File System), 266
AGP (Accelerated Graphics Port), 85
Algorithm
  distance vector algorithms, 180
  hierarchical routing algorithms, 179
  link-state algorithms, 180
  Source Routing, 177
  Spanning Tree, 177
Amplitude modulation, 91
ANSI (American National Standards Institute), 66, 231, 305
ANSI X3.135
  SQL (Structured Query Language), 67
ANSI/IEEE 802.3
  CSMA/CD
  (Carrier Sense Multiple Access/ Coll, 67

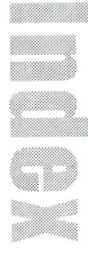

API (Application Programming Interface), *271*
Apple, *134*
AppleTalk, *227, 235, 302*
    EtherTalk, *227*
    TokenTalk, *227*
Application layer, *64*
Architecture
    RISC (Reduced Instruction Set Component), *181*
Archiving, *18*
    strategies, *43*
ARCnet (Attached Resource Computer Network), *133, 229, 235, 355*
ArcNet bus, *355*
ARP (Address Restitution Protocol), *262*
ARPANET (Advanced Research Projects Agency), *256*
ATM (Asynchronous Transfer Mode), *233, 297, 306*
ATM transmission speeds, *235*
Attenuation
    linear attenuation, *103*
    Near End Cross Talk (NEXT) attenuation, *103*
Audit policy, *329*
AUI (Access Unit Interface), *217, 350*
Authentication, *35*

Backup
    differencial, *44*
    full, *44*
    incremetal, *44*
Backup operators, *326*
Backup strategies, *337*
Balanced circuit, *103*
    balun, *103*
Base memory address, *83*
BER (Basic Encoding Rules), *64*
BGP (Border Gateway Protocol), *179*
BNC (British Naval Connectors), *215, 350*
boot PROM, *88*

BOOTP protocol, *88*
Bottleneck, *333*
Bridge, *174, 184, 212*
    addressing, *175*
    capacities, *177*
    Ethernet, *177*
    filtering action, *175*
    filtering capacity, *177*
    frame translation, *177*
    functionalities, *181*
    learning, *175*
    local bridge, *175*
    remote bridge, *175*
    throughput capacity, *177*
    Token Ring, *177*
British Telecom, *297, 367*
Broadband ISDN, *297*
Broadcast oriented networks, *336*
Broadcast storm, *336*
BSD (Berkeley Software Development), *11*
Bus Mastering, *87*
Bus topology, *163*
Bus type, *86*
Bus width, *84*

# C

Cable testers, *347*
Cables, *100, 347*
    backbone, *162*
    coaxial, *79, 104*
    fiber optic, *79, 108*
    shielded twisted pair: STP, *108*
    thick coaxial, *108*
    thin coaxial, *108*
    twisted-pair, *79, 100*
    unshielded twisted pair: UTP, *108*
CB radio communication, *164*
CDDI, *160*
CDE (Common Desk Environment), *67*
CDROM, *84*
Cellular networks, *111*
CHAP (Challenge-Handshake Authentication Protocol, *302*

Cheap-net, *215*
Client for Microsoft Networks, *25*
Client for Novell Networks, *25*
Client service for Netware Networks, *26*
CLNP (ConnectionLess Network Protocol), *62*
Clustering with RAID hardware, *37*
CMIP (Common Management Information Protocol), *64*
Coaxial cables, *105, 164*
    ArcNet cable, *104*
    RG58, *104*
    RG59, *104*
    RG62, *104*
    RG8, RG11, *104*
    thin coaxial Ethernet, *104*
CODEC, *98*
COMBO cards, *350*
Communication modes, *164*
    full-duplex, *164*
    half-duplex, *164*
    simplex, *164*
Communication protocols, *32*
Communications management, *164*
Company networks, *15*
Complete encoding, *94*
Connection hardware
    choice of, *183*
Connections
    multipoint, *157*
    point-to-point, *157, 161*
Connectors
    AUI, *86, 132*
    BNC, *86, 132*
    DB-9, *68, 86, 223*
    DB25, *68*
    MIC, *87*
    RJ-11, *227*
    RJ11, *101*
    RJ14, *101*
    RJ45, *86, 101, 132*
    RJ45 connectors, *217*
    RS232, *68*
    ST, *87, 218*

CONS (Connection Oriented Network Service), *62*
Contention, *169*
    priority management, *168*
COS (Corporation for Open Systems), *68*
COSE (Common Open Software Environment), *67*
    HP, *67*
    IBM *67*
    Santa Cruz Operation (SCO), *67*
    SunSoft (Sun Microsystems), *67*
    Univel (Novell), *67*
    USL (part of Novell), *67*
CRC (Cyclic Redundancy Check), *33 - 34, 61, 175*
CSLIP, *300*
CSMA, *168*
CSMA/CA, *167 - 168, 227*
CSMA/CD, *167 - 168, 176, 214, 220*
Cut-through switching, *182*

DARPA (Defense Advanced Research Projects Agency), *11, 256*
Data encoding, *89*
    complete encoding, *92*
    encoding digital data into analog signals, *91*
    encoding digital data into digital signals, *92*
    encoding scheme, *91*
    encoding technique, *91*
    online encoding, *92*
Data exchange aspects, *33*
    connection-oriented protocols, *34*
    context backups, *34*
    synchronization points, *34*
Data integrity, *33*
Data link layer, *61*
Data redundancy, *338*
Data server, *22*
Datagram, *171*
Datapoint Corporation, *229*

DCE (Data Communications Equipment), *97, 210, 304*
DECnet, *9*
Demand Priority Access Method, *226*
Department of Defense, *10*
    See also DoD
DFS, *266*
DHCP (Dynamic Host Configuration Protocol), *260*
DIGITAL, *9*
Digitized binary signals, *99*
Digitized signal, *99*
Direct Memory Access (DMA) channels, *83*
Disk mirroring, *38, 338*
Disk striping, *41*
Disk striping with parity, *40*
    RAID 3, *41*
    RAID 5, *40*
Distributed computing, *12*
DIX (Digital Intel Xerox), *217*
DLC (Data Link Control), *278*
DMA channel, *87, 133*
DNS (Domain Name System), *258*
DNS server, *259*
DoD (Department of Defense), *255*
Domain
    broadcast, *173*
    collision, *172*
DPAM (Demand Priority Access Method), *168*
DQDB (Distributed Queue Dual Bus), *224*
DTE (Data Terminal Equipment), *97, 210, 304*

Echo server, *138*
EEPROM, *351*
EGP (Exterior Gateway Protocol), *179*
EIA (Electronic Industries Association), *68, 209*
EISA (Extended Industry Standard Architecture, *84, 87*
    bus mastering, *84*

Encoding
    biphase FM-0 type encoding, *227*
    NRZI -4B / 5T type encoding, *232*
Encryption, *35*
Environment protection, *32*
ES-IS (Intermediary System and
End System), *179 - 180*
Ethernet, *167, 173, 175 - 176, 181 - 182, 184, 235, 336, 350 - 351*
    backbone, *185*
Ethernet fiber optics standards
    10baseF, *218*
    10baseFB, *219*
    10baseFL, *218*
    10baseFP, *219*
Ethernet LAN, *106*
Ethernet networks, *212*
Event Viewer, *331*

# F

Faraday cage effect, *103*
Fast Ethernet, *219*
    100BaseFX, *220*
    100BaseT4, *220*
    100BaseTX, *220*
Fast Packet Switching, *305*
Fault tolerance, *338*
FDDI (Fiber Distributed Data Interface), *67, 87, 160, 218, 222, 231, 235, 354*
FDM (Frequency division multiplexing), *95*
Fiber Backbone, *218*
Fiber optics, *105, 225*
Fiber Passive, *218*
Fibers
    graded index fibers, *106*
    step index fibers, *106*
File server, *23*
File sharing, *266*
File timestamps, *43*
File transfer, *16*
File update synchronization, *17*
Files
    Microsoft Access database, *18*

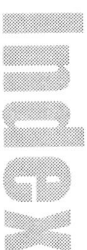

FOIRL (Fiber Optics Inter Repeater Link), *218*
Frame relay, *305*
Frame Relay Forum, *305*
Frequency modulation, *91*
FTAM (File Transfer Access and Management), *64*
FTP (File Transfer Protocol), *24*, *267*
FTP client, *26*
Full-duplex mode, *165*, *185*, *210*, *213*

Gateway Service for NetWare, *183*
Gateways, *183*, *185*
    SNA (Systems Network Architecture), *279*
Global group accounts, *327*
Global networks, *15*
Global One, *304*
    Deutsche Telekom, *304*
    France Telecom, *304*
    Sprint, *304*
Groupware, *20*

Half-duplex mode, *164*, *213*
Hardware aspects, *32*
Hardware fault tolerance, *36*
HDLC (High-Level Data Link Control), *62*, *213*
High level layers
    Server Message Block to
    Netware Core Protocol, *183*
Home Directory, *323*
HOPS, *179*
Hot plug, *36*
HTML (HyperText Markup Language), *64*
HTTP (HyperText Transfer Protocol), *24*, *268*
Hubs, *158*, *182*
    intelligent, *159*, *181*
    passive, *159*
    stackable hubs, *217*
Hybrid network, *161*

IAB (Internet Architecture Board), *256*
IBM, *9, 11, 62, 266*
IBM XT, *84*
ICMP (Internet Control Message
Protocol), *260*
ICS (IBM Cabling System), *102*
IEEE (Institute of Electrical and
Electronics Engineers), *12 - 13, 69, 133*
IEEE 10 Mbps standards
    10base2, *215*
    10base5, *216*
    10baseT, *217*
IEEE 1394, *86*
IEEE 802.12
    100VG AnyLan standard, *225*
IEEE addresses, *80, 350*
IETF (Internet Engineering Task Force), *305*
Implementation
    10BaseT, *185*
Infrared, *109*
Input/output address, *82, 132, 137*
Intelligent hubs, *226*
Interconnection, *365*
Interface cards, *181*
    3C509B, *181*
    3COM, *181*
Interfaces
    RS232-C, *98*
    RS232C, *61*
    V24, *61*
Internet, *11, 46 - 47, 256, 267*
Internet protocols, *255*
    suite, *257*
IP address, *259*
    classes, *264*
IP addressing, *263*
IP protocol (Internet Protocol), *11, 62, 134, 256, 263, 302*
IP telephone gateways, *368*
IPX (Internetwork Packet eXchange), *62, 134, 271, 273, 302, 351 - 352*

IRQ (Interrupt ReQuest lines), *81, 132, 137*
IS-IS, *179 - 180*
ISA (Industry Standard Architecture), *84*
ISDN (Integrated Services Digital Network), *46, 297*
ISO (International Standards Organization), *13, 57, 69, 231*
ITU (International Telecommunications Union), *67*
ITU model, *62*
ITU-T, *297, 305*

Jabber, *351*
JAM, *167*

Kings analogy, *58*

LAN, *109, 182, 185, 303, 306, 348*
    extended LANs, *111*
    wireless LAN, *109*
LAP-D (Link Access Procedure, D channel), *297*
LAPB (Link Accessed Procedures Balanced), *303*
Laser, *110*
LCC, *273*
Link-state algorithms
    Netware Link State Protocol, *180*
    Open Shortest Path First, *180*
LLC (Logical Link Control), *79, 213*
Local Area Network (LAN), *12, 14*
Local group accounts, *325*
LocalTalk, *227*
Logon Script, *323*
Loop management, *176*
Lotus Notes, *20*

MAC (Media Access Control), *79, 133, 174 - 176, 178, 181, 184*
MAC addresses, *262, 350*
MAC sublayer, *220*
MacOS, *271*
MAN (Metropolitan Area Network) networks, *14, 224*
Manchester differential encoding, *223*
Manchester encoding method, *214*
MAP, *63*
MAU (Multistation Access Unit), *159, 221*
MAU connectors, *354*
MAU hub, *157*
MBD files, *18*
MCA (Micro Channel Architecture), *84, 87*
Media type
    broadcast infrared, *112*
    laser, *112*
    narrowband radio, *112*
    point-to-point infrared, *112*
    satellite microwaves, *112*
    terrestrial microwaves, *112*
    wideband radio, *112*
Medium level layers
    IPX/SPX, *183*
    NetBEUI, *183*
Mesh, *161*
Mesh topology
    Internet, *161*
Message switching
    store and forward, *170*
MHS (Message Handling Systems or X.400), *64*
MIC (Modulation by Impulse and Coding), *298*
Microsoft Exchange Server, *20*
Microsoft LAN Manager
    Windows 3.1, *63*
    Windows 95, *63*
    Windows NT, *63*
Microwave systems, *112*

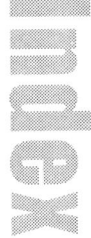

MIME (Multipurpose Internet Mail Extensions), *64*
Mirroring controllers, *39*
    duplexing, *39*
Mirroring servers, *40*
Mobile computing, *111*
Mobile networks, *367*
Modem, *97*
Monomode fibers, *106*
MSB, *81*
Multi-protocol router
    DECnet, *179*
    IP, *179*
    IPX, *179*
Multimode fibers, *106*
Multiple servers, *37*
    data mirroring, *37*
    with data duplication, *37*
Multiplexing, *95*
My computer, *142*

NC (Network Computer), *367*
NCP (Netware Core Protocol), *24, 270, 272*
NDIS (Network Device Interface Specification), *134, 136*
NET USE, *63*
NetBEUI (NetBIOS Enhanced User Interface), *273, 302*
NetBIOS, *260, 271, 273*
NetBox, *367*
Netware, *270*
Network
    access checking, *23*
    heterogeneous, *12*
    interconnecting, *172, 177*
    items of a, *23, 47*
    monitoring, *333*
    peer-to-peer, *27*
Network Interface Card, *79, 347, 351, 355*
    adding, *142*
    configuring, *137*
    installing, *136*

Network layer, 62
    best route, 62
    logical address, 62
Network management, 369
Network Monitor Agent, 334
Network monitoring tools, 333
Network Neighborhood, 142, 278
Network Operating System, 27
    AppleTalk, 31
    Banyan Vines, 31
    LANtastic, 31
    Microsoft Windows 95, 31
    Microsoft Windows NT, 31
    Novell Netware, 31
    Novell Personal Netware, 31
    Open VMS, 31
Network performance, 87, 335
Network protocol stack, 146
Network topology, 163
Neutralizing bad sectors, 43
NFS (Network File System), 24, 258, 266
NLMs (Netware Loadable Modules), 270
Novell, 43, 80, 134, 352
Novell Group Wise, 20
Novell Netware, 28, 33, 38, 40, 43
NTFS, 34
Null-modem cable, 211

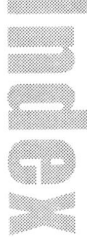

ODI (Open Datalink Interface), 134, 136
Ohmeters, 347
OMA (Object Management Architecture), 69
OMG (Object Management Group), 69
Online encoding
    Manchester, 92
    Manchester differential, 93
    NRZ1
    (Non Return to Zero, Invert on One), 93
Operating mode
    store and forward, 174
Optical fiber, 33
OSF (Open Software Foundation), 67, 69

OSI (Open System Interconnection) model, *57, 65, 70, 79, 183, 209, 227, 255, 257, 270, 297*
    encapsulation, *60*
OSPF (Open Shortest Path First), *179*

PABX (Private Automatic Branch eXchange), *299*
PAD (Packet Assembler/Disassemblers), *304*
PAP (Password Authentication Protocol), *302*
Parity, *41*
Path
    multipath, *179*
    single path, *179*
PC Card (PCMCIA), *85*
PC XT, *11*
PCI (Peripheral Component Interconnect), *85*
Peer-to-peer architectures, *321*
Performance Monitor, *333*
PGP (Pretty Good Privacy), *366*
Phase modulation, *92*
Physical address, *80, 133*
Physical layer, *61*
Physical layer standards
    100baseT, *214*
    10base2, *214*
    10base5, *214*
    10baseFL, *214*
    10baseT, *214*
PING (Packet InterNet Groper), *261*
Plug and Play, *134*
Plug and Play cards, *131*
Point-to-point, *213, 218, 235*
Port
    DB25, *179*
PPP (Point-to-Point Protocol), *158, 302*
PPTP (Point to Point Tunneling Protocol), *35*
Presentation layer, *64*
Primary rate access, *299*
Print Operators, *326*

Programming languages
    C, 67
    COBOL, 67
    FORTRAN, 67
PROM (Programmable Read Only Memory), 88
Protocol analyzers, 349
    LAN Analyzer for Windows, 349
    Network Advisor, 349
    Sniffer, 349
Protocol standards, 57
Protocols, 65
    ARCNet, 209
    ATM, 209
    FDDI, 209
    IEEE, 212
    LocalTalk, 209
    routable protocols, 179

QSPX (Queued packet and Synchronous exchange), 224

Radio, 110
    narrowband, 110
    wideband, 110
Radio-communications
    by packets, 111
RAID (Redundant Array of Inexpensive Disks), 33, 36, 338
RAID hardware, 37
RARP (Reverse ARP), 262
Recovery plan
    choosing, 337
Redundancy, 33
Reflectometers, 348
Remote fault diagnostics, 219

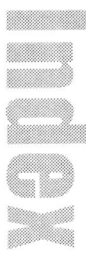

Repeaters, *173, 183*
    10base2, *174*
    10base5, *174*
    10baseFL, *174*
Resource level security, *28*
Responder, *138*
RFC (Request For Comments), *256*
RFS (Remote File Sharing), *266*
Ring topologies, *163*
    FDDI, *169*
    IEEE 802.5, *169*
    IEEE802.4, *169*
    Token Ring, *169*
RIP (Routing Information Protocol), *179, 258*
Routable protocols
    IP, *179*
    IPX, *179*
Routers, *178, 184*
    bridge-router (brouter), *184*
    dynamic routers, *180*
    static routers, *180*
Routing
    dynamic routing, *178*
    static routing, *178*
RPC (Remote Procedure Call), *266*
RS232 cable, *211*
Rules
    5-4-3 rule, *216*

SAG (SQL Access Group), *70*
SAMBA, *269, 276*
SAP (Service Advertising Protocol), *273*
Satellites, *112*
SCSI interface, *66*
SDLC (Synchronous Data Link Control), *62*
Security
    management, *328*
Server
    dedicated, *25*
    non-dedicated, *25*
    Print, *27*
Server mirroring, *37*

Server operators, *326*
Server power supplies, *337*
Server service, *24*
Services
    acknowledged connectionless, *213*
    application, *20*
    connection oriented service, *213, 234*
    connectionless service, *213, 234*
    database, *21*
    Mail, *20*
    printing, *19*
Session layer, *63*
SFT III (System Fault Tolerance III), *40*
SGML (Standard Generalized Markup Language), *268*
SID (Security IDentity), *324*
Signal conversion, *97*
Signals
    analog, *89*
    digital, *90*
    multiplexing, *94*
Simplex mode, *164*
SLIP (Serial Line IP), *158, 300*
SMB (Server Message Block), *23, 26, 276*
SMTP (Simple Mail Transfer Protocol), *258*
SNA (System Network Architecture), *62*
SNMP (Simple Network Management Protocol), *260*
Software fault tolerance, *36*
SOLARIS, *266*
SONET (Synchronous Optical NETwork), *297*
Source Quench, *261*
Spanning Tree Algorithm, *176*
Specialized network interface cards, *88*
Sperry Corporation, *231*
SPX (Sequenced Packet eXchange), *270, 272*
SSL (Secure Sockets Layer), *36, 366*
Standards
    802.5, *209*
    ANSI 87.1 standard, *229*
    CSMA/CD, *212*
    de facto, *66*
    de jure, *66*
    IEEE 802.1, *212*

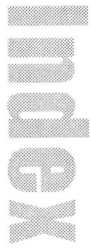

IEEE 802.10, *225*
IEEE 802.11, *225*
IEEE 802.12, *225*
IEEE 802.1D, *212*
IEEE 802.2, *213*
IEEE 802.3, *209, 212, 214*
IEEE 802.4, *212, 220*
IEEE 802.4 standard, *229*
IEEE 802.5, *212*
IEEE 802.5/Token ring, *221*
IEEE 802.6, *224*
IEEE 802.7, *225*
IEEE 802.8, *225*
IEEE 802.9, *225*
RS232, *209*
Token Bus, *212*
Token Ring, *212*
Standards organizations, *65 - 66*
Star topology, *163, 219, 226*
    twisted-pair Ethernet, *159*
STP (shielded twisted pair), *100 - 101, 222, 227, 235, 352*
Subnet mask, *265*
SUN, *258, 266*
Switches, *185*
Switching techniques, *170*
    circuit switching, *170*
    message switching, *170*
    packet switching, *170*
    store and forward, *182*
System Network Architecture, *9*
Systems
    baseband, *94*
    broadband, *95*

# T

TCNS (Thomas Conrad Network Systems), *229*
TCP (Transmission Control Protocol), *11, 255*
TCP/IP, *9, 11, 46, 57, 65, 71, 179, 255, 273, 300*
TDM (Time division multiplexing), *96*
TELNET, *179, 257*

Terminator plug, *348*
TFTP (Trivial FTP), *267, 268*
Thick Ethernet, *216*
Thick-net, *216*
Thick-wire Ethernet, *216*
Thin coaxial Tee-connector, *347*
Thin-net, *215*
TICKS, *179*
Token loss detection, *223*
Token Ring, *102, 133, 157, 160, 173, 176, 181, 184, 221 - 222, 235, 352 - 353, 355*
Topologies, *157*
    logical topology, *157*
    physical topology, *157*
TP, *350*
Transactional file systems, *33*
Transceiver, *87*
    thin-wired Ethernet, *87*
    cable, *217*
Transmission
    asynchronous, *165*
    synchronous, *165*
Transmission media, *100*
Transport layer, *63*
    connection oriented, *63*
Tree topology, *217*
Twisted pair, *214*
Twisted-pair Ethernet, *161*
Types of security
    security at resource level, *322*
    security at user level, *322*
Types of topology
    bus, *157 - 158*
    ring, *157, 159*
    star, *157 - 158*
    star bus, *162*
    star ring, *162*
    tree, *157, 161*

UCL, *11*
UDP (User Datagram Protocol), *255*
Unix, *9, 43, 258, 265 - 266*
Unix BSD, *256*
UNO (United Nations Organization), *67*
UPS (Uninterruptible Power Supply), *33, 337*
USB (Universal serial Bus), *85*
USENET, *15*
User accounts, *323*
User level security, *30*
User Profile Path, *323*
UTP, *217, 222, 227, 235*
UTP (Unshielded twisted pair), *100*
UUCP (Unix to Unix CoPy), *158*

VCI (Virtual Channel Identifier), *233 - 234*
Virtual circuit, *171, 181*
VLBus (Video Electronics Standard Association), *85*
Voltmeters, *349*
VPI (Virtual Path Identifier), *234*

WAN (Wide Area Network), *14, 15, 306*
Web server, *22*
Windows 3.x, *29*
Windows 95, *28, 135, 139, 141 - 142*
Windows NT, *35, 134, 139, 144 - 145, 322*
Windows NT Diagnostics, *140*
Windows NT NTFS, *33*
Windows NT Server, *38*
WINS (Windows Internet Naming Service), *259*
Wireless bridge, *111*
Wireless media, *109*
Workgroups, *28*
Workstction, *25*
World Wide Web, *161*

X Series
    X.200, *68*
    X.25, *68*
    X.400, *68*
    X.500, *68*
X.25, *171, 304 - 305*
X.25 PLP (Packet Level Protocol), *62*
X.500, *54*
XDR (eXternal Data Representation), *266*
XNS (Xerox Network System), *270*

▲ Quick Reference Guide ▲ Practical Guide ▲ Microsoft Approved
▲ User Manual ▲ Training CD-ROM Publication

VISIT OUR WEB SITE http://www.editions-eni.com

Please affix stamp here

## Ask for our free brochure

**For more information on our new titles please complete this card and return**

Name: ..................
..................
Company: ..................
Address: ..................
..................
Postcode: ..................
Town: ..................
Phone: ..................
E-mail: ..................

**ENI Publishing LTD**

500 Chiswick High Road

**London W4 5RG**